Acknowledgments

This volume arises out of a one-day symposium on nationalism and post-nationalism in Asia convened in Toronto in September 1996. It was the third in a series of annual conferences at which the Joint Centre for Asia Pacific Studies of the University of Toronto and York University brought together scholars of the Lake Ontario region and beyond to discuss issues of significance to the contemporary understanding of Asia.

In addition to the authors represented in this volume, papers were presented on that occasion by Ping-chun Hsiung, Diana Lary, Bernard Luk, Jeremy Paltiel, Robert Perrins, Janet Salaff, and Renita Wang. We are pleased to acknowledge their contributions to the process of thinking through the issues on the historical formation of nations in Asia that run through this book. Subsequent to the conference, we asked Susan Burns to contribute an essay on the shaping of the nation in early modern Japan both to extend the analytical range of the volume and to strengthen the representation of Japan within it.

The original conference was made possible by the financial support of the Department of History and the School of Graduate Studies of the University of Toronto, both of which are gratefully acknowledged. A more personal debt is owed to Carol Irving and Lynne Russell, whose unstinting enthusiasm for the academic work of the Centre made the tasks of organizing the conference and creating this book both possible and pleasurable. We thank Lynne in particular for sharing the editorial labors and compiling the index.

This book is the second time that the Joint Centre has had the privilege of working with the University of Michigan Press, which published the first of our conference volumes, *Culture and Economy: The Shaping of Capitalism in Eastern Asia*. Susan Whitlock has been unwavering in her enthusiasm for both projects, despite the challenges of publishing multiauthored manuscripts, and we are pleased to be able to thank her once again for her patience and encouragement. Thanks are due as well to Kevin Rennells for overseeing production, and to Janet Opdyke for her careful work copyediting the manuscript.

Contents

Introduction: Nations and Identities in Asia

Timothy Brook and Andre Schmid

The nation has dominated the organization and identity of polities and peoples in the twentieth century with an authority and force greater than those of any other concept and unlike any other time. Securely installed as one of the foundational ideas through which we construct our understanding of ourselves and our world, the nation is now tightly entwined in contemporary consciousness, so much so that it is difficult to conceive of a time when attachment to the nation was not celebrated as a primal urge or moral incumbency. Standing at the close of a century in which nations, armed with righteous convictions, have raged so frequently against one other, we can barely conceive of the world in any but national terms nor imagine our places on the globe within anything other than national units. The triumph of the nation has been to confirm its power to organize the world, to confine social collectivities within its boundaries, and to block awareness that things were not always what they now seem.

In recent years, however, the explosion of globalizing forces has caught the attention of even the most devoted advocates of the nation. Globalization per se is not new—forces beyond the nation have long influenced national possibilities prior to the twentieth century—but its current power is of an undeniable intensity. With capital circulating around the globe without regard for national borders, with peoples in various diaspora fashioning identities no longer congruent with national territories, and with such issues as human rights and ecological spoilage transcending the purview of any single nation, the national unit appears to be coming face to face with its irrelevance, some would even argue death, within the larger context of the world economy. Nations have become decreasingly capable of maintaining barriers to trade and information within their boundaries. Goods and services, as well as their providers and consumers, flow across national boundaries as much as they flow along them. Those who operate within the world economy are not indifferent to national boundaries. They work with national institutions of financial accounting and regulation to organize capital and labor when such coordination is beneficial, but they can just as easily disregard them when evasion is more profitable. The constantly enlarging presence of transnational corporations, currency blocs, and free trade zones further weakens the salience of the nation as the unit within which wealth is generated, accumulated, spent, and accounted. As the nation's economic significance wavers, so too does its power to act as the primary locus of human identity. Streams of immigration, following the flows of capital as well as the channels of old colonial connections, have made Chinese-Cuban restaurants in New York as unremarkable as Sikh-guarded Korean barbecue restaurants in Hong Kong.

But does all this mean that nations are really fading? Were we to line up these incongruous realities in a different way—looking not from the West to Asia but the other way around—we might begin to see that such predictions of the declining relevance of the nation reflect the concerns and perspectives more of Western than of Asian critics. This is not because globalization is having little effect in Asia—quite the opposite is the case—but because the world economy has long shaped the nations of Asia. Indeed, for the last two centuries, in particular, Asian nations have been enormously subject to the flux of globalizing forces. The ideal of the nation as something that exists within a hard shell of sovereignty may be a popular fiction among certain Asian elites, but beyond the sheltered realm of official rhetoric this ideal has been realized in only a few Asian countries for short periods, as in China during the 1950s and 1960s or in North Korea today. Throughout the nineteenth and twentieth centuries, the boundaries of Asian nations have been perforated in many ways: by the military incursions of imperialist powers, by the colonial imposition of alien administrative infrastructures, by the proselytization of protected missionaries, by the tremendous trade regulated by foreign tariff schedules, and by the appropriation of foreign vocabularies. These forces have drawn boundaries even as they have perforated them, shaping the territorial spaces within which national identities have taken form—at times resisting those global forces and at times acting in complicity with them but never indifferent to them. In Asia, the history of modern nations is inseparable from the history of imperialism, and it is far from over.

Asia's vulnerability to global pressures does not mean that an East-West relationship has been the sole dynamic in the emergence of Asian nations and nationalisms. The well-told tale of struggles for national self-determination arising from the conflict between a colonizing West and a colonized Asia is not repeated in this volume. Instead, we focus more on the historical processes within Asia that have shaped the formation of national identities—processes that have included a far wider variety of actors and ideas, both internal and external to any single nation within Asia, than is generally acknowledged in accounts of Asian responses to Western intrusions. In Japan, South India, Korea, and China, the subjects of the essays in this book, different groups of elites employed often competing strategies to fashion alternative senses of their national selves, often with only secondary reference to the West. The notion of an East-West divide, though often present in the historical process of modern nation formation, just as often remained in the background, eclipsed in particular historical moments by cleavages and fissures within Asia. The East-West division, famously seen by Edward Said (1978, 2) as an "ontological and epistemological distinction" underlying our knowledge of the Orient, recedes in this volume as the authors forefront the intra-Asian dynamic to Asian nationalism.

Fissures in National Formation

Asian nations have gained their particular modern forms in the context of the world system but only to the extent and in the way that Asian elites interested and able to affect national policy and identity have worked to make this happen. By investigating the writings and actions of individuals or groups engaged in this work within the world capitalist system, the contributors trace the processes through which identities favorable to the rallying of public opinion and the mobilizing of resources were formed (and reformed) during specific moments in the course of Asia's realignment in the world system. To catch sight of this work—what in this volume we call nation work—it is necessary to shift our gaze from the conventional East-West axis and consider three other sets of fissures internal to Asian nations.

First, there are the cleavages of gender, class, region, and ideology. These fissures have molded national identity as factions and shifting coalitions of elites have sought to mobilize populations behind their particular visions of the nation, almost always at the expense of rival groups offering competing ideals of the national self. Here the question of what the nation becomes (or what becomes the nation) has to do with power formations at the local level, not merely "who speaks for the nation?" as has often been asked, but which groups can wrestle their way onto the stage to speak. These power formations can at important historical junctures outstrip in significance the more diffuse power considerations of the global system so often cited in postcolonial studies. If all politics is local, so must be the politics of the nation, even within the global system. As most of the essays show, at least implicitly, urban, educated men dominated public articulations of national identity in the late nineteenth and early twentieth centuries, making public utterances about the nation largely an elite male enterprise. With their control of the means of knowledge production and, in some cases, with their positions in state bureaucracies, elite men could make sweeping claims for the nation, often conflating their own group needs with particular definitions of the nation and leaving little room in public forums for alternative voices.

The second set of fissures are those among the nations in the multinational world order in which Asian elites have found themselves negotiating the positions of their nations over the past two centuries. For these states' elites, their Asian neighbors—whether adjacent sovereign entities or internal groups struggling to attain that status—often played large roles in their self-understanding. Transcultural representation has a long history in Asia, as seen for instance in the "foreign people biographies" (*waizhuan*) of the Chinese dynastic histories. Modes of representation of Asian Others, which are usually seen as part of the arsenal of Western orientalism, had been fine-tuned by Asian writers for centuries before the Western powers arrived. Since the nineteenth century, this history of representation has proven useful to elites, as those same modes of representation, often with their content and purpose altered to fit the new contingencies of the period, could be employed in making new claims for their nations. Although previous scholarship has privileged the West as the primary Other for modern Asian nations, at least half of the essays in this volume locate this role with an Asian neighbor—Japan for Chinese reformers, China for Japanese, Brahmans for Dravidian activists in southern India, and China for Korean journalists. Newly incorporated into a world system with its center in the West, Asian elites still invested heavily in representations of their neighbors in order to articulate just what it was that marked their nations as different and therefore worthy of national celebration.

The third set of fissures, also internal to Asia, have been those separating the present from multiple pasts. Nation work regularly renders the past into a history that can serve the present goals of nationalist elites. Each of the contributors to this volume focuses therefore on specific moments in which individuals or groups worked at rethinking aspects of national identity through the filter of historical temporality while at the same time seeking, consciously or not, to distract attention from their efforts by rhetorical means, be it with the vocabulary of rediscovery and resurrection, evolution and progress, or essences and spirits. History served this purpose by lending the nation a seamless narrative and thereby linking the present to an ancient past, such that movement from the former to the latter had to be seen as a natural progression through historical time, not just of their nation but of all nations. As the subjects of historical narratives, nations were not themselves seen as products of history; rather, history was made to seem the medium through which the nation revealed itself. All the contributors to this volume address the cleavage of past from present by examining the work of historicizing that essayists, politicians, scholars, and journalists found necessary to make the nation appear. Through close examinations of nationalist texts, they demonstrate not only the historical contingency of nations and identities but also how historical interpretations work to conceal the process. These interpretations were not restricted to complex narratives stretching over long periods of historical time but could be worked through the manipulation of old language to stake new claims. The creation of a new word-concept out of a pair of venerable characters, the invocation of an ancient phrase infused with new meanings, the radical reading of a classical text, the appeal to, or even occupation of, a geographic location with symbolic resonance to past events—all these devices could be used to lend the nation the authority of history. The novelty of certain aspects of national identity could thus be overshadowed by carefully cultivated linkages, and ruptures, with the past.

To emphasize the local features of national identities in Asia, as we do in this volume, is not to posit an irreducible polarity between Asian and Western nations. Nor is it to imply an imagined Asian unity among these identities or the processes that created them. As the essays in this volume demonstrate, although Asian nations share features resulting from their shared experiences of colonialism, nationalist elites have registered and organized that experience in diverse settings and various ways. In this sense what they may nonetheless be said to have in common historically is the paradox of having struggled for independence from the West while at the same time fashioning the forms and identities of their nations within a world system dominated by the West. While these various visions of the nation were articulated within local Asian contexts, the outward forms of these articulations were marked by standards and expectations promoted by the Western ideologies dominant in the world system. What heroes were hailed, how language was conceived, whether territorial conceptions were invoked, what content was given to historical narratives—in short, the entire panoply of symbols and themes that provided the material around which national identity was articulated—varied greatly from nation to nation and even among groups within a single nation. However, the very impetus for elites to write so widely and prolifically of a nation-centered identity was itself part of the historical process of being incorporated and actively participating in a world system in which the nation is the fundamental unit.

It is the intense work required of nationalist elites who negotiated the complex interactions between the local and the global, the self and the other, and the present and the past that constitutes the central core of this volume. As the essays each show in different and context-sensitive ways, at any one moment this nation work could entail a broad variety of related and simultaneous activities: acts of interpretation, the careful scholarly study required for cultural inheritance and continuity, the creation of new symbols and their infusion with national meaning, the construction of representations, the appropriation of national forms and ideas from abroad, struggles against rivals—and always the effort to disseminate and instill the results of their work in as wide an audience as possible.

Rethinking the Nation

As entities linked to communities that existed prior to Western colonialism but still derivative to varying degrees of their colonial experiences, Asian nations have proven a fruitful site for rethinking many of the truisms in the earlier body of scholarship on the nation, which was based primarily on European case studies. This rethinking emerged most strongly in the scholarly literature on South Asia in the 1980s. Well before the breakup of Yugoslavia and the Soviet Union, Western scholars of Asia such as Benedict Anderson ([1983] 1991), Asian scholars in Asia such as Partha Chatterjee (1986, 1993), and Asian scholars in the diaspora such as Homi Bhabha (1994) sought to expose the colonial/creole nature of the nation in the modern world and to point out the ambivalent role of the nation in the world beyond the West. Their interventions, which grew out of the particular circumstances of Asian nations under difficult world conditions, have led to a reinvestigation of the multiple relationships between the metropole and the colony, and between modernity and the nation, not just in Asia but worldwide.

The instinct to problematize the nation is a recent phenomenon in Asia. For much of the last century and a half, neither nationalist elites nor scholars of nationalist movements questioned the relationship between the nation and the imperialist forces against which independence struggles were directed. The nation, according to the teleological narratives of modernity to which both activists and scholars subscribed, appeared as the sole appropriate unit for gaining liberty from imperialism as well as for recapturing the wealth that the colonial administrations channeled back to metropoles outside Asia. If nations, defined by international law as sovereign units, formed the fabric of international relations that governed global exchanges, then colonial elites aspired to organize their realms as sovereign nations in the hope that they too could participate in the world system on equal terms. For participation, as the phrase "the family of nations" implies, seemed to offer security and wealth on top of the vaunted freedom of independence.

For nationalist elites, the path to participation was developmental, entailing often radical changes in the ways in which they sought to represent themselves and their nations. In the late nineteenth and twentieth centuries, such changes were usually framed in the vocabulary of "civilization," which provided a measurable standard of all the globe's nations according to criteria as varied as literacy rates, rail-track mileage, industrial output, how well men could waltz while wearing morning coats, or how thoroughly they engaged social Darwinian theories of progress. Such self-proclaimed universal standards became part of the repertoire of Asian nationalist rhetoric. Defined largely in Western terms but presented as culturally unspecific, such notions and practices were used by elites to launch appeals for the right to national independence and to mobilize popular support when that right was denied. As various groups sought to negotiate which of these criteria to appropriate for their own individual and national purposes, they rarely questioned the narratives of progress that impelled such decisions. In their turn, historians busied themselves with revamping the past to fit the present. New national histories, which linked nations to post-Enlightenment narratives of progress, became common weapons in the struggle. Written so as to provide a teleological momentum that would carry their nations beyond a colonial past toward a future of wealth and power (Brook 1999; Duara 1995), history brought all nations into one metanarrative while still trumpeting their individual idiosyncrasies as evidence of cultural distinction and independence. Such was the persuasiveness of what from at least the beginning of the twentieth century can be seen as the global notion of national sovereignty.

This impetus for independence was never an uncontested process, however. Besides the reluctance of metropolitan powers to concede sovereignty—such as the French in Vietnam, the Dutch in Indonesia, and the British in India—competing nationalisms rose up (and continue to arise) within nations, challenging the vision of the nation proffered by the elites who first mobilized and dominated nationalist sentiment. One person's nation could turn out to be another's colonizing master. And when the masters were made to appear as comprador or otherwise compromised, the legitimacy of the existing polity could be challenged by calls for other types of nation. Some calls have been for class nations, as in China, North Korea, and Vietnam at midcentury, where communist parties established people's republics. Some calls were for communal nations bound by a single religion, as in South Asia where postwar India was rapidly divided into India and Pakistan and then further subdivided into

Pakistan and Bangladesh. As well, there continue to be calls for nations based on ethnic exclusion, as in Sri Lanka with Tamil nationalism or in Xinjiang where Uyghur nationalists challenge the hegemony of the nation. Whatever their outcomes, the national liberation struggles in Asia, even while challenging local power formations, have served to confirm the desirability of the nation as the unit through which the colonized subject presumably will find emancipation for the self as well as power and wealth for the nation.

The assumptions linking history, progress, and freedom to the nation that have underpinned nationalist movements in Asia have been shared by many of the scholars who have examined these phenomena. Whereas nationalist elites appealed to notions of national self-determination by wielding self-proclaimed "characteristics" that in their eyes "proved" the existence of their nations, scholars such as Hans Kohn (1944) and Hugh Seton-Watson (1977) sought to identify what these characteristics were by asking what combinations provided the necessary and sufficient conditions to explain the rise of nations. Though one called for political engagement and the other claimed political distance, both the national activist and the scholar of the nation held a fundamental assumption in common: whether for the purpose of asserting sovereignty or distinguishing an academic taxonomy, the nation was seen as an objective entity shown to exist by virtue of a handful of defining elements, be it territory, language, shared culture, or some other common characteristic. In this way, earlier academic writing on the nation, not unlike nationalist movements, served to reinforce the apparently natural role and objective claims of the nation in global modernity.

As elites in the newly sovereign nations of Asia struggled to attain the targets of modernization, many found their expectations for their postcolonial societies difficult to meet. In particular, the vaunted freedom and wealth expected of independence were found to be tempered, if not compromised, by the political and economic demands of the world system. The very global processes that had originally offered and reproduced a vision of liberation and bounty for the nation served to undermine their realization. Out of this ironic dilemma arose a critique of the relationship between modernity and the nation offered by a number of scholars interested in probing the global dimensions and paradoxes of the nation in the modern world. Prominent among these was Partha Chatterjee, who tackled this problem by examining the enduring conceptual hold that the metropole held over its former colony, argued that there is "an inherent contradictoriness in nationalist thinking, because it reasons within a framework of knowledge whose representational structure corresponds to the very structure of power national thought seeks to repudiate" (1986, 30).

Following this lead, a number of scholars have sought to make a break with this framework of knowledge by rejecting the widely accepted notion that the nation is a necessary vehicle for the teleological unfolding of modernity. Instead, nations are seen as ideological entities constructed in a specific historical milieu by specific historical actors. By questioning the structures of knowledge underpinning the claims made for nations, this critical perspective sees nationalism as what Chatterjee has famously called "a derivative discourse," disciplining newly self-determined nations into particular modes of political and international conduct favorable to continuing Western dominance. In their derivation and construction, both nationalism and nations are thereby tied to the hegemony of the West well after the heyday of formal colonialism. Both are interpreted as means by which the West sustains a privileged position in the world economy. In the course of challenging the assumptions shared by both the nationalists themselves and the early students of the nation, the newer critical scholarship has begun to examine the operations and mechanisms of nationalist discourse in terms of the historical processes that have shaped nations in Asia. Asia is now providing a fertile ground for questioning nationalist narratives about the origins and growth of nations. Moreover, in what is perhaps the most ironic twist, these lines of inquiry are increasingly being turned back against the metropole to raise similar questions about nations in the West.

Globalizing the Nation

Asian nations have been appropriate sites for this rethinking because of both their complex colonial histories and their long experience with precolonial state formations. States existed in most parts of Asia for millennia before the elaboration of a Europe-based capitalist world system and the installation of colonial regimes over the past few centuries. Many of these states manifested features often prescribed for the modern state, such as extracting revenue, patrolling borders, and dominating the ideological terrain within which people have located themselves, stored wealth, and organized economic transactions. Some early Asian states deployed such "modern" techniques as cadastral registration or the promotion of uniform language long before Europeans developed them to serve state-building projects (contrary to the assumptions in Foucault 1977 and Bourdieu 1991, 47–49). State elites in Asia that faced integration into the world system did so with a long experience of working within state structures. Although imperialist efforts were often directed at dislodging these elites and their institutions, many survived or became associated with new elite groups and institutions grounded in the old. The story of the Asian nation is never one of merely rising in "reaction" to the "impact" of Western imperialism, therefore, but rather is one of complex interactions between Western and indigenous practices and discourses, as elites deployed the language, territorial claims, and ideology of both old and new with the objective of fashioning a favorable place for themselves in their nations and in the world system.

The articulation of indigenous national identities is accordingly less an internal process of revealing a true national self than a transnational process of selecting indigenous and external cultural elements and endowing them with particular nationalist meanings through contrastive reflection with other groups, both internal and external to the nation. These identities are often being made and remade as the field of referents and pressures within which elites are situated change. And yet national identities resist purely random mutation. They unfold only within a field of culturally given possibilities, a field bounded by shared notions among these elites of what seems to be plausibly familiar and what looks hopelessly foreign. Yet the verities displayed by these apparent certainties can shift with remarkable speed, especially when external pressures seem to threaten what are perceived to be a nation's sanctity and safety. The boundaries of the familiar operate, nonetheless, even when political and cultural leaders struggle in the presence of external pressures to remake the people of their nations into New People guided by New Policies, New Culture, or New Thought, as Asian elites have often done during the past century.

Despite this rhetoric, the process of national identity construction generally favors a conservative alliance with the past. To make the present explicable, Asian elites have often turned to questions of origins. In every case in this volume, old empires and kingdoms that no longer survive furnish significant predecessors for notions of state power, racial longevity, or cultural self-sameness, which get invoked as fundamental to modern identities. Elites in Japan, India, Korea, and China have all undergone some form of national revival or national revolution in the context of having to engage with new political and economic technologies introduced during the last century and a half. To make sense of this experience they have selected elements of what they regard as their cultural heritage that seem best to express their nation's uniqueness and irreducibility. But that selection has gone on within global processes of ideological production that are universal. Nations may display tremendous variety—and in doing so frustrate taxonomic attempts to pinpoint just what a nation consists of—but the acts of display are part of the same logic. "The very act of possessing uniqueness," as Schmid points out at the beginning of his essay, "was universalized."

The last two essays of the volume, by Xiaoping Li and Thomas Keirstead, highlight the constructed nature of nations in Asia and the power of global forces by considering the recently coined concept of postnationalism. The term poses a self-conscious challenge to the paradigms of historical necessity and completion built into nationalist discourse and questions the privilege that the concept of nation enjoys in defining the twentieth-century world. Like its various "post-" cousins, postnationalism is a rhetorical device that indicates less a temporal shift than an attempt to reveal the mechanisms by which modern nationalist discourse conceals countervailing and destabilizing factors in people's everyday experience of the nation. The claim embodied in the concept of postnationalism alleges not just that global economic forces have come historically to override national determinations but that the nation has been displaced as an ultimate source of meaning now that the expansive phase of nation building has dissipated under the pressure of globalization. This is not to say that nations disappear within what some have called the postnational condition. They do continue to exist, but they confer meaning at best intermittently (Davey 1993, 266). Within the postnational condition, *where* something happens is no longer of overwhelming significance to *what* happens.

The Work of Making Nations

Nations do not exist merely by virtue of their prior existence but are sustained and reproduced by a combination of internal and external interventions. So too nationalism does not simply arise but requires work to make it happen. What that work involves depends on the political and cultural context in which it is carried out. If that context is the emerging modern nation-state, the intense moral commitment of the sort we associate with nationalism may not yet be present. In that situation, work of a basic constructive kind is required to produce national meanings: establishing policies that redirect state undertakings into nation-making exercises; or refashioning the categories of daily life through which social and political control is exercised; or formulating ideologies that plausibly rewrite the fundamental allegiances to which people devote themselves. These transformations have to be locally fashioned, but they cannot be wrought in national isolation. Rather, they must be worked out in relation to the complex nexus of local, regional, and global forces to which every nation finds itself subject.

The first three essays in this volume examine three separate instances of work undertaken to fashion modern nations in Japan, South India, and Korea. The first essay, by Susan Burns, treats the development of public health policy by the fledgling national government immediately before and after the time of the Meiji Restoration in 1868, when Japan moved rapidly to establish new forms of the nation. She finds that disease is particularly amenable to national usages, for the weakness of the individual body, particularly when it contracts diseases such as syphilis that were identified as foreign, can be regarded as evidence of the weakness of the national body. Vulnerability to disease is thus made into a sign of national failing, and its control conceived of as a necessary element in the work that has to be done for the aspiring modern nation to take its place on the world stage. As Burns demonstrates, public health policy can be used to sustain and enlarge the presence of the nation as it comes into the view of ordinary people and to induce their acquiesence to an identification with this nation.

Another realm in which work must be done to make the nation appear is the realm of ideology. The nation is only of consequence to the extent that it is apprehended as having immediate personal importance to those within it. That sense of consequence—of belonging—is usually best communicated in terms of a foundational ideology, whether of race, religion, or some other primordial identity. In many Asian societies, although the logic of national belonging tended to be arranged according to Western discursive models, the content of national identity was always worked up from the cultural materials at hand. The second and third essays in this volume provide instances of this sort of ideological work to fashion a nation. V. Ravindiran traces the formation among Tamils in South India in the latter half of the nineteenth century of a new identity termed "Dravidian." This identity, he discovers, owes its original formulation to the work of Scottish missionaries. Their purpose in isolating and celebrating a Dravidian identity was to dislodge Brahmanical authority in South India so as to facilitate a readier acceptance of Christianity there. Tamil scholars followed their lead by adopting Saiva Siddhanta, the worship of Siva, as the religious foundation of Dravidian identity. Once this identity was recognized as legitimate and as rooted in a religious worldview that could claim deep historical traditions, early Tamil nationalists could take it up as an ideology of cultural distinctiveness for the Tamil people. What is striking in this instance of nation work is that the scholarly foundations for this ideology were laid by Scots, not Tamils, and that the opposition that this national identity exploited was not with the distant West, but with Sanskritic Hindu culture.

Andre Schmid explores the ideological refashioning of Korean identity at roughly the same time. His essay presents a very different sort of ideological work through which Korean journalists strove to uncover deep historical rather than religious underpinnings, though, like the Tamils, their Other was not the West but a power closer to home, in this case China. Through their efforts to select and rework cultural forms as specific to the Korean peninsula, they aspired to create a national identity that marked Korea off from the Confucian impositions of the old Chinese empire. Schmid traces this work through the newspapers they used to disseminate their views between 1895 and 1910, showing the difficulties these writers encountered in reforming what had previously been considered the universal culture of East Asia into the national categories of the new world system. They discovered that formerly shared beliefs, symbols, and practices linked to the East Asian regional order were not so easily reappraised according to the logic of nationalization. This dislocation meant that nation work was not straightforward in Korea—as it rarely is anywhere—for the nationalists found themselves tangled in divergent impulses to incorporate into their Korean identity inherited symbols that could as easily be excluded as alien and Chinese if they so chose.

Once the process of modern national formation was well underway in twentieth-century Asia, the challenges of nation work became more varied and complex. For instance, Chinese elites found that they too were obliged to struggle with and select from their cultural heritage in the turnover in 1911 from empire to republic, although their dilemma was strung across a different divide. R. Bin Wong analyzes the conundrum of Chinese nationalism in the twentieth century by looking at the foundations on which the Manchus built their rule in the Qing empire. Contrary to the assumptions of Ernest Gellner and John Hall regarding the uniqueness of the modern nation as a fusion of culture and politics, Wong sees the legitimacy of the Qing empire as relying on a cultural unity that was lost once the Manchu throne was overturned. China thus came to experience "two kinds of nation," one rural and still ordered by Confucian duties, the other urban and understood as a "racial" unity necessitated by competition with other powers. This bifurcation still rests on a widening, even antagonistic, set of cultural fissures: between urban and rural, Dengist and Maoist, maritime and continental, Han and non-Han. Wong's analysis suggests that much more work remains to be done to ensure the viability of the Chinese nation.

One notable attempt to operationalize an urban vision of the Chinese nation through economic policy was the industrial development program that Chen Gongbo sought to mount between 1933 and 1935. With Margherita Zanasi's essay on this program we move from an abstract appreciation of the challenges of modern Chinese nationalism to a concrete case study of how a minister of industry strove to fashion an economic definition of the nation. He did this by combining self-strengthening visions of the nation inherited from the late nineteenth century with the international trend in the postwar years to create autarkic economies. Zanasi shows that Chen's vision of the nation directly shaped his attempts to develop the cotton industry within the bureaucratic and political constraints of the Guomindang state. His purpose in creating an autarkic economy under central command was primarily to wrest control back from Japan, but Guomindang factionalism undermined his efforts. As Zanasi shows, different visions of the nation had profound consequences for the distribution of political and economic resources at the local level, and these struggles often had important ramifications for the success or failure of rival definitions of the nation. Although Chen failed to install his plan as a permanent feature of the Guomindang regime, his vision of a centralized economy controlling the linkages between rural and urban producers became the model that the Communist state would successfully impose after 1949 by linking the economy to the fate of the nation.

Timothy Brook moves forward half a decade to examine the formation of what he terms "collaborationist nationalism," an ideology developed by Chinese political leaders who chose to collaborate with Japan after its invasion of China in 1937. This type of nationalism may not have been highly persuasive at the time, nor remembered once the war was over, but it accepted the nation as the key conceptual category under which collaboration had to compete with the anti-Japanese resistance. The resistance invoked the nation to unify the people to fight against Japan, the collaborators to mobilize them to work with it, and both claimed to represent the nation. The early collaborators of the late 1930s sought to strengthen their argument in favor of recuperating and celebrating ancient cultural traditions by picturing the Nationalists as having turned their backs on the nation when they allied themselves with an alien West. Neither Communist nor Nationalist historiography has deigned to credit collaboration with a coherent ideology of the nation, but collaborators did work to develop such an ideology in order to make sense of the largest invasion in modern Asian history. Japan's demands for East Asian co-prosperity placed the collaborators in what Brook calls a "hegemonic trap" from which they could not escape. Still, the effort to appreciate collaborationist nationalism as nationalism is repaid to the extent that it exposes the politically contingent nature of any nationalist claim, as well as its vulnerability to popular rejection.

Xiaoping Li completes the set of essays on China by examining the fragmentation of the Maoist vision of a fully unified and essentially rural nation with the dismantling of Maoist ideology and policies in the 1980s. Her attention is on the work that artists and intellectuals have undertaken to assemble a conception of China's national identity separate from the totalizing claims of the Communist Party. Whereas the 1980s cultural project was fruitful in borrowing from Western cultural discourses to reformulate cultural identities that defy national borders and put into question Maoist perceptions of "national culture," she finds that border crossing in the 1990s has operated more as a strategy employed by the state and its political and economic elites to dissipate the tension between the demands of global capitalism and the local necessity to maintain self-coherence. Li invokes the concept of postnationalism to name the method that artists used in the 1980s to make sense of living in the real world of the global economy and no longer inside the fictive shell of Maoist national autarky, but she uses it as well to identify the condition of formulating national identity under global capitalism in the 1990s. "The 'nation' remains significant in postnationalist constructions of self-identity," she argues, "yet belief in the nation is driven by the knowledge that to reproduce oneself locally (i.e., nationally) one must act globally. The nation survives in the age of globalization only by its reinvention through close integration into global structures. The postnationalist condition is thus schizophrenic: a tension between promoting globalization and manufacturing national cohesion runs through its structure." Li's analysis complements Wong's to the extent that the schizophrenia she has identified maps onto the cultural gap between urban and rural that he poses as the greatest ongoing challenge to nation work in China. Both scholars go back to the first high tide of nationalism in the May Fourth Movement (1919) to trace the roots of what Wong sees as the crisis of Chinese nationalism, and Li sees as China's postnational dilemma.

Thomas Keirstead continues the theme of postnationalism in the essay that concludes the volume. Like Li, he challenges the popular notion that nation and global capitalism are in competition and sees them instead as being in collusion. To investigate the effect of global context on national formation in Japan, he, too, returns to a foundational moment of transition, not in 1919 but in 1868, the Meiji Restoration. Keirstead chooses as his example the creation of modern history as a new, Western-derived discipline of knowledge used to narrate the nation in Meiji Japan. Noting that history was made to do the contradictory work of recording how things changed over time while at the same time remaining the repository of an unchanging national essence, Keirstead shows that, despite debates over divergent historiographical methods, all the various histories produced in this period unproblematically used the nation as the subject of the past. "Seen in this light, history's emergence in the Meiji period appears less as a battle between East and West than as an effort to displace older habits of reading and writing and substitute for them a narrative understanding of the past" that was conducive to bringing Japan into the world economy. His observation that global capitalism conceals the work of making nations by fetishizing them, just as it does any commodity, provides an appropriate analytical fulcrum for all the studies in the book.

In most cases examined in this book, Asian nationalists enunciated their appeals for national identity in terms of cultural ideals that predated the influence of the West. Of course, the arrival of westerners did initiate a period of transition, bringing diseases, knowledge, economic possibilities, and political threats of a new order. Inherited visions of the self had to be integrated with the new assumptions of nationalist discourse if they were to survive the pressures of the world system. Each of the contributors to this volume acknowledges the power and pervasiveness of nationalist discourse underpinning the world system, but all avoid in various ways the modernist argument that the origins of Asian nations are to be located solely in the West. Even though the incursions of militaries, capital, and knowledge from Europe and America contributed to the general conditions out of which modern nations arose in Asia, the processes of identity formation were particular to the Asian localities where they occurred. Nationalist enterprises found their distinctive voices more often in relation to tensions within Asia than because of the more generic strain between Asia and the West. The world system may have set the struggle for modern national identities in motion, but it did not determine its outcome. Only by attending to the local politics and indigenous languages of nationalist elites in Asia can these processes begin to be unveiled as historically contingent on the efforts of those who make their nations appear.

Constructing the National Body: Public Health and the Nation in Nineteenth-Century Japan

Susan L. Burns

The Body in Question

In 1883, Nagayo Sensai, who headed the Board of Hygiene within the Home Ministry of the Japanese government, wrote a short article entitled "Correcting the Mistaken Understanding of Hygiene." In this work, Nagayo attempted to clarify the meaning of the term *eisei,* which, while usually translated as "hygiene," is also part of the compound *kōshū eisei,* or "public health." He had chosen the compound *eisei* from the Chinese classics a little more than a decade before to translate the German term *Gesundheitspflege,* and it had quickly become one of the most popular of the Meiji neologisms, appearing in the titles of a host of health handbooks and in the advertisements of patent medicines.[1] Nagayo, however, was not pleased with the popular understanding of this term. Throughout his short piece, he emphasized the social benefits, rather than the individual pleasures, of hygienic practices. Hygiene, he asserted, did not refer to the pursuit of "easy living, delicious foods, or luxury," as many people seemed to think. Rather, its aim was "to discipline the body," "to strengthen the soldiers' vitality," and "to make the flesh able to withstand bad weather and humble living" (Nagayo 1883, 32–33).

Nagayo's concern for the public understanding of *eisei,* which had come to signify a wide range of "healthy" practices from brushing one's teeth to quarantining the sick, is revealing of the Japanese government's interest in the bodies of its citizens, an interest that was intimately tied to the pursuit of the new national goals of "Increase Production and Promote Industry" and "Rich

17

Nation, Strong Military," as popular slogans of the day put it. A subordinate of Nagayo's made this relation even more explicit when he declared, also in 1883, that "healthy bodies and active spirits are the single great foundation of Japan's wealth and power" (Matsuyama 1883, 2).

This essay explores the place of the body in the Japanese government's project of nation building in the last decades of the nineteenth century. Soon after its establishment in 1868, the new government of the Meiji emperor made improving the health of its citizens a state priority, and to that end it began not only to exercise its authority over medical knowledge, practice, and institutions but also to create a system of public health. Bureaucrats in charge of state medical policy such as Nagayo Sensai viewed sickness and disease as threats to the well-being of the "national body"—the literal rendering of the Japanese term *kokutai,* or "national polity," which had a central place in the ideology of the emperor-centered state (Gluck 1985, chap. 5). The medical system that emerged in the 1870s and 1880s was organized around the principles of policing and confinement, as the primary means of dealing with the "danger" that disease posed to the creation of a large healthy population of potential workers and soldiers. The process of constructing the new medical and public health system was, however, not easy. The government in articulating state medical policy made reference to notions of social benefit and national necessity, but popular contestation greeted attempts to implement the new public health policies, which suggests that the notion of an easy metonymic relationship between the "national" and individual bodies was one not shared by all Japanese. The debate over the nature of the relation between individuals and the national body is the subject of this essay.

I begin by exploring the rise of public health as idea, policy, and administrative system and then turn to examining how the concept of public health was applied to two very different diseases, syphilis and mental illness. I have chosen these two diseases out of the many that were addressed by public health policy in the nineteenth century for several reasons. First, in early modern Japan the "culture" of both diseases differed dramatically from the understanding of them that emanated from the Meiji state. By examining them, we can catch a glimpse of how the new medical policy entered into popular culture and with what consequences. Second, the two allow us to explore how public health discourse intersected with other discursive forms that also emanated from the state. For example, as we shall see, public health discourse on syphilis was never purely "medical" but was also implicated in and ordered by notions of sexuality and gender roles. Finally, the different natures of the diseases themselves make them useful for purposes of comparison and contrast. Proceeding in this way, I hope to expose the terms and the limits of the debate on the nature of the body. By the end of the Meiji period, the concept of "public health" had to some degree been naturalized but not in ways that clearly confirmed the relation between the individual and national bodies that the state envisioned.

The Meiji State and Medicine: Rendering Health "Public"

The new Japanese government's first statement on medical policy was issued in December 1868, only two months after the emperor's triumphant entry into his newly renamed capital of Tokyo. A proclamation of the Council of State announced that because of his "benevolence and affection" the emperor could no longer ignore the abuse of human life that characterized much of contemporary medical practice and thus he had decided to regulate the practice of medicine (Kōseishō imukyoku 1955, 1). The evocation of the emperor's interest and concern is significant because throughout the Meiji period the government legitimated reform efforts by identifying them with the imperial will—and by extension with the national good. But what this early proclamation also reveals is the extent to which concern about health and disease was shaped by the political dynamics of the last decades of Tokugawa rule. While the leadership of the Meiji government looked to Europe for models of how to construct a modern medical and public health system, the impetus for such reforms was quite different.

In Europe, public health became the object of popular and political discourse in the early nineteenth century, articulated in response to a rising concern about the poor health, sickness, and diseases that resulted from industrialization, urbanization, and the rise of capitalist economies.[2] The leaders of the public health movement were social reformers, including physicians, lawyers, clerics, and bureaucrats, many of whom saw the prevention of disease in ethical terms: it was part of a larger humanitarian program for ending poverty and despair. This was also the moment when campaigns to regulate prostitution and for prison reform and workplace improvements were taking place. The social reformers in Great Britain, France, and the German states were in agreement that health should be a right of citizens of modern states, but there was profound disagreement about what role the government should play in regulating and policing matters of health. In the case of France, the strong tradition of political liberalism mitigated against central government control of medical and sanitary matters, so that much authority remained in the hands of local and civic leaders. In Great Britain in the first half of the nineteenth century, there was a similar debate over the question of how and to what degree the state should concern itself in medical matters. The period from 1848 to 1871 has been characterized as the heyday of state medicine, but parliamentary and professional critiques of governmental intervention in matters deemed "local" and "medical" led to its gradual eclipse in the 1870s.[3] Even in the German states, some of which had made use of a system of medical police from the 1760s on to regulate sanitation, the nineteenth century saw the rise of civil reformers, many of them physicians, who worked to take power over medical matters away from government bureaucrats (Rosen 1993, 135–38, 253–59; Weindling 1994).

In Japan, in contrast, public health discourse predated industrialization and its attendant health problems, and it emanated not from civil society but from the new central government. If public health discourse in Europe emerged in response to industrialization, in Japan it took form in response to concerns about imperialism. In the early 1850s, the Bakufu, the government of the Tokugawa shogun, reluctantly signed a series of treaties with Western nations, "opening" Japan to foreign contact after more than two centuries of a Bakufu-imposed policy of limiting foreign trade to a single country, Holland, and a single port, Nagasaki. These treaties gave rise to what has been termed a system of "informal imperialism" through the creation of a number of so-called treaty ports in which citizens of the Western powers had special rights and privileges, in particular freedom of entry and extraterritoriality, which compromised the sovereignty of the non-Western countries where the ports were located.[4] The outcry that greeted the opening of the country strengthened the growing anti-Tokugawa movement, which coalesced around the cry "Revere the Emperor, Expel the Barbarians."

The creation of the treaty ports in Japan brought not only political and economic turmoil but also an epidemiological crisis. In 1858, the American naval ship *Mississippi* sailed into Nagasaki, one of the new treaty ports, with seamen infected with cholera aboard.[5] It was not long before cholera broke out among the Japanese population of that city and then spread through Kyushu and Shikoku to Kyoto, Osaka, and Edo, eventually reaching as far north as Hakodate in Hokkaido. During the three years of the epidemic, an estimated 280,000 people died; there were more than 100,000 dead in Edo alone.[6] Contemporary accounts of the epidemic paint a chilling picture of the social havoc and human suffering that the outbreak of the acute infectious disease brought. Funeral processions filled the streets, the air was thick with the smoke of crematory fires and the stink of decaying bodies, and coffins were stacked as high as mountains. In their desperation to ward off the evil spirits that many thought had brought the disease, people beat drums, fired guns, and carried out other exorcising rituals.[7]

As these activities suggest, the contagious nature of cholera was then poorly understood. The contemporary Japanese conception of disease derived from Chinese medical theory, which held that the main cause of illness was an imbalance in the body's *ki,* the "fundamental energy" that flowed through channels within the body. This imbalance was seen as having both endogenous and exogenous causes. The former included the failure to moderate the desires of the body—to overeat, overdrink, or partake excessively in sexual pleasures; all had the potential to upset the body's *ki.* The latter referred to environmental causes, such as bad air or water, that were specific to certain locations. Regional outbreaks of disease were often explained in this way by those knowledgeable in medical theory. But for many in early modern Japan it was neither immoderate habits nor bad air that caused disease but rather the dangerous presence of supernatural spirits, who had to be placated or frightened away for health to be recovered.[8] Thus, a common response of domainal officials to epidemics was to require the distribution of amulets and to order shrines and temples to conduct rituals to ward off the spread of the disease.[9]

In the aftermath of the 1858 epidemic, after the threat posed by contagious diseases such as cholera was recognized, the Bakufu would press for the right to deny foreign ships entry into the ports if it was thought that they might be carrying infected people—a request that the European nations would resist by citing their treaty rights.[10] But even in the absence of an understanding of the principle of infection, almost immediately the cholera outbreak of 1858 was linked in the minds of many Japanese to the unwanted foreign presence in Japan. Katsu Kaishū, the Bakufu official who negotiated the end of Tokugawa rule ten years later, was in Nagasaki in 1858 and wrote later of the popular theory that "officers from British ships had come ashore, sought out wells, and poisoned the water within them," thereby causing the epidemic (1971, 174). A Dutch naval officer in Nagasaki recorded a similar theory of origin: "it was rumored that Buddhist priests had declared that the disease of the sick was caused by poison that had been dumped into the wells and used this to inspire among the people the notion of expelling all foreigners" (Tatsukawa 1979, 184). It was in the context of this kind of cultural tension that a critical rethinking of notions of health and disease began to take place. At the center of this set of transformations was a group of medical practitioners who became extraordinarily influential in the Meiji period. These were the students of the medical school (*Igaku denshūjo*) attached to the Bakufu naval training school in Nagasaki, the *Kaigun denshūjo,* which had been created in 1855 to strengthen Bakufu defenses against the West by training retainers of the Bakufu and the various domains in navigation and other forms of maritime technology.[11]

The medical school, like the *Kaigun denshūjo* itself, brought together bright and ambitious young men from around the country for training in Nagasaki, a city where the unequal relations of power—political and technological—that shaped Japan's contact with the West were clearly on display.

Their teacher was Pompe Van Meedervort (1829–1908), a Dutch naval medical officer. During the five years he remained in Japan, Pompe, as he became known in Japan, taught medicine to a total of 133 students, one of whom was Nagayo Sensai.[12] His classmates included Matsumoto Ryōjun, who later became surgeon general of the armed forces and an official in the Central Hygiene Society; Ogata Koreyoshi, later founder of the first public hospital in Osaka and the head of the army's medical school; Seki Kansai, who was to head the Naval Hospital; and Iwasa Jun, who would serve as the personal physician to the Meiji emperor for thirty years.

In his memoirs of his years in Japan, Pompe wrote at some length of the cholera epidemic of 1858 and his efforts to instill in his students the concepts of contagion and sanitation, principles that he noted with pride were well understood in "my home land which is known to be a civilized country." In contrast, he stated, he had great difficulty in conveying both ideas to his students because "in Japan the horror of infectious disease seemed to be completely unknown. . . . As for the people of the city, they were at a loss to deal with this kind of disease." As a result, as cholera swept through Nagasaki, the Japanese "began to say that the cause of the disease was that Japan had been opened by the foreign countries, and soon they even regarded foreigners like myself as the enemies."[13] According to Pompe, he lectured extensively on theories of public health and also took his students on walking tours of Nagasaki, during which he tried to point out examples of a bad sanitary practice such as contaminated water supplies, poor waste disposal, and so on. At last, he believed he had conveyed to his students the basic concepts of public health:

> I explained many times the importance of hygienic principles and during the time of the cholera epidemic I lectured on hygiene, and gradually they began to understand the importance of these ideas. At last the students came to recognize that the cause of much human suffering was infectious disease and that the cure for this lay in the progress and principles of hygienic science. (Numata and Arase 1968, 59)

A tone of self-satisfaction pervades this section of the memoirs, and Pompe presents his lectures on the "civilized" and "progressive" concept of hygiene as an easy counter to the theories of the origin of the epidemic that some Japanese embraced. But another perspective of Pompe's achievement is offered up by his student Matsumoto Ryōjun, who dealt with the cholera epidemic at some length in his own memoirs.[14] Among the students at the Naval Training School, Matsumoto figured prominently, in part because of his status as a Tokugawa vassal and Bakufu official but also because he, unlike many of his fellow students, had some knowledge of Dutch and thus was responsible for taking notes of Pompe's lectures and translating them for his fellow students.

To some degree, Matsumoto's memoirs, composed in 1904, intersect neatly with Pompe's account of the same events. Matsumoto, too, identifies this period in Nagasaki as a point of origin for Japanese "public health," the discourse with which he would become closely associated in the Meiji period. Yet the cultural tensions of which Pompe speaks condescendingly have a different status in this text. Matsumoto's narrative of his training as a physician is ordered by the notion that the body was profoundly implicated in the relations of power that shaped Japan's contact with nations of the West. A case in point is Matsumoto's description of his attempts to facilitate Pompe's desire to give lectures on anatomy accompanied by dissections. According to Matsumoto (1980, 13), "at that time the theory of 'expel the barbarians' was very popular, so to take the corpse of a Japanese, even that of a criminal, and give it to a foreigner so that he can divide the entrails and cut up the eyes was something of consequence to the honor (*taimen*) of the nation (*kokka*)." Here the practice that Pompe viewed as unproblematically scientific is perceived in very different terms—the "Japanese" corpse functioned metaphorically to represent "Japan" itself. Significant, too, is the Japanese term that I have translated as "honor" in this passage: the two characters *tai* and *men* mean literally "body" and "face" and thus evoke the nation in corporal terms. When Matsumoto describes the cholera epidemic, the cultural dynamics at work in the dissection debate become overt again. Cholera is described as something that "invaded" Nagasaki from Shanghai and India, and it is the harbor area through which foreign ships passed that is specifically identified as a site of contagion. Matsumoto describes how he himself was infected while cruising aboard ship one hot summer evening (17–18).

The memoirs of Matsumoto, Pompe, and others reveal that in the final years of the Tokugawa Bakufu, the body was already being refigured as the object of social and political concern. It was in response to the 1858 cholera epidemic that the Bakufu rescinded its 1849 prohibition on the practice of Western medicine and began to encourage its diffusion. It even established a school of Western medicine in Edo, with Matsumoto Ryōjun as its head. And in 1862 the Bakufu sponsored the publication and distribution of a manual entitled "How to Prevent Infectious Disease" (*Ekibyō yobō setsu*), which addressed the problem of contagious disease as a "public" issue (Yamamoto 1982, 539). This refiguring of the body took place in a period of turmoil, as Bakufu authority disintegrated in the face of antiforeignism and pro-emperor fervor. As a result, the body came to be implicated in a new and not necessarily coherent set of meanings, becoming "social" at the same time that it was being demarcated as

"Japanese." Similarly, sickness and health were subject to redefinition: no longer merely individual concerns, they became implicated in emergent notions of national power and prestige.

The imperial proclamation of 1868 on the need for medical reform signaled the Meiji government's awareness of the significance the body had acquired. Only a few months later, in January 1869, two officials were appointed to take charge of the process of building a new medical system. They were Iwasa Jun (1836–1912) and Sagara Chian (1836–1906), both of whom had been students of Dutch Learning at the Juntendō and had studied Western medicine with Pompe and Matsumoto in Nagasaki. Matsumoto had remained loyal to the Bakufu during the wars of the Restoration period and so played no role in the early reform era. The first task that Sagara and Iwasa took up was the establishment of a medical school in Tokyo, the purpose of which would be to train a new medical elite and diffuse Western medical knowledge throughout the country. The question that most concerned Sagara and Iwasa initially was which European country should supply instructors for the school, an issue that was debated at some length among the Meiji leadership.

The proposal eventually submitted by Sagara reveals just how great a role notions of nationness played in even this kind of question. Sagara argued against hiring physicians from Holland because the "national strength" (*kokusei*) of that country was weak. French physicians were deemed unsuitable because its "national wealth" was insufficient. Great Britain was dismissed as a source because the British "despise our nation's people." Sagara's eventual conclusion was that German doctors should be hired to staff the new medical school because Germany's "national polity somewhat resembles our own; moreover, it is still not experienced in Asia" (Naimushō eiseikyoku 1925, 7–8). What these characterizations reveal is that Sagara envisioned a clear relationship between the nature of a country's medical system and its status as a nation measured in terms of wealth and power. The valorization of German medicine rested upon just such an assumption of causality. As Miyamoto Shinobu has suggested, to the Japanese leadership of the 1870s Prussia in particular seemed to present a model of nation building worth emulating (1975, 392). It was a monarchic state with a strong military that had succeeded in industrializing rapidly. Also viewed with much favor was the fact that the German states had not exhibited any colonizing ambitions in Asia, something that had led some within the Meiji government to regard Great Britain with suspicion. Sagara's proposal was accepted, and in 1871 two army doctors arrived from Prussia to begin teaching at the new school, which eventually became the Department of Medicine of Tokyo Imperial University.

Like Sagara, Nagayo Sensai came to feel that Japan had much to learn from

Prussia. In 1871, he was appointed a member of the Iwakura mission, the Japanese delegation dispatched to the United States and Europe to undertake the task of renegotiating the treaties of the 1850s and to gather information on Western institutions. Nagayo was initially assigned the task of investigating systems of medical education. In his memoirs, he recalled his experiences abroad with decidedly mixed emotions. He was painfully aware of how outlandish the Japanese—some in traditional garb, others wearing Western clothes for the first time in their lives—appeared to the Americans and Europeans they encountered, and he remembered that "people on the streets stopped and pointed and together whispered something that was clearly about us. Not understanding the language was a blessing." And he was frustrated that some of those he tried to interview "treated me like a child" (1980, 129–30). At the same time, he was exhilarated by the discovery of ideas and institutions that he came to feel would constitute a plan for "the expansion of a new imperial state." Writing in 1913, Nagayo remembered his "discovery" of a new relation between the nation and the body:

> While investigating various medical systems as I was touring England and America, I often heard such words as "sanitary" and "health," and when I came to Berlin I heard terms such as "Gesundheitsphlege" many times as I was conducting interviews. At first I just took them at face value and did not think deeply about them, but as my investigation continued I realized that they did not simply mean preserving one's own health. Gradually as I became more concerned, I began to pursue their meaning and I discovered that they referred to a special public administrative system that was responsible for the protection of the health of all citizens of the nation. Its foundation rested upon medicine, but it also drew upon physics, meteorology, statistics, and other disciplines and made use of them governmentally in order to remove hazards to human life and devise means to promote the welfare of the nation. (1980, 133–34)

What Nagayo recounts here so vividly is the moment when he began to conceive of health in radically new terms. No longer was it merely an object of individual concern but something the state had a profound interest in promoting, protecting, and regulating. Nagayo states that he immediately realized the importance of these concepts for his own country and made "public health" the focus of his investigations for the remainder of his stay in Europe.

Upon returning to Japan, Nagayo was given the responsibility of setting up a public health system when he was appointed head of the new Bureau of Medicine, established within the Ministry of Education in 1872. The early years of his tenure were devoted to drafting what became known as the "medical policy" (*isei*), a plan for the construction of a nationwide public health system. Drawing upon a draft authored by Sagara Chian, Nagayo's "medical policy" consisted of seventy-six articles and envisioned the reform of all aspects of medical practice in Japan. The medical policy addressed the roles of doctors, midwives, and pharmacists by calling for the establishment of a licensing system. It advocated the creation of a network of schools to train the new medical elite and the formation of public hospitals where the poor could seek treatment. The pharmaceutical industry, too, was to be brought under control through a system of testing and regulation of the distribution of drugs. But the foundation of Nagayo's medical policy was to be the creation of a Bureau of Hygiene, a central administrative body with authority over matters of health. Under the bureau, the entire country was to be divided into a system of seven public health districts. A public health office was to be established in each district and empowered to direct local authorities in the enforcement of health directives issued by the central government. Moreover, physicians in private practice were to be required to report all cases of contagious disease to these local authorities.[15]

The medical policy of 1874 was a plan for reform rather than a formal body of laws, but its promulgation reveals the Meiji state's profound concern for regulating and managing the bodies of its citizens. Perhaps the best indication of the state's commitment to realizing the plan was the transference of the Bureau of Hygiene from the Ministry of Education to the Home Ministry. The latter also housed the Police Bureau, and the goal of the transfer was to coordinate the activities of the two administrations so as to better enforce public health laws. Soon the Bureau of Hygiene, now with policing power, began to issue a series of laws designed to improve sanitation by regulating drinking water, removing human waste from privies, mandating that the dead be buried, and so on. After 1875, a licensing system for physicians was instituted, first in Tokyo and then gradually in the rest of Japan.

The pace of institutional change quickened in 1877 when cholera struck again. The new epidemic spread from Yokohama and Nagasaki, two treaty ports to which foreign ships had carried the disease from China. The Bureau of Hygiene soon issued a series of laws, entitled "Information on Preventing Cholera," which put in place a variety of strategies for containing the spread of disease, including the examination of ships entering the treaty ports, the creation of a system of quarantine hospitals to isolate those affected, limitations on travel and the transference of goods from infected areas, restrictions on public gatherings, and requirements for notification of the authorities and the compilation of statistics on the sick and the dead (Yamamoto 1982, 251–54).

How successful these measures were in controlling disease is difficult to measure: according to government statistics, more than thirteen thousand people were infected and more than ten thousand died. But the impact of this first "modern" epidemic was great. Speaking in 1906 before a meeting of local officials, Nagayo Sensai stated that "it was during the cholera outbreak of 1878, when the work [of the Bureau of Hygiene] suddenly expanded that society began to have a little awareness of the necessity for hygiene" (356). The cholera outbreak also hastened government efforts to extend the public health administration to the local level. In 1879, a Central Sanitary Committee was established within the Home Ministry. It then began to appoint Local Sanitary Committees and sanitary officers in towns, villages, and districts, drawing upon private physicians, police officers, and other members of the local elite to administer public health laws. By 1880, then, a functioning public health system was in place.

What this overview of the rise of public health from an institutional perspective fails to convey is the popular contestation that emerged in response to the Meiji state's efforts to bring health—and its lack—under governmental control. But, as Nagayo Sensai's words in the 1883 article with which I began this essay, as well as those from the 1906 address, suggest, the efforts of the public health officials met with a lack of understanding and in some cases overt resistance on the part of the Japanese people. The establishment of the new public health system required the reordering of the sociocultural understanding of sickness and health, of the body and the practices to which it was subject. This process was neither smooth nor easy, but rather it led to a series of confrontations between the government and the people over the question of "whose body is it?" A case in point is the violence that greeted government efforts in 1877 to enforce the new regulations designed to stop the spread of cholera. In Okayama Prefecture, when police attempted to quarantine those who were ill and forbade the sale of fish and shellfish, villagers rose up in protest, attacking police and physicians. The prefectural authorities dispatched more police, but even so it took seventeen days to restore order. In that same year in Chiba Prefecture, villagers attacked a doctor who was treating—and also reporting—cases of cholera. He was beaten to death and his body thrown into a river. Throughout the Meiji period, each time there was a cholera outbreak the authorities' efforts to enforce the quarantine laws met with popular violence, as police, doctors, and the quarantine hospitals themselves were attacked (Tatsukawa 1971, 191–92).

I want to look more carefully at popular responses to the rise of public health by examining the discourse that emerged in relation to two other diseases that were targeted by the public health and medical establishments in the early Meiji period, syphilis and mental illness. In epidemiological terms, the two could not be more different, but both became the object of the intertwined policies of policing and confinement. These efforts at regulation did not pass unnoticed by the Japanese public but rather were taken up, questioned, and to some degree subjected to a process of interpretation and appropriation in the popular discourse of newspapers, magazines, fiction, and advertisements. By exploring such works, we can catch a glimpse of how nationness came to be inscribed upon the body and with what consequences.

Syphilis and Public Health: Engendering the Nation

The issue of syphilis takes us back to the treaty ports of the 1860s, to imperialism and its impact on the understanding of disease. In June 1860, two years after the outbreak of cholera in Nagasaki, the *Posadnik,* a ship of the Russian navy, sailed into the harbor of that city. The commander of the ship applied to the local authorities for permission for his crew members to put ashore for a period of several months of rest and recreation while the ship was repaired, restocked, and refueled. Permission was quickly granted by the Bakufu magistrate of Nagasaki, a man named Okabe Suruga no mori, and the sailors moved into Goshinji, a local temple complex near the harbor. However, within days local residents began to complain that the Russian sailors were molesting Japanese women and girls in the area. When Okabe in turn complained to the Russian commander, the Russian applied for permission for his men to visit the area of Nagasaki designated as the *yūkaku,* the so-called pleasure quarters, where officially authorized brothels were segregated from the rest of the city. Again, permission was granted, but negotiations came to a standstill when the Russian commander then insisted that the women in the quarters be subjected to genital examinations to discover whether they were suffering from syphilis before they engaged in sexual relations with his sailors. This suggestion met with dismay on the part of Okabe and outrage on the part of those within the quarters, and they turned to Matsumoto Ryōjun, in his capacity as Bakufu official and Pompe's student, to mediate this new crisis.

Unlike cholera, a "new" disease to the Japanese in the 1850s, syphilis was well known. The disease is generally thought to have been introduced to East Asia early in the sixteenth century by Portuguese seamen trading with the Chinese. From China, syphilis was transmitted to Japan, where it was initially known as *tōkasa,* or the "Chinese pox," reflecting the same strategy of naming that occurred in Europe, where Italians had termed it the "French sickness" and the French called it "the pox of Naples." Later, the disease came to be referred to colloquially simply as *kasa,* while in medical texts it was referred to as *baidoku* and *baisō*. By the end of the sixteenth century, syphilis had spread throughout Japan. An illustration of how common the disease was is a statement by the physician and Dutch Learning scholar Sugita Gempaku, who wrote in 1810 that of every thousand patients he saw each year, perhaps seven or eight hundred suffered from syphilis (Tatsukawa 1979, 145). Unlike the case in Europe, however, where syphilis because of its sexually transmitted nature evoked intense political, religious, and ethical scrutiny and was the object of shame, fear, and disgust, it was in Japan perhaps "just" a disease. European missionaries and traders active in Japan late in the sixteenth century have left numerous expressions of astonishment over the fact that infected Japanese made no attempt to hide the disfigurement that resulted from the disease in its tertiary stage (Kariya 1993, 25–29).

The Russian demand that the Japanese prostitutes be examined for syphilis was in keeping with a policy in place in many European countries by the mid–nineteenth century. The tendency to identify cultural Others as the source of syphilitic infection lasted only a few decades, and thereafter, from the seventeenth century to the nineteenth, it was the Woman as Other who began to figure in discussions of the origin and transmission of the disease. According to Winfried Schleiner, Renaissance physicians believed that women were the agents responsible for producing the disease as well as the active infectors. They argued that the disease was produced in the "filth" of menstrual blood and the heat of female genital organs or resulted from mixing the semen of multiple men in the vagina of a promiscuous woman. And, as Mary Spongberg has demonstrated, such theories continued to circulate in medical discourse in Great Britain well into the nineteenth century. Similarly, Sander Gilman in his study of the European iconography of syphilis argues that in visual images of the disease men are overwhelmingly represented as the sufferer or victim, while women appear as its corrupt and venal source. In the late-eighteenth and early-nineteenth centuries, this gendered discourse on syphilis came to be mediated by the rise of public health policies, which were then taking form (Schleiner 1994; Spongberg 1997; Gilman 1988, 252–56).

The result of this series of conjunctions was a new concern in the nineteenth century for limiting and treating the spread of syphilis by controlling those seen as primarily responsible for its transmission, prostitutes, who were now conceived of as threats to men, the family, society, and ultimately the nation. The first country to attempt to regulate prostitution in order to control syphilis was France. The system, which was implemented in 1810, required that every prostitute register with the police. Inscription meant that the prostitute would now be free from police harassment, but in return she had to submit to regular medical examinations for syphilis and, if found to be infected, had to agree to confinement in a prison hospital for treatment. Russia followed the French model in 1843, when the Ministry of Internal Affairs began to regulate commercial sex in the Russian empire. Medical police committees oversaw the operation of brothels and issued licenses to prostitutes, obligating them to appear for periodic medical examinations. Authorities were authorized to incarcerate in hospital wards prostitutes believed to suffer from syphilis (Harsin 1985, 6; Bernstein 1995, 2).

Matsumoto Ryōjun discusses the issue of syphilis at some length in his memoirs. He notes that initially the Japanese in Nagasaki were indignant at the Russian request. Okabe, the Bakufu magistrate, is quoted as stating that this was "something that has never occurred in our country." And when the owners of the various brothels were approached by Okabe, they "complained bitterly and expressed their indignation" (Matsumoto 1980, 24). What is clear is that it was not sexual relations with the foreigners that was the object of their protest—Dutch and Chinese traders at Nagasaki had long been allowed to frequent the quarters—but rather the understanding of syphilis and the identification of the women within the licensed brothels as a source of infection. Although some scholars have argued that the creation of the "pleasure quarters" in Japan in the early seventeenth century was a strategy to contain the spread of the disease, there is no explicit mention of it in the various laws and edicts that established these districts.[16] Matsumoto's solution to the Russian demand for examinations was a curious one, which reveals a lack of awareness that syphilis constituted a problem except in terms of foreign relations. He proposed recruiting poor women from Nagasaki to work as prostitutes for the foreign sailors. In return for good compensation, these women were asked to accept not only the attentions of the Russian sailors but also frequent medical examinations by Pompe and his students. In short order, Matsumoto's plan was put in place. The structure where the women received their customers became known as the "Russian Sailors' Brothel" and the women as the "Russian whores." The syphilis examinations came to be referred to colloquially in Nagasaki as "viewing the whore's private parts" (Kariya 1993, 111).

Matsumoto reports that his solution to this crisis was well received by all. The brothel owners were greatly pleased because they pocketed the profits from running the foreigner's brothel. Likewise, Magistrate Okabe, upon hearing of the happy resolution of the plan, is described as laughingly declaring, "how wonderful indeed that the people in my jurisdiction can profit off these foreigners" (Matsumoto 1980, 25). But after leaving Nagasaki Matsumoto began to perceive the examination procedure not merely as a way of appeasing foreigners in the treaty ports but as a necessary and vital technique that had implications for Japan as a whole. Upon his return to Edo, the seat of Tokugawa power, he began to serve in a variety of medical positions within the Bakufu: he became the head of the newly established Bakufu school of Western medicine, the physician to the shogun's household, and later the chief medical officer of the Bakufu army. It is from a position of authority that he initiated attempts to control the spread of syphilis based upon his Nagasaki experience. Noting that licentious behavior had become common in Edo following the opening of the country, Matsumoto declared that "the failure to regulate syphilis is worse than allowing arson. Fire just destroys property, but the spread of syphilis continues without limits from children to grandchildren, and thus it is the most serious of all diseases. By killing people, it destroys the strength of the nation" (42–43). With this thought in mind, he launched a campaign to begin syphilis examinations in the pleasure districts of Edo, approaching brothel owners as well as Bakufu officials. However, the resistance was such that he eventually abandoned the notion of regulating the preexisting quarters, and—drawing upon his Nagasaki experience—he formulated a plan to create a new brothel district premised upon the goal of a syphilis-free zone in the area of Edo known as Nezu, well-known as a place where unlicensed prostitutes gathered. When this new district was authorized, it initially consisted of twenty-one brothels. On the entrance gate to the quarters a large sign was posted, which declared it to be the Syphilis Hospital District of the Bakufu medical school. However, the examinations for syphilis never got under way, for, as Matsumoto notes ruefully, "suddenly the Bakufu fell, and so we couldn't do the examinations, and all I succeeded in doing was creating another brothel district" (45).

The plan for the syphilis-free brothel district was only one way in which Matsumoto gave form to his new concern about this disease. More successful, ultimately, was another approach. In 1862, Matsumoto authored a very popular health handbook called *Methods for Preserving Health* (*Yōjō hō*). Such works had a long tradition in Japan, but Matsumoto's innovation was to abandon the principles of Chinese medicine in favor of those of Western medicine. In this work, Matsumoto explicitly attacks the principles of Chinese medicine, labeling them "childish" and "difficult to accept," and describes "how to prevent disease before it manifests itself" by means of such new concepts as contagion, sanitation, and hygiene. Matsumoto devotes an entire section, entitled "Matters of the Bedroom," to delineating the social threat posed by syphilis:

> Syphilis spreads from person to person, and gradually its poison increases. Because of this not only is one's own life lost, but also the poison is spread to one's children and this gives rise to every kind of terrible illness. Indeed,

it is impossible to know how many thousands of people are infected from one syphilitic woman. (Nihon gakujutsu gakkai 1965, 40–41)

The answer to the syphilis problem was clear to Matsumoto. He described the policies of licensing brothels, examining prostitutes, and confining those infected as the norm in "all the countries of the West" and called upon the authorities in Japan to emulate this system.

In the aftermath of the Meiji Restoration, the refiguring of syphilis as a social problem continued—but now the participants included the leaders of the new central government. Like public health authorities in Europe, the Meiji government took the stance that prostitutes were primarily responsible for the spread of the disease. Thus, in 1871 the Council of State ordered the Home Ministry to direct the local governments to establish examination centers for syphilis. The text of the directive that was issued reads as follows:

> In recent years in every area, the number of prostitutes has increased and they cause much harm. Because of them men in their prime enter into lives of dissolution and entire families are ruined. Moreover, they spread syphilis and thus harm the bodies of many, and in some cases that disease is spread to the next generation. This is a most unfortunate thing. . . . Therefore, no new brothels can be opened. Nothing can be done about those already in existence, but each district must establish an examination center for syphilis. (Yamamoto 1994, 25)

In response to this directive, the cities of Tokyo, Kyoto, and Osaka began to require that prostitutes submit to medical examinations. Government support for the plan to control syphilis by policing prostitutes was further strengthened when in 1873 Kawaji Toshiyoshi (1836–79), who had been given the job of surveying the police systems of the European nations, returned from a year abroad. He provided Ōkubo Toshimichi, then governor of Tokyo Prefecture, and the Home Ministry with a detailed account of how the cities of Berlin and Paris made use of police authority to require licensed prostitutes to submit to syphilis examinations (Tome 1994, 463–64). Drawing upon these European examples, in 1873 the government created five districts in Tokyo where brothels could carry on their trade. In each district, a "hospital" was established, and the women who worked in the licensed brothels were required to submit to medical examinations at these institutions (Yoshimi 1982, 227).

Just how much attitudes toward syphilis had changed is perhaps best illustrated by quoting a government directive of 1876 that was issued by the Home

Ministry to the local police bureaus, which in that year gained authority over matters of public health:

> Of the infectious diseases, there is none more virulent than syphilis. And the source of this plague is none other than prostitution, and so there is no better way to prevent it than examining prostitutes for the disease. In those areas where there are brothels, these inspections must take place.... From the perspective of public health, there is no more urgent matter. (Yamamoto 1994, 25)

As Narita Ryūichi (1982, 105) has noted, while public health discourse identified prostitutes as the source of infection, it also regarded their profession as necessary from the perspective of male sexuality. Thus, in public addresses, health handbooks, and other texts, men were advised to avoid unlicensed prostitutes in favor of licensed ones, to keep sexual contact to a necessary minimum, and to wash their genitals well after sex. In keeping with this strategy of containment, between 1878 and 1884 ever more stringent laws were issued requiring the obligatory examination of all prostitutes for syphilis and their confinement if infected in what had come to be known as "prostitute hospitals." These hospitals became part of the urban landscape, not only of Japan's major cities, but also of the provincial towns where inductees into the imperial army were stationed. Soon after the promulgation of the medical policy of 1874, the government began keeping records of the number of hospitals that were established as tangible proof of how "modern" the country was becoming. These numbers are suggestive of how pervasive the examination system soon became. In 1878, there were 40 venereal disease hospitals in Japan; by 1882, that number had more than tripled, to 130. This meant that of 626 institutions identified as hospitals in 1882, a full 20 percent were syphilis treatment centers located in or adjacent to the brothel districts (Kōseishō imukyoku 1955, 820).

As government policy was involved in identifying the prostitute as responsible for the plague of syphilis, the disease came to be referred to popularly as *karyūbyō*, which means "disease of the pleasure quarters." The policy of licensing brothels to facilitate the inspection process was not without its critics. The newspapers of the 1870s and 1880s contain many articles on syphilis. A substantial number of these merely publicized the new laws and policies that the central, prefectural, and municipal governments were putting into effect. Others, however, took the form of commentary or reportage on the effects of the new policies and adopt a critical tone toward government policies. The journalists who authored these articles exposed the harsh reality of the examination system and its effect upon the women who were subjected to it. For example, in 1872 the *Osaka nippō* (Osaka daily news), reported that a young prostitute named O-Raku had committed suicide rather than submit to the indignity of the genital examination. The article went on to describe the examination procedure that took place in Osaka under the direction of the students of the Naniwa Medical School: in the presence of four or five doctors, the woman was required to hitch up her skirts, and sit on a specially designed chair which had a round opening in it. The doctors then examined her by peering beneath the seat of the chair. The article draws a pointed contrast between the women, who cry and try to run away, and the doctors, who smoke, smile, and laugh (Nakayama 1982, 2:472). Another article, this one published in *Shimbun zasshi* (News magazine) in 1873, suggests how the women—and presumably some of the readers of the newspaper—viewed the examination procedure. It quotes a poem written on the wall of the examination room, presumably by one of the prostitutes, which stated, "instead of looking at the pictures in pillow books, they want to see the real thing, these stupid officials" (Nakayama 1982, 1:493). The suggestion, of course, was that it was prurient curiosity, rather than concerns about the health of Japan's citizens, that motivated official enthusiasm for the examinations. Another mocking commentary on the government obsession with syphilis is offered by an illustration that appeared in *Tōkyō nichinichi shimbun* (Tokyo daily newspaper) in 1876. According to the text, the man depicted in the illustration as lying upon a futon is a Yokohama merchant who, after suffering from syphilis for thirteen years, has become delusional. His friends have gathered around him to carry out *tsukimono-barai*, an exorcism of the spirit that has possessed him. The merchant tells them "you must be possessed by a badger or a fox. It is the disease called syphilis that has a hold on my body. If you don't leave me alone, I will report you to the Kanagawa authorities" (Nihon ishi gakkai 1979, 180).

What is remarkable about the critical discourse on syphilis and prostitution is how quickly it came to an end. After 1890, there were no more newspaper articles of the kind just described. The medical examination of prostitutes had been rendered routine and commonplace with an ease not replicated in other aspects of the new public health system. This was because the articulation of the prostitute as something outside of, and a potential threat to, the new national culture was taking place through multiple and overlapping discourses. While public health authorities and the medical establishment were labeling her a source of disease, the Japanese state was addressing her through the writing of family law, which valorized female chastity, and by the articulation of "good wife and wise mother" as proper female roles. In state discourse, women were exhorted to contribute to the nation through hard work, frugality, the management of the household, and the care of children and the elderly (Matsumoto 1975; Nolte and Hastings 1991). In relation to this conception of female roles, prostitution was situated as a "shameful profession" (*shūgyō*), so much so that *shūgyōfu* ("the woman of a shameful profession") became another word for prostitute.

Perhaps nothing is more indicative of how stigmatized prostitution had become than the discourse that emanated from the prostitution abolition movement that took form in the 1880s. Originating as local groups, the mainstays of which were Christian reformers and "peoples' rights" advocates, the movement gave rise in 1890 to the National Association for the Abolition of Prostitution. The name of this movement is something of a misnomer because the object of its attack was not prostitution itself but the system of licensed prostitution that existed in Japan. As Tome Yuki has noted, the abolitionists attacked prostitution on ethical grounds, charging that it encouraged immorality, led to wasteful spending and laziness, and was the origin of a variety of vices. The state's regulation of prostitution, they charged, constituted de facto authorization of such immoral behavior. In fact, far from viewing state regulation of prostitution as the exploitation of the women, the abolitionists attacked it as something that besmirched the national honor. Their call was for the criminalization of the prostitution. Thus, the rhetoric of the movement was ordered by attacks upon the prostitutes themselves. They were "criminals from the perspective of ethics" who do not deserve "protection under the nation's law," according to one editorialist. Another member of the movement declared that the prostitutes should be moved to the villages of the outcaste people known as *burakumin* so as to "keep separate the education of daughters of good people and those of prostitutes." In keeping with this view of prostitution, the abolitionist movement did not attack the compulsory syphilis examinations of prostitutes in the brothel districts but rather argued that these should be required of unlicensed prostitutes and geisha as well (Tome 1994, 475–79; Garon 1993).

The public health policy on syphilis thus authorized the marginalization of the prostitute in order to validate another vision of the "Japanese woman." As this suggests, public health discourse was not only for and about the nation; it was also a significant factor in the production of a new national culture, one feature of which was a striking asymmetry in gender roles. To put it bluntly, the national body was a male body. But the very fact of the prostitutes' marginalization in relation to state-sponsored notions of national culture led some to idealize them. Early in the 1920s, a new discourse of nostalgia for the brothel districts emerged, a literature perhaps best represented by the works of Nagai Kafū—this in spite of the fact that these areas were by now routinely referred to as "public latrines" by health officials (Garon 1993, 721). In a series of short stories published in popular literary magazines such as *Shinshosetsu* (New novels), *Chūō kōron,* and *Mita bungaku* (Mita literature), Kafu described the brothel districts as sites where an authentic Japanese sensibility survived as a remainder or trace of pre-Meiji culture that had somehow eluded the formation of "modern" notions of gender, marriage, work, success, and happiness authorized by the nation-state.

Mental Illness and the Nation: Contesting Confinement

The Bureau of Hygiene justified its policing of prostitutes for syphilis as necessary to protect the health of the nation's youth and innocent women and children from a virulent infectious disease. From the perspective of the end of the twentieth century, mental illness is a disease of a very different nature, one that calls for a strategy other than the regime of policing and confinement that was applied to syphilis. But in fact mental illness came to be viewed as a threat to the national body that rivaled syphilis in its potential for harm. In keeping with this perspective, early in the Meiji period the mentally ill became the focus of national policy.

In 1883, the Ministry of Education of the Meiji government dispatched a young man named Sakaki Hajime, a recent graduate of the medical school of Tokyo Imperial University, to Germany to study psychiatric medicine (Kaneko 1982, 72–75). During the four years he spent in Germany, Sakaki attended lectures by such figures as Karl Westphal and Kurt Mendel at the University of Berlin and toured many of the state-supported asylums in Germany and Austria. Upon his return to Japan in 1887, Sakaki assumed the first chair in psychiatric medicine at the Tokyo University Medical School and became the director of the Tokyo Public Asylum. The origins of the latter institution date back to 1873, when an institution called the *Yōiku-in* was established to house the elderly, orphaned children, and the mentally ill, members of an indigent population in Tokyo that had grown during the first troubled years of the new government. In 1879, the mentally ill were removed and placed in a separate facility. With no physicians then on staff, the facility's purpose was confinement rather than treatment (Kawakami 1982, 307–8).

The psychiatric discourse that Sakaki studied in Germany, which formed the basis of his lectures at Tokyo Imperial University, was the biological psychiatry that predominated in Europe in the late nineteenth century. Associated with figures such as Henry Maudsley in Great Britain and Richard von Krafft-Ebing in Germany, biological psychiatry held that all mental illness was physical in origin and that mental defects and weakness had a strong hereditary component. As Elaine Showalter has suggested (1985, chap. 4), this biological model of madness was shaped by Darwinian notions of evolution. Physicians inspired by theories of evolution in biology and the social sciences maintained that a hereditary organic taint compounded by bad habits (widely defined to include masturbation and homosexuality as well as laziness and reading too many novels) caused madness. For the biological psychiatrists, insanity came to represent a genetic reversal, a regression to a lower nature. Using the term *degeneration,* they asserted that mental illnesses got worse as they were passed from generation to generation, causing progressive decline within families and the population as a whole. As this last phrase suggests, biological psychiatry transformed insanity from an individual or family tragedy into a profound social problem. In the late nineteenth century, the concept of degeneration was picked up by eugenists, social hygienists, and politicians in the West, who began to argue that European society and culture were doomed unless action was taken to control the poisoning of society by the insane.[17]

Even before Sakaki's return to Japan, the discourse of biological psychiatry had been introduced to Japan's medical establishment by means of translations of British and German psychiatric texts that had been published in the mid-1870s.[18] The first of these was Henry Maudsley's *Body and Mind,* which was published in Japanese in 1876 under the title *Seishinbyō yakusetsu* (A theory of mental illness).[19] In the 1880s, several German psychiatric texts were also adapted, translated, and published, including Heinrich Schule's *Clinical Psychiatry* and Richard von Krafft-Ebing's *Erotomania* and *Handbook of Psychiatry.* All of these works introduced their Japanese readership to an exotic new vocabulary and a series of complex systems of classification that drew upon notions of both origin and symptom to categorize and thereby explain madness. However, the diffusion of the new psychiatric discourse required more than the mere translation of Western medical texts. In fact, it required as well the disestablishment of the theory of madness that was already in place.

When we examine the medical journals that began to be published in Japan in the 1870s, we discover that the most pressing problem for the emergent psychiatric discipline was how to account for the phenomenon of *monotsuki,* or "possession," the notion that the body of a subject could become an agent of an other, an other that was identified as a deity, the spirit of someone who had died, or most often the spirit of animals such as foxes, badgers, snakes, and dogs, which were associated with the divine. As Hiruta Genshirō, Oda Susumu, and Tatsukawa Shōji have demonstrated, in early modern Japan it was the theory of "possession" that was used to explain madness (Hiruta 1985; Tatsukawa 1986; Oda 1990). The body in this theory of madness differs profoundly from that upon which biological psychiatry relied. In the discourse of "possession," the corporal limits of the body are represented as fluid and traversable, capable of being breached not only by other forms of consciousness but by other bodies as well.

The earliest text that articulates the emergence of a medical assault on the explanatory power of the notion of possession was a short article by one Ezawa Tamamaro, a native of Kōchi, which appeared in the *Tōkyō iji shimbun* (Tokyo medical newspaper) in 1879. Ezawa notes that "in my homeland there is a kind of illness. We natives call it dog-deity possession or badger-deity possession. . . . I have witnessed it many times, however I cannot understand the source of this illness."[20] Over the course of the next year, the pages of this journal were filled with a series of attempts to explain this phenomenon. The first response came from Oike Masanao, a student of medicine at Tokyo Imperial University, who wrote that he immediately recognized that this was clearly a case of mental illness but was unsure of its cause until he consulted with Erwin von Baelz, one of the German physicians employed by the Japanese government to teach at the school. Baelz had begun lecturing on psychiatry that very year, 1879. According to Oike, Baelz told him that a similar form of madness was known in Europe, where, for example, those who called themselves witches claimed to be possessed by demons. But Oike reported that in Europe "since today this is clearly recognized as a pure case of mental illness, the afflicted one is always placed in an asylum and made to be treated."[21]

This initial effort to insert possession within the paradigm of biological psychiatry was not particularly well received. One physician, writing from Tokyo, questioned the validity of labeling *monotsuki* as "mental illness," arguing that it seemed to be more prevalent in some areas than in others, which suggested the influence of climate or environment. Another doctor asserted that "this sickness is an issue of knowledge and ignorance. Therefore, even if one speaks of Shikoku, this is not to say that everyone is stricken with this illness. It is common among the foolish and the stupid people who live in backward areas. And one rarely hears of it in areas where human knowledge is advanced."[22] The definitive psychiatric theory of possession was provided by Baelz in 1885. This article, entitled "The Disease Theory of Fox Possession," was published in four Japanese journals that year, ensuring the widest possible readership.[23] Working within the discourse of biological psychiatry, Baelz argued that "possession" was nothing other than a symptom of a "mental defect." His explanation ultimately rested upon a theory of the binary nature of the brain. He stated:

> Based upon observations, what is called fox possession occurs when the two halves of the brain become independent while simultaneously continuing to perform their respective functions, although the stronger half tries

to control the tongue. When we view the condition of the patient some-times it seems that the fox is speaking and other times that the patient himself is speaking normally. I have observed that this is just as if the two halves of the brain were struggling for the control of speech.

The cause of this division within the brain was attributed to a "disruption of thought"—the result of some shock to the mind of either a physical or an emotional nature. However, Baelz noted, it was those who were already sus-ceptible because of poor health, heredity, or "weak nerves" who fell victim to this disorder.

It was Baelz's image of the body as the subject of a defective "mind" that was deployed against the early modern conception of madness. In the period after 1890, this assault took the form of a particular mode of practice. Medical students from the Psychiatry Department of Tokyo Imperial University, now under the direction of Sakaki Hajime, were dispatched to conduct fieldwork in rural areas. There, with the help of local officials and physicians, they subjected those afflicted with possession to interviews and examinations, thereby bring-ing them physically under the authority of the new psychiatric discourse. The first of these expeditions took place in 1892 under Shimamura Shun'ichi in Shi-mane Prefecture; then in 1897 Kure Shūzō did fieldwork in Hiroshima and Shi-mane Prefectures. Similarly, in 1900, Aragi Sotarō was ordered to undertake a survey of Tokushima Prefecture, and in 1904 Morita Masatake published the results of his work in Tosa Perfecture.

The published reports of these surveys reveal the nature of the new regime of description and classification that was brought to bear on those afflicted with possession. There is, for example, the case of a young woman in Shimane, which appears in Shimamura's report (1892, 981–82). In his case study, Shima-mura begins by detailing the event that preceded the onset of the girl's symp-toms: a high fever that resulted from an infected wound. This, however, is situ-ated within a description of the body that suggests a predisposition to mental aberration: generally poor physical health, slow development, a father with a liking for sake, and a brother who suffered from "brain" disease. Ultimately, Shimamura—carefully noting that the girl complained of stomach pains—classified this as a case of hysteria, which according to the biological psychia-trists was a "nervous disorder" of the womb. Thus, a classificatory system, drawing on notions of sexuality, heredity, and physiology, was used to decon-struct the explanation of the girl's condition that she and those around her had embraced: that her father had borrowed five yen and failed to return the sum to a neighboring family, which in revenge had cursed the girl with fox possession. What Shimane and the others who carried out the fieldwork were honest enough to admit is that those who became the objects of the new psychiatric discipline were not particularly cooperative. In the published accounts and field notes of these expeditions, we see again and again the difficulties the doctors and officials encountered: local families hid their afflicted members, refused to cooperate with the interview process, and questioned the diagnosis.

The popular contestation of the biological model that is hinted at here becomes far more apparent when we examine the popular discourse on confinement that emerged in the 1880s. The institution of the asylum was intimately linked to the rise of biological psychiatry in Europe. As late as 1800 in Europe, there were only a few hundred individuals confined in a handful of asylums. However, as biological psychiatrists began to valorize the asylum as the model institution for diagnosing and treating patients, and also for preventing them from infecting the larger society, they began to be constructed in far greater numbers and on a greater scale. According to an 1891 directory of asylums in Germany, there were no fewer than 202 public facilities and at least another 200 private ones. In Great Britain, the number of asylum patients doubled between 1859 and 1909 (Shorter 1997, 34, 47).

A most passionate advocate of the asylum in Japan was Kure Shūzō, a student of Sakaki's and one of those who engaged in fieldwork in the 1890s. In 1898, when Sakaki died prematurely at the age of forty, Kure was chosen to be his successor. Like his teacher before him, he was dispatched by the government to Germany, where he studied with Krafft-Ebing and Emil Kraepelin, then the premier figures in German psychiatry. Even before his departure for Germany, Kure had made a name for himself as an articulate proponent of the notions that mental illness was a pressing public health problem and the establishment of asylums offered a solution to it. In 1898, he published *Seishinbyōgaku shuyō* (the essentials of psychiatry), a thousand-page compendium of contemporary European psychiatric literature. In it, Kure cites some twenty-two works by authors such as Maudsley, Krafft-Ebing, and—interestingly—Kraepelin. Kraepelin "revolutionized" European psychiatric theory when in the 1880s he abandoned the elaborate classification systems of his predecessors, which focused on presumed physical causes and symptoms, and began to classify illnesses according to prognosis or the course of their development.[24] Kraepelin did not deny the possible validity of biological psychiatry, but he declared that it was not demonstrable. It was this new concern for the clinical observation of patients over time that allowed Kraepelin to identify diseases such as schizophrenia and manic depression. However, while Kure made use of Kraepelin's classifications, he adhered rigidly to the biological model of psychiatry that Kraepelin questioned.

This is nowhere more apparent than in the lengthy preface to the *The*

Essentials of Psychiatry. In it, Kure declared that psychiatry was important not only as a scholarly endeavor but also for Japan as a nation. Why? In Kure's words,

> Public health is of great importance to the nation. Whether a country is weak or strong, rich or poor, depends greatly on whether its people are healthy or not. The most important thing for the nation is to avoid those diseases that are of a hereditary or deviant nature. It is estimated that in countries where there is much insanity, one in five hundred people is afflicted. If we apply this to our country, it means that there are 80 million madmen among our population. The disease of madness destroys the nerves which are the sacred place within every human being and these deviant nerves are in many cases passed down to descendants. If we allow this to go on, then every year the decline will continue, until it has a great effect upon the productiveness and merit of the whole country.[25]

For Kure, the asylum became the solution to the problems posed by the mad, whose behavior certainly, and more importantly whose reproductive potential, posed such a threat to Japanese society. After his return to Japan in 1903, he published a series of articles in medical journals, declaring the need for asylums. Typical of these is one entitled "Why Do We Hesitate to Establish Asylums?" In it, Kure revised his statistics—now it was one in three hundred people who was insane—and declared again that the insane inflicted great harm upon both their families and the nation (1902, 4–5).

In Japan, too, the rise of biological psychiatry was accompanied by the establishment of asylums, an institution that had no counterpart in the premodern period. By 1900, there were a host of public and private mental institutions in Japan, including eight in Tokyo alone. But the asylum was not the only or even the most common means of confining the mentally ill. In 1879, the Metropolitan Police Headquarters of Tokyo established procedures for private confinement for purposes of "nursing the insane and controlling wayward children."[26] Basically, all that was required was that parents or guardians petition the local police office for permission to confine in the home or elsewhere those under their authority for an indefinite period, with no provisions made for medical examination or treatment. Nor were procedures for release put into place. As this suggests, mental illness was viewed by the police authorities not as a medical issue but as a threat to social order, a perspective that was enhanced, not challenged, by the rise of biological psychiatry in the 1880s and 1890s. The Tokyo procedure was replicated in other localities until in 1901 the government established uniform national laws for in-home confinement.

The medical profession's embrace of confinement as the strategy necessary to protect the individual, society, and the nation from the disease of madness emerged as the most controversial and contested aspect of the new psychiatric discipline. The best evidence of popular resistance to the new regime of confinement is the series of events known as the Sōma Incident, which held the Japanese public enthralled from 1884 until 1896. The central figures in the Sōma Incident were Sōma Tomotane (1852–92), son and heir of the last feudal lord of Nakamura Domain, and Nishigori Takikiyo, a former low-ranking retainer of the Sōma family.[27] In 1884, Nishigori went public with charges that members of the Sōma family together with senior retainers had illegally confined Tomotane for more than five years in his home by falsely claiming that he was mad. The Sōma family would contest these charges in the press and later in court, but what they did not dispute was that beginning in 1879 Tomotane had been confined in a specially prepared room in the Sōma mansion. The family pointed out that Tomotane had been examined and diagnosed as insane by a number of prominent physicians and that they had followed the legal procedures defined by the police code.

Initially, the Sōma family attempted to respond to Nishigori's charges. They submitted a letter from Iwasa Jun, now physician of the Imperial Household Ministry, which stated that Tomotane "suffered from insanity, his mind is completely deranged, and at times he is in a frenzy. In light of this, he should be confined and receive careful treatment." However, when Nagatanigawa Tai, the former director of the Tokyo Public Asylum and the current head of the medical bureau of the Tokyo Metropolitan Police, together with Nakai Chōjirō, the current director of the Tokyo Public Asylum, examined Tomotane in response to Nishigori's charges, they declared that he was suffering from "episodic erotic monomania" and should not be confined. In response, the Sōma family moved Tomotane into the Katō Mental Hospital, the first private asylum in Japan, which had been established in 1878. Four months later, he entered the Tokyo Public Asylum. There, his treating physicians diagnosed him as suffering from "manic depression characterized by periods of dementia" said to be the result of heredity, social change (which seems to have referred to the Meiji Restoration and its aftermath), and marriage to an unsuitable partner.[28]

Even after Sōma Tomotane's move to the asylum, Nishigori's complaints continued. Then, in January 1887, after bribing one of the nurses, Nishigori illegally entered the asylum and left with Tomotane. Incredibly, their first night after the escape was spent in the home of none other than Gotō Shimpei (1857–1912).[29] Gotō was then a promising young official in the Bureau of Hygiene. He would become the head of that office in 1892, and this became a stepping stone to even more prestigious posts: in 1898, he became the governor-general of Japan's colony, Taiwan; in 1906, the president of the Southern

Manchurian Railroad Company; in 1916, home minister; and, in 1918, minister of foreign affairs. Nishigori found a powerful advocate in Gotō, and even after he and Tomotane were discovered Gotō continued to follow the case. He eventually identified numerous irregularities, including the fact that Iwasa Jun had issued a diagnosis without examining Tomotane. In the meantime, however, Tomotane was returned to the Tokyo Public Asylum, where he was again examined by a panel of distinguished physicians. The new diagnosis was "violent dementia" characterized by delusions and periods of frenzied activity. The doctors stated that confinement was not appropriate. In the aftermath of the failed rescue attempt, Tomotane's plight became the object of intense public scrutiny. Nishigori went from newspaper to newspaper, arguing that the charges of madness were a ruse concocted by the Sōma family, which, with the aid of the medical establishment, the police, and the courts, were trying to gain control of the family fortune. Then, in February 1892, Sōma Tomotane died at the age of thirty-nine.

Even after his death, however, newspaper coverage continued unabated as the police investigated charges by Nishigori that Tomotane had been poisoned, the Sōma family sued Gotō and Nishigori for slander, and Gotō Shimpei openly criticized prominent physicians and police officials for their actions in relation to Tomotane. During the ten-year period in which the Sōma Incident was unfolding, Japan's mass media focused obsessively on questions of Tomotane's medical status and the validity of his confinement. In 1889, for example, a book on the topic went through seventeen printings; this was followed by at least ten other works by 1896.[30] The media coverage was overwhelmingly sympathetic to Tomotane, who appears as a tragic hero, championed by Nishigori, a loyal vassal. In contrast, the psychiatric establishment, together with the police and other public officials, were portrayed as cruel and corrupt, capable of imprisoning a man for more than ten years and then perhaps killing him. An object of particular scorn on the part of journalists was the series of conflicting diagnoses that were applied to Tomotane's condition, which were accompanied by differing explanations of the origin of his illness and his prospects for recovery. It was this ambiguity, situated against the claim of "scientific" objectivity, that led journalists to suggest that motives of profit and politics, rather than medical treatment, had led to the confinement of Sōma Tomotane.

Gotō Shimpei explained his championing of Nishigori, a problematic figure that some observers came to view as either a con man who was out to swindle the Sōma family or as delusional himself, as in keeping with his duties as a public health official. He argued that, Nishigori's motives aside, it was necessary for the Bureau of Hygiene to root out corruption within the medical profession, to influence police and judicial procedures that impacted upon medical matters, and to protect individual rights. In 1890, Gotō wrote "Policy toward Mental Illness," in which he argued that the psychiatric profession should be independent of the police and that there had to be legal protection of the rights of the insane (1890). While serving as head of the Bureau of Hygiene in 1892–93 and 1895–98, however, Gotō did nothing to change laws that related to in-home confinement. When the Diet took up the issue of a national law on confinement in 1900, he played no role in the debate, a stance that has led some scholars to argue that Gotō's involvement in the Sōma Incident had more to do with self-promotion than concern for protecting individual liberty (Okada and Yoshioka 1966, 990–92). Certainly Gotō's view of the relative priority of the national body in relation to the individual body is clear. Soon after being appointed head of the Bureau of Hygiene, he gave a speech before a graduating class of medical students in which he declared, "there are three kinds of doctors. The best doctors are those that care for the nation, the middle group care for the medical profession, those at the bottom, care for sick people. You graduates will become the kind of doctors who treat the sick . . . but those like myself care for the nation" (Sawada 1929, 104).

The popular discourse on the Sōma Incident notwithstanding, confinement continued to be posed as the solution to the social problem of madness. The number of mentally ill people subject to home confinement rose dramatically, as did the number of psychiatric hospitals. In 1910, Nagao Setsuzō, writing in the *Tōkyō asahi shimbun* (Tokyo Asahi newspaper), made note of a new development in the urban landscape of Tokyo—the sudden proliferation of new private institutions that billed themselves as "psychiatric hospitals" (*seishin byōin*). This he related to yet another curious new sight. In major train stations such as Shimbashi and Ueno, one often encountered people who had come to the capital from the countryside, leading their mad son or daughter, husband or wife, in order to install them in one of the new asylums of the city. They were met, he noted with irony, by barkers in the employ of these institutions, which competed for this valuable new commodity (1983, 2:173). Nagao's report is only one of many accounts of the asylum that appear in popular discourse after the turn of the century. In 1904, for example, for almost two months, *Yomiuri shimbun* (Yomiuri newspaper) serialized a report entitled "The Darkest Place of Mankind: The Madhouse," which not only detailed conditions within the asylums but also provided graphic descriptions of those within it. Popular magazines, too, offered up the experience of the asylum for the perusal of their readers with articles such as "A Visit to the Tokyo Asylum and the Female Psychiatric Patients I Saw There" and "A Visit to a Psychiatric Hospital."[31]

What is striking about the descriptions of the mad that appear in these articles is how little they seem to rely upon the biological paradigm of madness that had authorized the regime of confinement. A case in point is the description of women patients that appears in the exercise in reportage entitled "A Visit to the Tokyo Asylum and the Female Psychiatric Patients I Saw There," which appeared in *Fujin sekai* (Women's world), a periodical that had an urban, educated, middle-class female readership in 1910. The female asylum residents the author describes bear little resemblance to the hereditary degenerates of biological psychiatry. Rather, one is described as an educated and elegant woman, another as "a graduate of a girl's normal school," and a third as a "graduate of Nihon Jogakkō," a prestigious women's college. And their psychiatric difficulties are related not as the consequence of brain disease, weak nerves, or bad habits but as the understandable response to difficult social situations—an unhappy marriage, a taxing job, or the death of a child.

In works such as these, we discover the emergence of a popular discourse on mental illness that countered what was emanating from the state and psychiatric establishments. Authored by general practitioners, doctors of Chinese medicine, journalists, and laypersons and diffused by means of magazines, newspapers, and the health handbooks known as *eiseibon,* this discourse put forth the notion that modern life—the very modernity the state was pursuing—itself constituted a kind of illness, chronic and debilitating. Modernity, it was said, was the source of a whole range of health problems for the populace, particularly those that had a psychiatric component, with education, factory work, riding in trains, and indeed urban life itself all described as the causes of a decline in health and vitality (Tatsukawa 1986, 53). A similar understanding of mental illness—albeit now rendered in a highly commercialized mode—also ordered the many advertisements for patent medicines found in the popular magazines and newspapers of this period, which claimed effectiveness in treating fatigue, depression, hysteria, and nervousness. Many of these advertisements were directed at students, office workers, and bureaucrats, the elite of the modern age but also those who seemingly suffered most under its weight (Kawamura 1990, 100–121).

In the context of this popular psychiatric discourse, the asylum, too, was subject to reinterpretation. In the fiction of the early 1900s, the asylum and the hospital are represented in terms that contest the view that this institution was necessary to protect the nation from the masses of madmen who threatened it. Rather, it is represented as a place of refuge, a haven, a retreat from the larger society. For example, in "The Story of a Certain Woman," a short story by Shimazaki Tōson, O-Gen, a woman in her sixties, exhausted by the difficulties of family life and feeling herself falling into a state of mental confusion, retreats to an asylum, which she comes to call her *kakurega* (literally, a "hidden home").

Similarly, in the story "The Hospital Window," Ishikawa Takuboku narrates the confusion and isolation of a young man in the city. A newspaper reporter and aspiring poet, he feels increasingly alienated from the world of work and social relationships. Throughout the story, as the man's paranoia and confusion grow, he looks again and again to the window of a certain hospital, which becomes a symbol of comfort and relief. Here, then, the asylum becomes that which protects not society from the madman but the madman from society.

Conclusion: Recovering the Private Body

By the turn of the twentieth century, public health policy in relation to both syphilis and mental illness was firmly in place, and other diseases were now preoccupying the officials within the Bureau of Hygiene, among them tuberculosis and leprosy. But even as names such as O-Raku and Sōma Tomotane passed from the pages of Japan's newspapers, the struggle to define the relationship between the individual body and the nation continued. Beginning around 1900, a new form of popular discourse emerged to contest the public health view of sickness and disease. Authored by some of Japan's most prominent intellectuals, this discourse took the form of what I have termed a "literature of the hospital" (Burns 1997). The texts that comprised this discourse took a variety of forms. Some were posed as sickbed journals or diaries, such as Ozaki Kōyō's *Byōkotsu roku* (A record of my sick body, 1905) and Kunikida Doppo's *Byōshō roku* (A sickbed journal, 1910). Other texts took the form of narratives, such as Tokutomi Roka's *Hototogisu* (The cuckoo, 1899–1900) and Shimazaki Tōson's *Byōin* (Hospital, 1913). A third category of texts includes Nakae Chōmin's *Ichinen yūhan* (A year and a half, 1903), Tsunashima Ryōsen's *Byōkanroku* (A record kept while ill, 1907), and Taoka Reiun's *Byōchū hōrō* (Wandering while ill, 1913). These texts differ from the others in that thematically they do not deal directly with the experience of illness. For example, although the "year and a half" of Chōmin's title refers to the length of time he is told he has to live after he is diagnosed with cancer, the work itself is a collection of essays on social and political topics. Thus, although these works do not attempt to explore the experience of illness, they evoke the hospital as the place of inscription to mark the text as somehow special.

Whatever their form, the texts that constitute the literature of the hospital are ordered by a view of bodily health that stands in marked contrast to that projected by the Bureau of Hygiene. Far from representing sickness as a threat to public order, the social good, and national wealth and power, these works characterize it as a privileged state that removes one from the mundane world of work and social responsibilities. Here the experience of confinement is not stigmatized but in fact valorized because it allows a measure of introspection and self-reflection not otherwise available. Thus, within the literature of the hospital the body is represented, or rather recovered, as a "private" space. It is precisely this notion of the "private body" that we discover in Masaoka Shiki's sickroom journal, which was originally serialized day by day in the newspaper *Nihon* (Japan). The journal opens with the words "this bed of mine, six feet long, it is my world" (1992, 106). A similar view of illness as liberation orders Kunikida Doppo's journal *Byōshō roku* (A sickbed journal), written within a sanitarium as the author was dying of tuberculosis. Doppo echoed Shiki when he declared, "the hospital is not a prison, it is a kind of small universe. It is the world. It is man no matter where he is who creates the world." It is the celebration of himself as subject that becomes the object of this text, as Doppo turns again and again to speak of "I myself," "my heart," "I Kunikida Doppo." "See me in your eyes, hear me with your ears, know me with your heart," he tells the reader at one point. "It is my body that rests grandly for all to see here upon this hospital bed" (1976, 19, 35).

The literature of the hospital, like the journalistic reports of the 1880s and 1890s, the reportage on the asylum, the health handbooks, and Kafū's stories, all reveal that the people of Japan were never passive before or merely subject to the discourse of public health and its vision of the national body. Rather, these texts engaged the state discourse on health and disease through overt critique, satire, and appropriation. By means of these strategies, the writers of these texts, as well as those who read them, succeeded in assigning to their bodies meanings that called into question and thereby subverted the state's attempts to say what the body was and what it could do. In the end there emerged no single "national body" but multiple visions of both "nations" and "bodies."

NOTES

1. William Johnston (1995, 179–80) notes that Nagayo chose the term *eisei* because the Chinese character for *ei* originally meant to "police" or "patrol." Thus, in his understanding, *hygiene* meant "to police life."

2. The classic works on the rise of public health are Rosen 1993 and Shryock 1948.

3. For comparative studies of the development of public health, see Fee and Porter 1992 and Ramsey 1994.

4. W. G. Beasley (1987) characterizes the treaty port system in this way. The term *informal imperialism* originated with Fray (1940, 399) and was adopted by Gallagher and Robinson (1953). It also provides the framework for Duus et al. 1989.

5. Nagasaki became an open port in 1855 when the Bakufu signed a treaty with Russia. This was the first treaty to include a provision for extraterritoriality. A second treaty

with Russia, signed in 1857, allowed for carefully regulated trade. The Harris Commercial Treaty of 1858 gave Americans access to trade at Nagasaki as well, and it was followed by similar treaties signed with the Dutch, Russians, British, and French. On the creation of the treaty ports, see Beasley 1989 and Hoare 1994.

6. The statistics are from Tatsukawa 1971, 179.

7. On the 1858 epidemic, see Tatsukawa 1979, 177–205, and Yamamoto 1982, 14–27.

8. In her analysis of bubonic plague in China, Carol Benedict (1996, chap. 4) notes a similar division between the "medical" and "popular" understanding of disease.

9. On such practices, see Hiruta 1985, especially chap. 3.

10. On this issue, see Yamamoto 1982, 552–84. It was not until 1899 that the Meiji government succeeded in securing the right to inspect incoming ships.

11. Holland, then the only country that had relations with Japan, donated a steamship and sent twenty-two officers and crewmen to teach at the school. The student body numbered about two hundred.

12. Nagayo was the son of a long line of physicians who had served Omura-domain in Kyushu. At age seventeen, he was sent to Osaka to study at the Tekijuku, the school of "Dutch Learning" (the term used to designate all forms of knowledge that originated in Europe) founded by Ogata Kōan in 1838. From Osaka, he traveled to Nagasaki to study with Pompe. For a biographical sketch of Nagayo, see Janetta 1997, 151–60.

13. Originally entitled *Vijf jaren in Japan* (Five years in Japan), Pompe's memoirs have been translated into Japanese (as Numata and Arase 1968).

14. Matsumoto was born in 1832 as the second son of a Tokugawa vassal named Satō Taizen. About the time of Matsumoto's birth, his father became interested in the new discipline of Dutch Learning. After a time studying in a school in Edo, he traveled to Nagasaki, the premier site for the study of Dutch Learning because of the presence of the Dutch traders there. Satō eventually founded his own school of Dutch Learning, the Juntendō, which together with the Tekijuku in Osaka was one of the premier schools of Dutch Learning. As a teenager, Jun, or Junnosuke, as he was then known, was adopted into the Matsumoto family, which for more than 150 years had served as physicians in the shogun's household. In 1858, he traveled to Nagasaki to receive medical training from Pompe. See Ogawa and Sakai 1980, 216–17.

15. The medical policy of 1874 is included in Kōseishō imukyoku 1955, 477–82.

16. A listing of the various laws and edicts associated with the establishment of the "pleasure quarters" in Edo can be found in Yamamoto 1994, 5–15.

17. On the concept of degeneration, see Shorter 1997, 93–99.

18. For an exhaustive survey of Meiji period works on psychiatry, see Kaneko Junji 1965.

19. Maudsley (1835–1918) was professor of psychiatry at University College Hospital, editor of the *Journal of Mental Science,* founder of the Maudsley Hospital, and a prolific writer on mental medicine. Showalter (1985) describes him as "dominating" English psychiatry.

20. *Tōkyō iji shimbun* 54 (Tokyo medical newspaper, 5 April 1879): 16.

21. Ibid., 65 (11 June 1879): 8–9.

22. Ibid., 85 (1 November 1879): 23–34; 89 (6 December 1879): 18.

23. These journals were *Iji shimbun* (Medical news, nos. 147–48); *Chūgai shimbō*

(National and international news, nos. 417–20); *Tōkyō iji zasshi* (Tokyo medical journal, no. 317); and *Kampō* (Civil service news, nos. 469–70).

24. The characterization of Kraepelin's thought as "revolutionary" is from Shorter 1997, 105. Kraepelin's work is discussed on pages 99–109.

25. An annotated text of Kure's preface is included in Kaneko 1965, 73–80. The quoted passage is from page 75.

26. For the text of this policy, see Kōseishō imukyoku 1955, 391–92.

27. The following summary of the course of the "Sōma Incident" and of Nishigori Takekiyo's charges is based on my reading of contemporary newspaper coverage, as well as the summary provided in Okada 1981, 117–24.

28. One of the strangest—and most hotly contested—aspects of the Sōma Incident was Nishigori's claim that if Tomotane was mad it was because his family had conspired to marry him to a woman physically incapable of engaging in sexual relations.

29. On Gotō's involvement, see Okada and Yoshioka 1966, 990–92; Sawada 1929, chaps. 5–6; and Fukuda 1943, chap. 6.

30. This popular work was Nishigori Takekiyo's *Kami mo hotoke mo nai yami no yō no naka* (In a dark world without god or buddha, 1889).

31. The former (Anon. 1910a) appeared in *Josei sekai* (Women's world) 4, no. 10, and the latter (Anon. 1910b) in *Jogaku sekai* (Women's study world) 9, no. 6.

Discourses of Empowerment: Missionary Orientalism in the Development of Dravidian Nationalism

V. Ravindiran

The mental eyes of everyone must be opened not only to see that the present miserable condition of their life has been due to the spell cast on them by Brahmin witchcraft, but also to realise the great truth common to all great religions, that is: all are the children of one Heavenly Father.

—Maraimalai Adigal (1925)

Edward Said's *Orientalism* continues to have a profound influence on recent conceptions of and scholarship on Asia and Africa. His thesis that European orientalism was more a discourse of European power over the Orient than a "veridic discourse about the Orient" (1978, 6) has gained many noted adherents (e.g., Viswanathan 1989; Inden 1990; Dirks 1987; Chatterjee 1986; Prakash 1990). While the work inspired by Said has yielded fresh insights, it has also tended to encourage a rather simplistic understanding of the European colonial encounter and the scholarly undertaking known as orientalism. In its crudest form, this analysis presents both the encounter and orientalism as nearly total hegemonic projects in which all classes of the colonized lost not only their self-determination but also, more importantly, their power to construct their own "true" identities or imagine their own "real" histories and nations, resulting in "errant" identities and "derivative" nationalisms (see Chatterjee 1986; also Nandy 1983). By foregrounding the interests and imperatives of the colonizers in the production of orientalist knowledge, this perspective serves to mask the interests and complicity of local power groups, the earlier histories of their dominance, and their discourses of power in the production of that knowledge. Thus, such scholarship unwittingly, and perhaps ironically, paints a view of colonized regions as culturally and socially homogeneous, with little internal cultural or class struggles and contradictions, at least until the advent of European hegemony.

Recent revisionist scholarship has noted that this approach affords little agency to the colonized and, more importantly, fails to take into account the collusion between orientalist knowledge and power that existed within the "Orient" long before European colonialism (see especially Pollock 1993; Irschick 1994). This essay contributes to this revisionist interrogation of the Saidian perspective by analyzing the role that missionary orientalism played in the development of Dravidian nationalism in South India. Through its efforts to subvert the dominant school of orientalism in Hindu India, missionary orientalism affords a particularly illuminating lens through which to observe the dynamics of orientalist knowledge production on India. Far from being a hegemonic "colonialist imposition" upon a passive "Orient," European orientalism was dependent upon and responsive to the discourses of locally dominant groups and reflected many of their visions and interests. Similarly, far from being passive victims of orientalism, dominant groups in the colonies actively participated in the construction, maintenance, and propagation of orientalist knowledge (see also Schmitthenner 1991; Trautmann 1997). "Local" power dynamics and struggles, and not only colonial imperatives, must be taken seriously when looking at the production of cultural knowledge, whether that knowledge be European orientalism, "pre-British Orientalism" (Pollock 1993), or even postcolonial scholarship. This chapter contends that European orientalism must be viewed as a more complex, multifaceted, and contradictory set of discourses than the Saidian perspective has acknowledged.

Discovering "Dravidian"

Dravidian nationalism[1] began gaining momentum in South India at the beginning of the twentieth century in opposition to the dominant discourse of Indian nationalism. Its emergence affords a significant example not only of the complicity of missionary orientalism in the process of identity construction and nationalism in South India but, more importantly, of its role in empowering subordinate groups or communities there. Ideologically, Dravidian nationalism posited a parallel but counter discourse to the dominant "orientalist" construction of India as Aryan and Sanskritic. Its ideological origins can be traced not only to the historical tensions that existed between Sanskritic and local vernacular cultures in South India but to the modern reconfigured articulation of these tensions inspired by missionary orientalism (Ravindiran 1996). The missionaries were impelled in this project by their belief that Brahmanism and the caste system posed the greatest obstacles to Christian conversion in South India. They drew both their inspiration and their justification for this project from earlier resistance to Brahmanical culture found in ancient and medieval Tamil literary works.

Missionary orientalism embraced and supported local vernacular languages and cultures of South India in opposition to those of Sanskrit, inspiring a significant body of scholarship that proposed the existence of an ancient and once "pure" Dravidian culture free from Brahmanism that needed to be recovered and reclaimed. Alleging that the Aryan/Sanskritic[2] culture of the Brahmans had corrupted this Dravidian culture, they called for the recovery of the latter. Many elements that now constitute Dravidian nationalist ideology derived from this anti-Brahman missionary orientalism.

There were at least two key "moments" in the evolution of Dravidian nationalist ideology. The first consisted of the efforts to present Tamil and other South Indian languages and speakers as having a genealogy distinct from those of the Indo-Aryan linguistic family and its speakers in India. It is exemplified in the pioneering philological work of Rev. Robert Caldwell (1814–91), *A Comparative Grammar of the Dravidian or South Indian Family of Languages* ([1856] 1974). Caldwell not only coined the word *Dravidian* to describe the languages and peoples of South India, but he also constructed, with the aid of the modern disciplines of philology, archaeology, and history, a genealogy for Dravidian languages, culture, and people marked by their opposition to their Aryan/Brahman counterparts. His work provided a significant "scientific" bulwark against the privileging of a Brahmanical vision of India prevalent in his time. It also provided the rising classes of non-Brahmans in South India with a significant ideological weapon against Brahman sociocultural and intellectual hegemony.[3] His use of the term *Dravidian* came to have an enormous appeal for these people by providing a single category under which all the linguistically disparate non-Brahman caste groups in South India could unite (Sivathamby 1993, 28).

Caldwell's work had a phenomenal impact, for aside from laying the ideological foundation for Dravidian nationalism it opened up a whole field of scholarly inquiry into things "Dravidian." After Caldwell's achievement, others launched a search for a distinctly "Dravidian" religion and culture. This was the beginning of the second key moment in the evolution of Dravidian ideology. European scholar-administrators and missionaries were again in the forefront in raising the issue of a distinctly Dravidian religion in the orientalist scholarship of the time. Although Caldwell had dismissed the religion of the Dravidians as "demonolatry" overlain with a thin veneer of Brahmanism, other European Christian missionaries and scholar-administrators searched for and found in the ancient Tamil and other vernacular religious and literary works evidence of an ethical and religious system that was in their eyes more compatible with the Christian tradition (Gover [1871] 1959).

The major impulse in much of the missionary support for a distinctly Dravidian religion, again, was their antipathy toward Brahmanism and what was considered to be its latest manifestation, neo-Vedantism. Neo-Vedantism by the late nineteenth century in South India had come to be considered by many Christian missionaries and Dravidian ideologues as the new liberal face of a resurgent Brahmanism in India. Working against the ascendancy of neo-Vedantism among English-educated Hindus that had been in part promoted by orientalist scholarship, some Christian missionary scholars working in South India sought to promote what they considered to be a distinctly Dravidian religious tradition.

This second key moment involved the identification and resurrection of a Dravidian religion, which came to be identified as Saiva Siddhanta.[4] It is best exemplified in the writings of pioneer revivalists who forged an "inviolable" link between Saivite and Dravidian identity. In the writings of advocates such as the Protestant missionary George Pope, pioneer Tamil ideologues such as P. Sundaram Pillai, J. M. Nallaswami Pillai, and Maraimalai Adigal, Saiva Siddhanta became the original and "true" religion of the Dravidians. In fact, the Dravidian ideology derived much of its indigenous impetus and resonance from its association with a Saivite identity. As most of the early indigenous intellectuals in South India who embraced the Dravidian ideology were Tamil Saivites, the Dravidian movement began largely as an integral part of the Saiva Siddhanta revival movement. These ideologues utilized the Christian missionary vision of a unique Dravidian language, culture, and religion to present Saiva Siddhanta as a distinctly Dravidian religion. In so doing, they clearly disrupted an earlier vision of a less racially defined or caste-bound Saiva Siddhanta tradition.

The First Key Moment: The Separation of Brahmans and Non-Brahmans

Although Caldwell was the first to give systematic articulation to Dravidian ideology, elements can be traced to an earlier missionary orientalism in South India, notably to the writings of European scholar-administrators associated with the "Madras school."[5] Early South Indian missionaries such as Abbé

Dubois (1816) had legitimized their staunch anti-Brahmanism by referring to evidence of anti-Brahmanism in the vernacular literary traditions of South India.[6] Dubois had once observed: "The Hindoos may be divided into two classes—the imposters and the dupes. The latter include the bulk of the population of India; and the former is composed of the whole tribe of Brahmins" (cited in Hough 1824, 2). Scholar-administrators associated with the Madras school of orientalism such as Francis Whyte Ellis (d. 1819) and C. P. Brown (1798–1894) also laid much of the groundwork for Caldwell.[7] In fact, it is becoming increasingly clear that South Indian missionaries and European scholar-administrators associated with the Madras school played a significant role in the modern renaissance of South Indian vernacular languages and their associated cultural nationalisms in general.[8]

Robert Caldwell was one of the most dedicated scholar-missionaries of nineteenth-century South India (Stock 1899, 319). Hailing from a Scottish Presbyterian family of fairly modest means, he joined the London Missionary Society (LMS) at the age of nineteen. After obtaining his B.A. from the University of Glasgow, he sailed for Madras in 1837 as a missionary for the LMS. From 1837 until his death in 1891 he toiled as a missionary in South India, working among lower-caste Hindus. In 1841, he left the LMS and joined the Society for the Propagation of the Gospel (SPG). It was also in that year that he moved to the southerly Tamil district of Tinnevelly and began working amongst a caste known as the Shanars, a people whose traditional occupation as climbers of the palmyra tree gave them fairly low status in the caste hierarchy.

Aside from his regular duties as a missionary, Caldwell spent a great deal of time and effort as a scholar. In fact, much of his missionary zeal seems to have been directed into his research.[9] Although there are hints of a Dravidian ideology in Caldwell's earlier work on the Tinnevelly Shanars (1850), it was through his *Comparative Grammar* that he systematically laid the foundation of Dravidian ideology. A painstaking and brilliant work, it reflects both Caldwell's knowledge of a vast number of languages and his wide knowledge of history, archaeology, and ethnology. It was not so much the philological findings in the work that had such a profound impact as the way Caldwell interpreted and expressed them in the lengthy introduction and appendix. He not only managed to erect a racial, linguistic, and religio-cultural divide between the minority Brahman and majority non-Brahman (Dravidian) population of South India, but also proposed a systematic project for reclaiming and recovering an ancient and "pure" Dravidian language and culture.

Caldwell's work was timely. Keenly aware of the "state of knowledge" about India at the time and sensitive to the great lacuna in that knowledge with regard to South India, he sought to fill this gap in a way that was acutely sensitive and responsive to the deep fissures and contradictions in South Indian society and culture. His theory of a separate and independent racial, linguistic, and cultural origin for the non-Brahman South Indians, whom he had styled the Dravidian people, served to defend and celebrate Dravidian languages, peoples, and cultures at a time when the Aryan/Brahman language, people, and culture held center stage as the sole custodians of Indian culture.

Caldwell justified coining the word *Dravidian* to denote both the South Indian languages and the non-Brahman peoples as follows:

> The word I have chosen is "Dravidian," a word which has already been used as a generic appellation of this family of tongues by the Sanskrit geographers. Properly speaking, the term "Dravida" denotes the Tamil country alone. . . . A Dravida is defined in the Sanskrit lexicons to be "a man of an outcaste tribe." . . . This name was doubtless applied by the Brahminical inhabitants of Northern India to the aborigines of the extreme South and is evidence of the low estimation in which they were originally held. ([1856] 1974, 26–27)

In coining the word *Dravidian,* Caldwell posed it in opposition to a northern Brahman identity and in the process highlighted the word's subaltern association, "a man of an outcaste tribe." By this very definition, Caldwell not only deftly established a divide between the Brahmans and the non-Brahman peoples of South India but also gave the term a subversive potential. He thus created the conceptual basis for a "Dravidian" cultural/religious identity with an accompanying history—and even for a Dravidian nation.

Caldwell's central argument was that Dravidian languages, peoples, and cultures had a genealogy independent of those of the Brahmans. This independence and difference followed, he argued, from the fact that the Dravidians were of a completely different racial stock, what he called a Scythian stock. Utilizing largely philological evidence, Caldwell asserted that the Dravidians were descendants of an ancient Scythian race from central and high Asia who had come to India long before the coming of the Indo-Aryans. This radical distinction underpinned Caldwell's celebration of Dravidian "identity." Like many of his contemporaries, he believed that the supposedly superior racial and intellectual ability of the Indo-Aryans made them responsible for the higher civilization of India. Nevertheless, in his view Dravidian languages and civilization were not as poor as previously considered by Western orientalists and Brahmans. Although the Dravidians may have obtained elements of their higher civilization from Brahman colonists, those benefits were far outweighed by the evil customs the Brahmans had brought with them. Writing of Dravidian civilization prior to the arrival of the Brahmans, Caldwell notes that the Dravidians "in many things were centuries behind the Brahmans whom they revered as instructors and obeyed as overseers: but if they had been left altogether to themselves, it is open to dispute whether they would not now be in a much better condition at least in point of morals than they are." He continues:

> The mental culture and the higher civilization which they derived from the Brahmins, have, I fear, been more than counterbalanced by the fossil-ising caste rules, the unpractical pantheistic philosophy, and the cumbersome routine of inane ceremonies, which were introduced amongst them by the guides of their new social state. ([1856] 1974, 79)

As we shall see later, Caldwell's attribution to the Brahmans of the evils of the caste system, together with the pantheistic and ritualistic aspects of Hinduism, were avidly taken up by later Dravidian ideologues.

Caldwell contended that Dravidians did have elements of civilization that, though simple, were free of many of the evils of Brahmanism. The religion of the ancient Dravidians, he argued, was demonolatry or a type of shamanism much like the religious practices associated with the ancient Scythians. It was a practice that he believed was later integrated into Brahmanism with the arrival of the Brahmans in South India:

> It is the peculiar policy of the Brahmins to render all the religious systems of India subservient to their purpose by making friends of them all. . . . Thus Brahminism yields and conquers, and hence, though the demon worship of Tinnevelly is as far as possible repugnant to the genius of orthodox Hinduism . . . yet even it has received a place in the cunningly devised mosaic of the Brahmins, and the devils have got themselves regarded as abnormal developments of the gods. (1857, 41)

This kind of missionary critique of Brahmanical Hinduism later became popular with many Dravidian ideologues.

Although the ostensible aim of the *Comparative Grammar* was to present Caldwell's philological research on South Indian languages, he also utilized the work to comment on Dravidian origins, literature, history, peoples, religions, and even physical types. When asserting the independence and purity of Tamil, he made use of the opportunity to introduce the idea that Brahmanism was alien to the Dravidians:

Tamil can readily dispense with the greater part or the whole of its Sanskrit, and by dispensing with it rises to a purer and more refined style. . . . Of the entire number of words which are contained in this formula there is only one which could not be expressed with faultless propriety . . . in equivalent of pure Dravidian origin: that word is "graven image" or "idol!" Both word and thing are foreign to primitive Tamil usages and habits of thought; and were introduced into the Tamil country by the Brahmins, with the Puranic system of religion and the worship of idols. ([1856] 1974, 32–33)

Caldwell colored his construction of Dravidian civilization with anti-Brahman sentiments. He argued that "few Brahmins have written anything worthy of preservation" in Tamil. "The language has been cultivated and developed with immense zeal and success by native Tamilian Sudras; and the highest rank in Tamil literature which has been reached by a Brahmin is that of a commentator" ([1856] 1974, 31–33). Caldwell chose to foreground what appeared to be an insulting *varna* designation given to the powerful non-Brahman Sudra castes of South India by the classical Brahmanical legal texts:

The application of the term "Sudra," to the ancient Dravidian chieftains, soldiers, and cultivators may prove that the Brahmins, whilst pretending to do them an honour, treated them with contempt. . . . The Brahmins who came in peaceably, and obtained the kingdom by flatteries, may probably have persuaded the Dravidians, that in calling them Sudras, they were conferring upon them a title of honour. If so, their policy was perfectly successful. ([1856] 1974, 77)

Caldwell's writings on the "Dravidian physical type" indicate his sensitivity to the aspirations of the rising non-Brahman, English-educated classes of South India as well as his desire to appeal to their sensitivities. Caldwell started his section on the Dravidian physical type by quoting at length the description of Dravidian physical features by B. H. Hodgson: "A practised eye will distinguish at a glance between the Arian and Tamulian style of features and form." According to Hodgson: "In the Arian form there is height, symmetry, lightness and flexibility. . . . In the Tamulian form, on the contrary, there is less height, less symmetry, more dumpiness and flesh" (Caldwell [1856] 1974, 506–7). After arguing against this sort of unflattering description of Dravidian physical features, Caldwell asserted:

When we compare the physical type of cultivated, high caste Dravidians with that of the Brahmins, no essential difference . . . can be observed. In many instances the features of the high-caste Dravidian women are more delicately formed and more regular than those of Brahmin women themselves, whilst their complexions are at least equally fair. . . . The Dravidian type of head will even bear directly to be compared with the European. (510–11)

Caldwell further used both philological and ethnological arguments for considering even the lowest-ranked groups of South India such as the Paraiyars to be of the same category as the Dravidians since they were the descendants of the same original race. Only the Brahmans were excepted (490–501).

Caldwell's National History

Caldwell's lengthy introduction to the *Comparative Grammar* reads like a national history of the non-Brahman peoples of South India. In subchapters with titles such as "Pre-Aryan Civilization of the Dravidians," "Political and Social Relations of the Primitive Dravidians to the Pre-Aryan Inhabitants of Northern India," and "Relative Antiquity of Dravidian Literature," Caldwell repeatedly conveyed his underlying message that the ancient Dravidian culture and literary works were more "pure" when compared with the contemporary state of Tamil language, literature, and culture, which had been "corrupted" by Brahmanical culture. Caldwell was essentially proposing a mandate for the "Dravidians" to reclaim their languages and culture from the "pernicious" influences of Sanskrit and Brahmanism.

Caldwell even used the word *nationalism* to describe earlier periods in the Tamil region. In a section entitled "Priority of the Literary Cultivation of Tamil," he privileged the "Shen Tamil," or high Tamil, of ancient times over contemporary colloquial Tamil. Describing "Shen Tamil," he observed: "High Tamil contains less Sanskrit, not more, than the colloquial dialect. It affects purism and national independence; and its refinements are all *ab intra*" ([1856] 1974, 54). Caldwell throughout the work exalted earlier Tamil eras, such as the Jaina period, as times free of Sanskrit and Brahmanism when "nationalistic" currents were ascendent:

The period of the pre-dominance of the Jainas (a predominance in intellect and learning—rarely a predominance in political power) was the Augustan-age of Tamil literature, the period when the Madura College, a celebrated literary association, flourished, and when the *Cural,* the *Chin-tamani,* and the classical vocabularies and grammars were written. Through the intense Tamilic nationalism of the adherents of this school, and their jealousy of Brahminical influence, the Sanskrit derivatives which are employed in their writings are very considerably altered. (56)

Caldwell's purpose in citing such examples was to convey an anti-Brah-man "Tamilic nationalism." Caldwell credited "the Jainas of the old Pandiya country" with "a national and anti-Brahmanical feeling of peculiar strength; and it is chiefly to them that Tamil is indebted for its higher culture and its comparative independence from Sanskrit" (84). His practice of utilizing earlier Tamil history to justify a Dravidian revival that was anti-Brahman became the model followed by later Dravidian ideologues. This strategy became increasingly effective and popular as more and more ancient Tamil literary works were rediscovered and published in the latter part of the nineteenth century. Caldwell ended with a hopeful message for the Dravidians, which sounds much like a call to arms:

> Now that native education has commenced to make real progress, and the advantages of European knowledge . . . are becoming known . . . it may be expected that the Dravidian mind will ere long be roused from its lethargy, and stimulated to enter upon a brighter career. If the national mind and heart were stirred to so great a degree a thousand years ago by the diffusion of Jainism . . . it is reasonable to expect still more important results from the propagation of the grand and soul-stirring truths of Christianity. . . . The hitherto uncultivated minds of the lower and far more numerous classes of the Hindu community, are now for the first time in history brought within the range of humanising and elevating influences. A virgin soil is now for the first time being ploughed . . . and in process of time we may reasonably expect to reap a rich crop of intellectual and moral results. (90)

The use of such terms as the *Dravidian mind* and the *national mind* and the references to the education of the "lower and far more numerous classes" suggest that Caldwell was writing with a certain expectant mandate for the "Dravidians."

Caldwell in his magnum opus thus managed to construct a genealogy for the non-Brahman peoples of South India that presented them as having an origin and identity different from those of the Brahmans. Moreover, he proposed to the Dravidians a mandate to recover their culture from the supposedly pernicious influence of Brahmans, Brahmanism, and Sanskritic culture—a people and culture that had been part of South Indian history and culture for at least a millennium. Caldwell's legacy to the rising non-Brahman, English-educated classes of South India was an orientalist foundation for their emerging identity as a nation.

The Second Key Moment: Linking Dravidian Ideology with Saiva Siddhanta

Caldwell's philological work had a tremendous impact on orientalist scholarship on South India. In the preface to the second edition of the *Comparative Grammar*, published in 1875, Caldwell provided a four-page list of books and articles "bearing directly or indirectly" on Dravidian philology that had appeared since the first edition ([1856] 1974, xxxvi–xl), evidence that a spate of ancient Tamil literary and religious works in translation were appearing in his wake. These rediscovered works were often presented in glowing terms and compared favorably with Sanskrit works and the best classical and religious writings in other languages. Many of the earliest endeavors were undertaken by missionaries and colonial officials (Gundert 1869; Gover [1871] 1959; Pope 1886, [1893] 1984). Most of these European exponents, apart from praising such works, also foregrounded them as the unique products of the Dravidian mind and civilization. Thus, by the late nineteenth century a solid scholarly foundation for a Tamil/Dravidian literary and cultural renaissance was firmly in place.

One of the earliest Tamil intellectuals to embrace and "indigenize" Dravidian ideology was P. Sundaram Pillai, who belonged to the higher non-Brahman Tamil/Saivite Vellalar caste. It was he, along with his missionary supporters and Saivite followers, who effected the second moment in the evolution of Dravidian ideology by forging an "inviolable link" between a Dravidian and a Saivite/Tamil identity. Their work played a crucial role in presenting Saivite religion—a religion strongly associated with the Tamils since at least the medieval period—as a uniquely Dravidian religion. But before we look at this indigenization of Dravidian ideology led by non-Brahman Tamils it would be instructive to look at the writings of a missionary orientalist who not only advocated Saiva Siddhanta as a Dravidian religion but played a significant role in entrenching and elaborating the Dravidian ideology proposed by Caldwell.

George Uglow Pope (1820–1907), also from Scotland, was one of the most prolific and influential missionary exponents of Tamil religious and literary works. He came to Madras as a Wesleyan missionary in 1839. Like Caldwell, Pope joined the SPG in 1841 and was assigned to work in the southerly rural Tamil district of Sawyerpuram. Pope, too, was a scholar-missionary who quickly mastered the Tamil language. He was in South India around the same time as Caldwell and at least on one occasion in the 1840s cooperated with Caldwell in opposition to the anti-Christian activities of a Hindu revivalist organization (Stock 1899, 319). Caldwell in turn acknowledged the valuable help of Pope in the *Comparative Grammar* (Caldwell [1856] 1974, xiv).

Pope left India in 1882 and from 1885 held the post of professor of Tamil and Telugu at Oxford University. It was after his move to England that he began to undertake in earnest the work of popularizing and disseminating Tamil religious and literary works through translation, in particular those that strongly endorsed and espoused a Dravidian ideology. The intellectual roots of Pope's espousal of the Dravidian ideology can be traced to his edited translation of the French missionary Abbé Dubois's pioneering critical study of Hinduism, first published in 1816. Pope published his own version of Dubois's famous work in 1879 under the title *A Description of the Character, Manners, and Customs of the People of India*. Dubois at the end of a long and largely fruitless career as a missionary had concluded that the prospect of converting the Hindus was bleak. He was particularly pessimistic regarding the conversion of higher castes and saw the conversion of the lowest or outcastes as the only prospect for Christianity. The resistance of the higher castes he blamed on resurgent intellectual Hinduism, which he termed "Brahminical prejudice" (Beauchamp 1906, xxv–xxvi).

Pope's edition of Dubois's work ends with a chapter entitled "On the Sect of the Jains and the Principal Differences between Them and the Brahmins." In this text, Dubois foregrounds the oppositional relationship between the Jaina religion and Brahmanism:

> In the progress of time, the true religion [Jainism] was gradually abused in different essential points; and abominations, corruptions and superstitions of every kind have usurped its place. The Brahmins who gained the ascendant, swerved from all the old religious maxims . . . substituting in their place a monstrous combination in which there cannot be seen a trace of the primitive doctrine. ([1879] 1989, 394)

Dubois's description of Jainism and its corruption by Brahmanism reads much like the explanations offered by later Protestant missionaries and Dravidian ideologues regarding the corruption of the "Dravidian" languages and religion by Brahmans. It confirms that missionaries such as Caldwell and Pope were following an earlier tradition of critical missionary scholarship on Hinduism. The Jains had opposed the Brahmanical innovations and so "preserved in purity the pristine religion of the country" (Pope 1879, 395). Dubois's writings on Jainism and its anti-Brahmanism resembled Pope's own later advocacy of Saiva Siddhanta and the Tamil language in opposition to Brahmanism and Sanskrit.

In his preface to Dubois's work, one can see Pope's awareness of the complex developments within Hinduism. He was willing to consider certain schools within Hinduism as either similar to Christianity or having had an original Christian inspiration. His awareness of such complex developments itself anticipates and explains the kind of intervention he hoped to make within Hinduism. It explains his later active support for Saiva Siddhanta in opposition to Brahmanism and neo-Vedanta as the "real" religion of the Tamils. He also emphasized dialogue with the Hindus, arguing that it was the lack of real knowledge and intercourse with the Hindus that had prevented Christianity from making a greater impact:

> I am not indeed disposed to consider the Hindus to be the apathetic, unchanging people they have often been represented to be. The career of Chaitanya in Bengal and of Nanak in Punjab . . . shew that the Hindus are not . . . by any means slow to take in new ideas and to attach themselves to new systems. We have found them apathetic, for we have not striven to interest and arouse them, and have not, in many cases, studied them or their books with sufficient care, to enable us to talk with them mind to mind. Between them and us there has been a great gulf fixed. How shall it be bridged over? (1879, xxiii)

Pope's reference to the reformist figures Chaitanya and Nanak reveals his admiration and support for this strand within Hinduism. Both had led movements that were anti-Brahmanical and to some extent anticaste. Pope's later encouragement of Saivite Bhakti literature and Saiva Siddhanta is understandable when seen in this light. Thus, as early as 1879 Pope believed that Christianity could make an impact through a deeper exploration and perhaps selective encouragement of certain strands within Hinduism. Pope ends his preface to Dubois's work with an earnest appeal, one that reveals not only his mission but his approach to reforming Tamil society:

> To revive a decaying civilization is confessedly difficult; yet with all the resources of Western science, all the means and appliances of British wealth, power and influence and, above all, with a religion which breathes into all who receive it in sincerity . . . we ought to—we certainly must—effect [this revival] among the races of whose manners and customs this work gives so true and lively a picture. (1879, xxi)

Pope's first major intellectual and cultural intervention in the Tamil religio-cultural world was through the English translation of a popular Tamil ethical treatise, *The "Sacred" Kurral of Tiruvalluva-Nayanar,* first published in 1886.
He began his introduction by observing that the fame of Tiruvalluvar, "the
weaver of Mayilapur," "belongs to South India alone and to only one great race
there. He is the venerated sage and lawgiver of the Tamil people," thereby linking the great *Kurral* to the "one great race," the Tamils. He also noted that "that
which above all is wonderful about the *Kurral* is the fact that its author
addresses himself, without regard to caste, peoples or beliefs, to the whole community of mankind; the fact that he formulates sovereign morality and
absolute reason" (Pope 1886, i). Pope thus attributed the *Kurral's* broad appeal
to all Tamils and its affinity with the ethical teachings of Christianity to its
absence of caste ideology. With the same kind of logic, Pope proposed a nationalistic mandate for Tamils:

> The Tamil race preserves many of its old virtues, and has the promise of a
> noble future. Their English friends, in teaching them all that the West has
> to impart, will find little to unteach in the moral lessons of the *Kurral*
> rightly understood.... So far, then, we may call this Tamil poet Christian.
> (xxi)

For Pope, the friends of the Tamils were the English, and it was the task of these
English friends to guide the "Tamil race":

> To understand [the] Tamil, to free him from mistaken glosses, to teach his
> works, to correct their teachings where it is misleading, and to supplement
> where it is defective, would seem to be the duty of all who are friends of
> the race that glories in the possession of this poetical masterpiece. (xxi)

Pope called on the English to support Dravidian civilization for what he
regarded as its Christian elements and its difference from Brahmanical ideology. As he wrote in the introduction to the *Kurral,* "The truth seems to be that
the Madura school of Tamil literature, now too full of Sanskrit influences, was
supreme till the advent of the St.Thome poet" (iv). Sanskrit culture is thus the
Other of Tamil literature, and Christianity is its ally. In this study, Pope also utilized the *Kurral* to promote the writing of "Pure Tamil," which meant ridding
the language of Sanskrit words that had accreted over the years. The *Kurral,* he
claimed, is "a well of Tamil undefiled" (xv–xvi).

Pope's next major work, published in 1893, was a translation with commentary of a popular ancient Tamil classic, the *Naladi-Nannuru* (Four Hundred Quatrains). He declared that the work "reflects the thoughts and ideas of a great mass of the Tamil people, and indeed of the yeomanry of India . . . and is often called the *Vellalar-Vetham*," that is, the "Veda of the Cultivators of the Soil" (Pope [1893] 1984, viii). The Vellalars were the most powerful non-Brahman landholding caste of the Tamil region and were the first to embrace the Dravidian ideology. By choosing a work that was popular with them, Pope aimed to have an impact on these powerful non-Brahman castes. In his introduction, he drew a parallel between the work of the Christian missionaries for the Tamil language and that of the Jains. He also identified the Saivite tradition as the most recent guardian and repository of the Tamil language:

> These verses, mainly but not, I think, exclusively of Jain origin, were doubtless expurgated by the Caivas [Saivites], under whose chief guardianship Tamil literature has since remained. . . . Perhaps the Jains fostered the vernaculars partly out of opposition to the Brahmins. Reformers and missionaries who generally address themselves to the intelligent middle classes, have often been the most assiduous students and promoters of the vulgar tongues. Quatrain 243 of the Naladi shows the feeling of hostility that existed between the North and the South: between Hindus and Jains. The great antiquity of Tamil which is the one worthy rival of Sanskrit, is abundantly plain. (x)

Here Pope carried the ideas of Dubois much further by identifying the Saivites as the "chief guardian(s)" of Tamil literature after the Jains. Indeed, Pope is best remembered for his vigorous support of Saiva Siddhanta as a uniquely Dravidian religion. He seems to have supported Saiva Siddhanta for the same reasons that he championed the Tamil ethical treatise, the *Tirukkural*. He saw in both an alternative religious philosophy to Brahmanism that had, in his mind at least, some earlier Christian inspiration.

Pope's most monumental undertaking was a translation of an important Saiva Siddhanta text, *The Tiruvacagam* (1900), in which he boldly asserted that Saiva Siddhanta was an exclusively Tamil religion:

> The Caiva Siddhantha system is the most elaborate, influential, and undoubtedly the most intrinsically valuable of all the religions of India. It is peculiarly the South-Indian, and Tamil, religion. . . . Caivism is the old prehistoric religion of South India, essentially existing from pre-Aryan times, and holds sway over the hearts of the Tamil people. . . . Its texts

books (probably its sources) exist in Tamil only.... (Classical Tamil is very little studied, yet this key alone can unlock the hearts of probably ten millions of the most intelligent and progressive of the Hindu races). (lxxiv)

Here Pope coupled his ardent endorsement of Saiva Siddhanta with his assertion that it was a "peculiarly South-Indian, and Tamil, religion." Interestingly, Pope shifted his earlier view, expressed in the preface to Dubois, that neo-Vedantism was the most influential religion in the Tamil region (Pope 1879, xxvii). Instead, he now endorsed Saiva Siddhanta, despite his knowledge that its revival had effectively curtailed the advance of Christianity in the neighboring Tamil region of Jaffna in present-day Sri Lanka.[10]

The ideological thrust of Pope's work on the *Tiruvacagam* becomes even more apparent in his call for a Tamil revival in what was essentially a religious work:

The speech of a dying people may, perhaps be allowed to die; but this cannot be said of the Tamil race. Heaven Forbid. Dead languages have great uses . . . yet, in many ways, the living tongues are better! One cannot tell what flowers may yet bloom, what fruits may yet ripen, on the hardy old trees. Let Tamilians cease to be ashamed of their vernacular! (1900, xii–xiii)

Pope's endorsement of Saiva Siddhanta as "a peculiarly Tamil religion" was implicated with his belief that the modern revival of the Tamil language and literature had much Christian inspiration and support. He provided a genealogy of this modern Tamil efflorescence in the introduction to *Tiruvacagam:*

There exists now much of what is called Christian Tamil, a dialect created by the Danish missionaries of Tranquebar, enriched by generations of Tanjore, German, and other missionaries; modified, purified, and refrigerated by the Swiss Rhenius and the very composite Tinnevelly school; expanded and harmonized by Englishmen . . . and finally waiting now for the touch of some heaven-born genius among the Tamil community to make it as sweet and effective as any language on earth, living or dead. (xii–xiii)

He credited this renaissance to "that unique genius Beschi," de Nobilibus, and more recently "Ellis and Stokes,—with a multitude of others, such as Drew, Caldwell, and Percival, who advanced Tamil culture, [of whom] space forbids me here to speak" (xii). In Pope's view, therefore, the Tamil revival was largely stimulated by the work of missionaries. At the end of his genealogy, he named "two recent works which seem to me to give promise of a veritable re-descent in more modern attire of the Tamil Saraswati [goddess of learning]," P. Sundaram Pillai's dramatic work *Manonmaniam,* and V. G. Suryanarayana Sastri's *Tani-pacura-togai* (Anthology of Solitary Songs). Both authors were English-educated Tamils whose writings reflected the spirit and impact of missionary writers such as Caldwell and Pope. A friend of Pope's, Sundaram Pillai, as we shall see next, was the first Tamil intellectual to embrace and expound much of Caldwell and Pope's Dravidian ideology. Suryanarayana Sastri (1870–1903), affectionately called "Dravidian Sastri," was the head Tamil pandit at Madras Christian College and a close friend of the great evangelist and principal of the college, Rev. William Miller. Sastri was an ardent Tamil revivalist and perhaps the first Tamil to initiate the practice of writing "pure Tamil" in the modern period.

The Indigenization of Dravidian Ideology

The men who came forward to embrace and "indigenize" Dravidian ideology were drawn predominantly from an English-educated, higher non-Brahman, caste of Tamil/Saivites of southern India. They became the spokesmen of the Saivite revival movement, which was beginning to gather momentum in Tamil Nadu by the latter part of the nineteenth century. Ironically, the Tamil/Saivite revival had begun in neighboring Sri Lanka as a response to Christian missionary proselytization. Led by the numerically strong and dominant non-Brahman Vellalar caste in Sri Lanka, it soon stimulated a similar revival among the higher non-Brahman castes in Tamil Nadu. Unlike the case in Tamil Sri Lanka, where the main contender to Saivism was an aggressive Christianity, the non-Brahman Saivites in South India faced the additional threat of the ascendancy of neo-Vedantism and Vaishnavism, which reinforced Brahman hegemony in South India.Their adoption of an anti-Brahman ideology therefore served not only to reclaim their sociopolitical power and position but to undermine the power and appeal of the predominantly Brahman advocates of neo-Vedanta and Vaishnavism in South India.

Prior to this modern Saivite revival, Tamil elites, both Brahmans and non-Brahmans, were intimately involved in the propagation and maintenance of Saiva Siddhanta. Saivites and their traditional religious institutions, the Saivite mutts, as the missionaries recognized, had served as the chief repositories of the Tamil language and literature from at least the medieval period. In addition to the Saivite Brahmans, the higher non-Brahman Tamils had a history of investment and participation in the Saiva Siddhanta school, which had begun with the Vellalar saint Meikanda Deva in the thirteenth century. The fact that there had been at least three powerful Saiva Siddhanta mutts in the Tamil region led exclusively by higher non-Brahman Tamil castes since the late-sixteenth century also attests to the elite Tamil involvement and investment in Saiva Siddhanta. These powerful centers of Saivite orthodoxy had earlier histories of contestations with the all-India Brahmanical dharmic norms—norms that were generally inimical to the "Sudra" leadership of Hindu religious life (Koppedrayer 1991). These contestations had not, however, sought to overturn Brahmanical norms (as the missionaries sought) as much as to justify the leadership of *sat sudra* or "clean Sudra" castes in Hindu religious institutions.

In addition, attempts had been made since the early medieval period to "Tamilize" the Saiva Siddhanta school of thought (Prentiss 1996), originally an all-India school (Davis 1991), by fusing its philosophy and practice with the earlier Bhakti traditions and histories of the Tamils, perhaps through the active participation of Tamils of the higher castes. Thus, the Saivite tradition had come to express a uniquely Tamil sense of culture and identity prior to the modern period, and it was this sense that revivalists of the late nineteenth century hoped to resurrect, with the help of missionary orientalism, to counter the rising hegemony of the Aryan/Brahmans in both the religio-cultural and the social spheres. Inspired by the Dravidian ideology of the missionaries, many non-Brahman Saiva Siddhanta revivalists claimed this tradition as a unique product of Dravidian civilization and denied the role that Brahmans and Sanskrit culture had played in its evolution. In the process, they were clearly disrupting not only an earlier vision and practice of a less "racially" or caste-defined Saiva Siddhanta tradition but also a Tamil tradition.

P. Sundaram Pillai

P. Sundaram Pillai (1855–97) was one of the earliest non-Brahman Tamil intellectuals to creatively embrace and extend Dravidian ideology. He, like many of the pioneer ideologues, belonged to the higher Tamil Vellalar caste. Born and raised in the region of Trivandrum, Sundaram Pillai received an excellent English education. He held both B.A. and M.A. degrees and taught history and philosophy at Maharaja's College, Trivandrum (K. K. Pillai 1957). Although disregarded by most current scholarship on the Dravidian movement, Sundaram Pillai's work needs to be located against the broader background of a Vellalar-led Saivite/Tamil revival originating in Sri Lanka, which was beginning to have an impact on Tamil Nadu by the latter part of the century. Sundaram Pillai was an English-educated spokesman for this revivalism in Tamil Nadu.[11]

One of the most influential of Sundaram Pillai's writings was a research article first published in the *Madras Christian College Magazine* entitled "The Age of Tirujnana-Sambhanda" (1891–92).[12] The article presented in a subtle and scholarly way Sundaram Pillai's adoption and translation of Dravidian ideology in the service of Tamil/Saivite nationalism. In the article, he established a close connection between Saivite religion and Tamil identity, subsuming both under a Dravidian identity. Although the essay ostensibly sought to assign greater antiquity to an important Tamil Saivite saint, Tirujnanasambhanda, Sundaram Pillai had a much wider mandate, as he made explicit in the conclusion of the article, where he listed the "main purposes subserved by the paper":

> It gives a birds-eye view of the sacred Tamil literature of the Saivas. It controverts the opinion of Dr. Burnell with regard to the antiquity and value of Tamil literature. It proves the utterly unfounded nature of the hypothesis advocated by Dr. Caldwell and Mr. Nelson with regard to the age of Sambandha. An attempt is made to trace the religious history of South India.... Facts are deduced to prove with the help of the latest archeological researches that Sambhanda could not have lived in any period later than the early years of the seventh century. (1909, 60–61)

In short, Sundaram Pillai was attempting to write a brief history of the Tamil people and their Saivite religion from a Dravidian perspective. To this end, he expanded with a much greater sense of authority on the conclusions first offered by Caldwell on the antiquity and greatness of Dravidian civilization and culture. In presenting a bird's-eye view of Tamil Saivite literature, Sundaram Pillai cleverly linked the Saivite and Dravidian identities:

> By the Saiva community, I mean the Hindus that regard Siva as the head of the Hindu trinity. Saivas, in this sense, form the bulk of the population ... in short, where ever Tamil is the prevailing tongue.... For all the Saivas, and particularly for the non-Brahamanical Tamil Saivas, Tirujnanasambandha is the highest authority.... The Tamil Saivas have their own system of sacred literature, compiled and arranged so as to match the Vedas, Puranas, and Sastras in Sanskrit. (1–2)

Although not expressed in the openly anti-Brahman manner characteristic of later ideologues, he repeatedly emphasizes the Dravidian identity of the Tamils.

Thus, the saint Tirujnanasambhanda is depicted as a "Dravida child" (47). Noting that the saint's hymns were originally set to "Dravidian" music, Sundaram Pillai regrets the loss of the original tunes and, much in the style of Caldwell, credits this loss to the introduction of music brought "by the Aryan musicians of the north. Some of the old names are still retained; but it is difficult to believe that they denote, in the new system, the same old Dravidian melodies" (5).

The strength of Sundaram Pillai's arguments rests on the use he made of ancient Tamil literary sources. As one of the earliest and most effective indigenous pioneers of Tamil literary history, he argued against the prevailing scholarly consensus that there could have been any significant Tamil literary production before the ninth century and that Dravidian literature was but a poor imitation of the Aryan literature. On some issues in this regard, he parted company with the orientalists. Besides demonstrating some of the "erroneous deductions" that Caldwell had made regarding the age of Sambhandha, he criticized the views of orientalists that Tamil literature was a poor source of history (1909, 27–29). Rejecting Caldwell's view "that these literary records are devoid of historical implications," he argued that they did provide "most reliable data for reconstructing extinct societies and social conditions"(27–29). Not unlike Caldwell, however, Sundaram Pillai maintained that exclusive reliance on Sanskritic sources to the neglect of Tamil led to a distorted view of Indian history and civilization. In particular, the Dravidian contribution to Indian history and civilization was belittled. Noting that "South Indian chronology has yet to begin its existence," he decried the fact that scholars did not yet have "a single important date in the ancient history of the Dravidians ascertained" (9). Sundaram Pillai's mission was to stimulate and encourage research in the realm of Tamil studies in order to lend substance to their claims of a distinctive national identity.

Sundaram Pillai did not live to articulate more forcefully or in a more elaborate fashion the ideas that he formulated regarding Dravidian civilization and culture. However, there is ample evidence that he was the major indigenous source and inspiration for later Dravidian ideologues. Sundaram Pillai's letters toward the end of his life to one of these, Nallaswami Pillai, as well as the testaments of some of his associates, position Sundaram Pillai as the foremost "brain child" in the indigenization of a Dravidian ideology. In one of the letters, Sundaram Pillai wrote:

> I regret I have not yet been able to formulate my theory for popular conviction; but am doing what I can to prepare the minds of gentleman like you from Ceylon to Bangalore for the full recognition of the truth when publicly announced. The Vellalas who form the flower of the Dravidian

race, have now so far forgotten their nationality as to habitually think and speak of themselves as Sudras. . . . In fact, to tell them that they are no more Sudras than Frenchmen and that the Aryan polity of castes was the cunningly forged fetters by which their earliest enemies—the Aryans of the North—bound their souls, which is worse than binding hands and feet, might sound too revolutionary a theory, though historically but a bare fact. I have converted privately several to this opinion among the leaders of the community here and there: and I must go on with the work, sometime more in the same noiseless fashion before I can trust myself to print.

He added, borrowing the ideas if not some of the very words of missionaries such as Caldwell and Pope, that "most of which is ignorantly called Aryan philosophy, Aryan civilization, is literally Dravidian or Tamilian at bottom." Similarly, "most of the great thinkers and great philosophers and even poets who pass for Aryan, are our men, as Europeans are now beginning to find out. Let the idea work in you and you will find enough of proof yourself. What a lamentable history is ours! It crushes my heart to think of it" (Subramania Mudaliar 1909, 2). Sundaram Pillai also claimed "the Saiva system of thought and worship" to be

> peculiarly our own. With our usual complaisance we have surrendered our right to it, no less than to the temples which, you know, were originally constructed by us and administered entirely by our *Kurrukal* [non-Brahmin priests] and which it is now a pollution for them to enter and worship. . . . "Karayan Purredukap Pambu Kudiyirukum" [when the white ants make a nest the snake moves in and takes over] is a significant proverb applicable in many ways to the history of the Dravidian race. (3)

His closing comment on Dravidian failings reminds us that while Sundaram Pillai indigenized and extended ideas originally articulated by Caldwell and Pope, he chose to render their nuanced praise of Tamil/Dravidian civilization in a more celebratory, nationalist manner. He also dropped Caldwell's vision of the Dravidian religion as "Demonolatry overlain by a thin veneer of Brahminism," proposing in its place the Saivite religion as the original and quintessential religion of the Dravidians.

J. M. Nallaswami Pillai

The most important Tamil contributor to the Dravidian movement after Sundaram Pillai was J. M. Nallaswami Pillai (1864–1920). Like Sundaram Pillai, Nallaswami Pillai also hailed from a Tamil Vellalar family and received an excellent English education. After completing his B.A., he obtained a law degree and for much of the remainder of his life worked as a district judge. Nallaswami Pillai's central concern was the revival of Saiva Siddhanta, and his success in this endeavor has earned him credit as one of the greatest pioneer Saiva Siddhanta revivalists of the modern period. Perhaps more than Sundaram Pillai, Nallaswami Pillai was intimately associated with many of the traditional Vellalar-led Saiva Siddhanta institutions and figures in the Tamil region. Like Maraimalai Adigal after him, he was a staunch disciple of the fiery but "traditional" revivalist Somasundara Nayakar (1846–1901). Nayakar belonged to the Vanniar caste, which is significantly lower than the Vellalar, but he played a powerful role in influencing the nature of the Saiva Siddhanta revival in Tamil Nadu.

Nallaswami Pillai's revival of Saiva Siddhanta went hand in hand with his efforts to recover and revive the Tamil language and literary works. Though Nallaswami Pillai did not embrace Dravidian ideology as entirely or thoroughly as Sundaram Pillai, his work nevertheless served to link the revival of Tamil with the revival of Saiva Siddhanta, an achievement that contributed immensely to the strength and appeal of Dravidian ideology. Nallaswami Pillai's writings not only illustrate the pioneer nature of the Saiva Siddhanta revivalist project but also show how much the revival of Saiva Siddhanta was aided by Christian missionary writings.

Nallaswami Pillai made his reliance on orientalist scholarship explicit in the first issue of the journal he founded in 1887, in which he regrets as shameful "that we should be coached in our Veda and Vedanta by German Professors on the banks of the Rhine and the Ouse and that an American from a far off country should be the first translator of the foremost work in Tamil philosophy and that an old Oxford Professor should sit poring over the Tamil 'word' and render it into English verse." These men were "noble examples," but a grander project was in sight. His aim, he declared, was "no less than to transplant on Indian soil some of those activities in the field of Indian Religion, literature and history which are carried on in far off countries by Western savants and to stimulate indigenous talent to work and achieve a moderate share of success in these departments" (*Siddhanta Deepika*, June 1897, 14–15).

His first major work was an English translation with commentary of the central text of the Tamil Saiva Siddhanta school, *Sivajnana Botham,* in 1895. A previous translation by the Rev. H. R. Hoisington (1801–58), an American missionary attached to the Vattukottai seminary in Jaffna, had been published a half century earlier in 1854. Nallaswami Pillai's introduction to his own translation revealed the pioneering nature of his project as well as his debt to earlier missionary writings:

Very few Pandits could be found in South India who are able to expound the text [*Sivajnana Botham*] properly even now. . . . When I had fairly begun my translation, I learnt from a note in Trubner's *Sarva Darsana Sangraha* that a previous translation of this work existed and hunting out for this book, I chanced upon an old catalogue of Bishop Caldwell's books and I subsequently traced out the possession of Bishop Caldwell's book to Rev. J. Lazarus, B.A. of Madras who very courteously lent me the use of the book and to whom my best thanks are due. I have used the book to see that I do not go wrong in essential points and in the language of translation. (1895, vii–viii)

In the same preface, Nallaswami Pillai also registered his awareness of working in an intellectual climate that European missionaries had made more conducive to the study of Tamil religious writings, for he mentioned having come across recent publications by Pope, Rev. G. M. Cobban, and Sundaram Pillai.

In the introduction to his English translation of another important Saiva Siddhanta work, *Sivajana Siddhiyar* (1913), Nallaswami Pillai took the time to reflect more generally on the genealogy of his revivalist efforts, which he referred to as "personal details":

The original translation of *Sivajnana Botham* and *Siva Prakasam* by Rev. Hoisington and that of *Sivajnana Siddhiyar* by Dr. Graul was published more than forty or fifty years ago, but they did not seem to have attracted the attention of European and Indian scholars. About the time I commenced my work Rev. G. M. Cobban was familiarizing the Madras readers with his translations from *Saints Pattinattar.* . . . Dr. Pope's long promised *Tiruvacagam* only appeared in April 1900. And since then, the subject has received considerable attention at the hands of Christian missionaries like Rev. Mr. Goudie, Rev. Mr. Goodwill and Rev. Mr. Schomerus and their contributions appeared in the *Christian College Magazine, Harvest Field, Gospel Witness,* etc. (1913, ii–iii)

This testimony indicates that if pre-Caldwellian attempts to introduce Saiva Siddhanta in South India in the mid–nineteenth century had largely failed to arouse much interest among both "European and Indian scholars," it was toward the latter part of the nineteenth century, after the publication of Caldwell's magnum opus, that the revival of Saiva Siddhanta and Tamil began to gain momentum in South India.

Nallaswami Pillai was a great friend and admirer of Pope. Pope had been a regular contributor to Nallaswami Pillai's Saiva Siddhanta revivalist journal

Siddhanta Deepika (Light of Truth) through which the latter attempted to attract greater attention to Pope's contributions, going so far as to serialize his life and work (Pope 1910, 1). Nallaswami Pillai announced Pope's death in his journal as "the passing away of this great Tamil scholar, missionary and Saint. . . . The loss to the Tamil land and literature is immense. He loved the Tamil people and their literature. He was the greatest living scholar, among the living or the dead. . . . If he was born in the old days," Nallaswami Pillai insisted, "he would have been catalogued with the 63 [Saivite] Saints. His service to the Saivite religion and Siddhanta Philosophy are incalculable as he was the first to bring its importance to the light of the English speaking world. May his soul rest in Sivam!" (Pope 1973, xx–xxiii).

Most of Nallaswami Pillai's writings first appeared in *Siddhanta Deepika*. Though the journal aimed principally at promoting the revival of Saiva Siddhanta, the project inevitably foregrounded many ancient Tamil religious and literary works. Nallaswami Pillai sought to highlight what he felt was the southern Hindu religious tradition, which had been overlooked by an exclusive reliance on North Indian sources:

> The wonder however is why in spite of the Antiquity of Religion and Philosophy, and the vastness of its literature in Tamil and Sanskrit, it [Saiva Siddhanta] has attracted the attention of so few Oriental scholars. The reason is not far to seek. Most of the European scholars from Sir William Jones lived in northern India, and the school of philosophy that was brought to their notice was that of Sri Sankara and that of Saktaism. . . . However the views of these Oriental scholars mainly influenced those in Europe so much so that in the course of time, Hinduism has been identified with the Vedanta of Sankara, in the European mind; and with the revival of learning in India itself, this has also acted on the Hindu mind. (1913, iv–vii)

Here, Nallaswami Pillai, apart from explaining how Saiva Siddhanta had come to be neglected, revealed his awareness that orientalist scholarship had "acted on the Hindu mind." Indian intellectuals appear to have had a kind of Foucauldian awareness of the power of orientalist writings to shape Indian perceptions of their own traditions and *Siddhanta Deepika* was launched in order to correct this one-sided and "erroneous" representation of Hinduism by paying greater attention to "the Languages and history of South India and the Dravidian Philosophy and religion," thereby supplying "a real and absolutely important want" (*Siddhanta Deepika*, June 1897). Prominent English-educated South Indian intellectuals wrote for the journal, as did Europeans, particularly Christian missionaries. Its contributors and contents reflected Nallaswami Pillai's own cultural hybridity and the complex genealogy of his Tamil Saiva Siddhanta revivalist efforts.[13]

Maraimalai Adigal

The missionary genealogy of the revivalist movement is most clear in the writings of Maraimalai Adigal (1876–1950), the man most popularly associated with Dravidian ideology. In his work the ideas that had been generated and shaped by figures such as Caldwell, Pope, Sundaram Pillai, and Nallaswami Pillai finally found expression in and for the Tamil intellectual and cultural milieu. Perhaps it is for this reason as well as for the boldness of his advocacy that Adigal is regarded as the central ideologue of the Dravidian movement. Unlike his predecessors, who wrote mainly for an English-reading or bilingual audience, Adigal wrote primarily in Tamil for a Tamil-reading audience.

Adigal's formal English education was more limited than that of Sundaram Pillai's or Nallaswami Pillai's. He completed only the fourth form at the Wesleyan Mission High School in his hometown of Nagapatinam. From a young age, however, he cultivated a sound knowledge of ancient Tamil literary, grammatical, and religious works from a local Tamil teacher. Many of his early patrons and friends were non-Brahman Saivites or Saiva Siddhanta revivalists. He also came under the powerful influence of his Saiva Siddhanta guru, Somasundara Nayakar, from an early age.[14] Adigal's interest in Tamil literary and religious works and Dravidian ideology, and his opposition to the claims of the neo-Vedantic Hindu revival, were inspired first and foremost by his early exposure to and interest in Saiva Siddhanta.

Adigal's writings and lectures first appeared in *Janacagaram* (Ocean of Wisdom), the Tamil monthly journal he founded in 1902. The journal was one of the earliest to systematically propagate Saiva Siddhanta and Dravidian ideology. In the first issue, Adigal betrays his intellectual debt to Caldwell in an article entitled "Tamil Vadamoliyil Iruntu Pirantatama" (Is Tamil Derived from Sanskrit?). The article reads as both an introduction to the basic principles of comparative philology and a systematic argument for looking at Tamil and Sanskrit as languages having independent origins. Nowhere are the debts to philology, Caldwell, or the orientalist debates directly acknowledged. Furthermore, the classical or archaic Tamil prose style that Adigal employs in his writings served to mask how much he relied upon and utilized the methodologies and conclusions derived from European scholarship, giving one the impression of reading the work of a "traditional" Tamil pandit rather than the research and conclusions of an intellectually and culturally hybridized Tamil intellectual.

This talent for selectively and covertly borrowing from European scholarship while conveying his message in a language and idiom suitable for the Tamil literary world of the time gave Adigal's writing its unusual power and appeal.

What also distinguished Adigal's writings from those of his predecessors was a more forthright, aggressive, and less nuanced advocacy of Dravidian ideology. Writing mostly for a Tamil reading public seems to have freed Adigal from much of the critical and sober constraints of scholarship directed primarily toward an English reading public. In the preface to his Tamil work *Sinthanaik katturaikal* (Reflective Essays, [1908] 1980), Adigal was particularly frank:

> Before the immigration of northern Brahmins . . . the Tamil people studied much, for their monarchs encouraged its learning in every way. . . . [There is an] entire absence from old Tamil literature of all mythical, romantic, libidinous, and indecent accounts about gods and sages which constitute an essential feature of Sanskrit works. . . . But from this sense of truth came a fall, the moment the Aryan Brahmins came from the north. . . . Since these Brahmins were very selfish, greedy and cunning, they did their best to keep the people in ignorance and illiteracy. . . . The people were forbidden to learn anything in general and Sanskrit in particular. (1980, 16)

Aside from the blatant condemnation of Brahmanical "imports" into Tamil culture, this passage also underlines Adigal's more far-reaching critique of Brahmanism, to which he attributed the "ignorance and illiteracy" of contemporary Tamil society. He warned in brazen terms:

> If the limited number of Hindu people who call themselves Brahmins . . . go on most unreasonably claiming all high privileges exclusively to themselves, to the detriment of the teeming millions . . . certain it is as night follows day, that this comparatively insignificant number of people would be wiped out of existence in a few centuries. (1980, 19–20)

This kind of strong critique of Brahmanical civilization, which had its seeds in missionary orientalism, would be taken to new heights under the later Dravidian ideologue E. V. Ramaswami and the Rationalist Movement beginning in the 1930s.

In 1916, Adigal formally launched the "Pure Tamil" movement, which was aimed at eliminating Sanskrit from the Tamil language. Here again the debt to missionary inspiration is clear. In a passage dealing with this subject, Adigal cited Caldwell and his assertion that Tamil can stand alone without the aid of Sanskrit. He then wrote:

> This impartial and candid, comprehensive yet discriminating view of the Tamilian languages and their relative merit put forth long ago by a great European [Caldwell] ought to open—if it had not already opened the eyes of the misled Tamils to see the youthful glory, richness, and virility of their mother tongue and advance its culture on quite independent lines. (38–39)

Adigal also boldly articulated the vision of a Dravidian nation implicit in the work of Caldwell:

> The Tamil, the Telugu, the Canarese, and the Malayalam people and other Dravidians living in the remotest parts of India, being the descendants of a single highly civilized ancestral race related to each other by the closest ties of blood and speech, should once more knit themselves together by eschewing the company of the Aryan intruder who harbours no goodwill towards them and should work harmoniously for promoting the common welfare of their several communities that live scattered all over India (39).

Adigal ended this passage with an almost Christian ethical maxim, that until the Aryan "treads the path of righteousness, until he learns to treat others with a kind and human heart, until he realizes the great benefit of living on a footing of equality with others and represses the feelings of selfishness, vanity, pride, and greediness, the company of an Aryan should be studiously avoided but not be hated" (39–40).

Like Pope and Sundaram Pillai, Adigal maintained that Saiva Siddhanta was a uniquely Dravidian religion. As he observed in one of his few English works, entitled *Saiva Siddhanta as a Form of Practical Knowledge,* "the religion and philosophy of Saiva Siddhanta, as has been pointed out by Dr. G. U. Pope, are, 'peculiarly South-Indian' and the Tamils who are the pre-Aryan inhabitants of India, are alone the sole and strict adherents of this system from times immemorial" (Maraimalai Adigal 1940, 13). In the same work, Adigal wrote of the difficult problem of recovering this Saivite religion of the Dravidians, which later accretions of "Aryan falsehood" had "corrupted":

> The modern Mayavada Vedanta and Vaishnavism which came to spread here after the eighth century A.D. achieved what their predecessors could not achieve, simply by fabricating fictitious, obscene and licentious

Puranic stories and thus catching the fancy of the Tamil people. This influx of the Aryan falsehood into Tamil led to the formation of a class of literature which is notorious for the most degraded type of Puranic religion. (1940, 6)

Writing of his efforts to recover the Saivite religion, he called for Tamils "to sift this mongrel mixture and disentangle the golden truths of Saiva religion. The task is no easier one and it cannot be further appreciated even by the Saivites whose mind is dyed deep in the Aryan myths" (Maraimalai Adigal 1957a, vii–viii).

Like many of his predecessors, Adigal blamed the Brahmans and the dominant school of orientalism for the neglect of Tamil and Saiva Siddhanta. "For this grievous ignorance of Tamil literature and the Saiva Siddhanta," he wrote, "it is the early contact of the western scholars with the Brahmins that is responsible" (1940, 47). However, what is especially interesting is his account of the process of reclamation and recovery of "Dravidian" culture, since it not only implicates the role of missionary orientalism but also his own unique role in that project:

> The knowledge of Tamil and Tamil classics had to lie concealed, or rather unrecognized for centuries, even from the searching eye of the European intellect, until a few learned and very painstaking Christian missionaries such as Dr. Caldwell and Dr. G. U. Pope ventured to turn their serious attention to Tamil classics and devote their whole life time to a deep study and correct representation of their nature and contents. . . . I consider my Tamil works to be more important than the work I intend to do in English. For my Tamil brethren are mostly illiterate and even the very few who are literate are unenlightened. . . . Therefore, I had to apply myself most strenuously for more than forty years to the hard labour of bringing enlightenment to my country men. (Maraimalai Adigal 1940, 49–50)

By implicating both missionary orientalism and his own unique role in the project of reclaiming Dravidian civilization, Adigal was able to represent that project as moving beyond its orientalist foundations into an indigenous form.

Concluding Remarks

This reconstruction of the role of missionary orientalism in the creation of Dravidian nationalist ideology enables us to make a few observations regarding the nature and role of orientalism in India, particularly as it pertained to South India. With reference to the work of Caldwell, one can observe that European orientalism played a powerful role in reconfiguring and rearticulating earlier tensions and contradictions within South Indian society in quite transformative ways. The ideas of figures such as Caldwell acquired their power and appeal not so much through radical transformations of the meanings of earlier categories but through strategic shifts in the meanings of key categories that appealed to emerging, potentially powerful groups. Figures like Caldwell and Pope were clearly cognizant of the internal dynamics and contradictions of South Indian society and culture and were sensitive to their emerging forces. Their work had the potential to disrupt and reorder previous sociocultural hierarchies and hegemonies in the South Indian "Hindu" order. This is particularly borne out by Dravidian nationalism's moderate success in disrupting the close alliance and cultural nexus between Brahmans and dominant non-Brahman groups such as the Vellalars, Nayars, and Reddis in southern India. It needs to be underlined, however, that this transformation was not accomplished by missionary orientalists through their "hegemonic" orientalism but rather by the dominant non-Brahmans who utilized the missionaries' ideas according to their own purposes and mandates. Yet by helping to empower local vernacular languages, religions, and cultures in South India the missionary orientalists laid the ideological basis for one of the most powerful critiques of the Hindu social order, its cultural practices, and its cosmology to appear in India in the modern period, leading to the anti-Brahmanical Rationalist Movement with its "Dravidian" preoccupations with Saiva Siddhanta and Tamil.

Far from being passive victims of an orientalist discourse, local figures and communities played a decisive role in the construction, maintenance, and propagation of orientalist knowledge. And they did so for a nationalist purpose that, as Benedict Anderson (1991) has observed, both drew from and superseded earlier identities and senses of community based on religion, caste, and language. Just as Indian nationalism drew from a transformed Brahmanical vision of India, Dravidian nationalism derived its peculiar resonance by invoking non-Brahman identities and histories. And just as missionary orientalism was dependent for its success on the participation and support of dominant non-Brahman groups in South India, so too a similar dependence and dialectic existed between the dominant school of orientalism and elite Hindu castes and classes in North India. Seen from this perspective, the Saidian thesis masks an altogether different and long forgotten "local" intellectual conquest, explaining perhaps why Said's thesis continues to be so attractive to many of the scholarly in Asia and the West.

NOTES

For their critical comments on earlier drafts of this essay, I would like to thank Tim Brook, Andre Schmid, and Milton Israel.

1. The term *Dravidian nationalism* is used here to include the anti-Brahman, anti-Aryan, anti-Sanskrit movement that began gaining momentum early in the twentieth century in South India, especially in the Tamil region. It led to the establishment of the various Dravidian political parties that have been in power in the state of Tamil Nadu since the 1960s. For a time, there were even calls for a separate Dravidian state.

2. For the sake of brevity, the term *Brahmanical ideology* is used herein instead of the more cumbersome *Aryan/Brahmanical/Sanskritic ideology* to describe the dominant neo-Hindu ideology that undergirds Indian nationalism and against which Dravidian nationalism was constructed.

3. South India, and more particularly the Tamil region, was an especially suitable site for such a religio-cultural intervention, for not only was the Brahman population fairly small but Brahmanism and Sanskritic culture had experienced substantial resistance in earlier times. The structural configuration of the system of social stratification in South India, with its unusual anomaly in the ranking of castes, was also favorable for such an intervention. The powerful landholding castes that were next in rank only to the Brahmans were assigned the fairly low and demeaning *varna* category of Sudra. Unlike the situation in North India, where the Hindu population had a fair distribution of the four *varna* groupings of Brahman, Kshatriya, Vaishya, and Sudra, South India had only two categories, Brahman and Sudra. The dharma, or duty, of a Sudra according to the classical Sanskritic legal texts was one of menial work and service to the three higher *varnas*.

4. The Saiva Siddhanta tradition in the Tamil region can be traced at least to the medieval period, when the Saiva Siddhanta school of thought was consciously fused with an earlier Saivite Tamil Bhakti tradition. In contemporary Tamil usage, Saivism and Saiva Siddhanta have come to mean the same thing and thus are used in this essay interchangeably.

5. The Madras school was founded in the early decades of the nineteenth century in imitation of the dominant center of orientalist researchers in Calcutta. Its scholars were primarily associated with the College of Fort St. George in the city of Madras. The Madras scholars, more in tune with missionary orientalism, claimed and asserted a superior knowledge of South India in relation to the Calcutta school, which conformed to the dominant pre-British Hindu traditions and ideologies that privileged a Brahmanical vision of India (Pollock 1993). Trautmann (1997) notes that the Calcutta school eclipsed the older missionary orientalism that had reigned before.

6. Dubois in his *Hindu Manners, Customs, and Ceremonies* (Pope 1879), while speaking of the heterodox and anti-Brahman Telugu poet Vemana, distinguishes the literary tradition of the Brahmans from the non-Brahmans in South India:

> Amongst the few Hindu works which are written in a free philosophical vein, and in which the Hindu religion and its customs are openly criticized, not one that I know of has been written by a Brahmin. All the works of this kind that I have seen

have emanated from authors who were not of this caste. Tiruvalluvar was a Pariah, Pattanattupillai and Agastya were both of the Vellala caste and their poems are written in Tamil. . . . One of the most famous is Vemana . . . of the Reddy caste. . . . It is to be noticed that the authors of all these satirical and revolutionary works belong to recent times. If in earlier days any enlightened writer published similar works, the Brahmins have taken care that not a trace of them shall remain. Nowadays they rage against the authors we have mentioned, and speak of their works with contempt. They cannot of course, succeed in destroying them, but they do everything in their power to prevent the reading of them.

7. Ellis was the first to demonstrate, in 1816, that the South Indian languages belonged to a family entirely different from the Indo-Aryan. C. P. Brown, son of a senior chaplain of the East India Company, played a key role in shaping the ideology of the modern Telugu renaissance and nationalism through his tireless efforts to restore a less Sanskritized Telugu. Brown was one of the first Europeans from Madras whom Caldwell met on his first voyage to India, and they remained life-long friends. Brown had a Christian antipathy toward Brahmanism and encouraged the non-Brahman elements of Telugu literature and culture (Schmitthenner 1991, 90).

8. The contributions of orientalists such as Rev. H. Gundert for Malayalam, C. P. Brown for Telugu, and Rev. F. Kittel for Kannada are striking examples.

9. Caldwell's most notable publications aside from his magnum opus on Dravidian grammar include *The Tinnevelly Shanars* (1849), *A Political and General History of the District of Tinnevelly* (1881), and *Records of the Early History of the Tinnevelly Missions* (1881). He also played a key role in the revision of the Tamil Prayer Book and the Tamil Bible.

10. Pope referred to the antimissionary Saivite of Jaffna, Arumuga Navalar, in the same work as "a zealous reviver of modern times of the Caiva system." After giving Navalar's account of a story in a Tamil work, he opined: "Of course recognizing the spirit of this teaching, it may be allowed us to doubt whether such explanations would ever have been dreamt of but for Western teachings; and whether myths like these are the appropriate means for imparting this instruction." Pope added a footnote to the last comment: "I write quite unreservedly, knowing full well the courtesy and candour of my Caiva friends, who will not question my love for them, and unfeigned respect for their cherished convictions" (1900, lxiii–lxiv).

11. A notice of an early Saiva Siddhanta revivalist association in Tamil Nadu, the Saiva Siddhanta Sabha of Trichirapally, named Sundaram Pillai as its patron, indicating his involvement in the emerging Saivite revivalism (*Siddhanta Deepika,* June 1897, 95–96). The editor of the most important English journal devoted to the propagation of Saiva Siddhanta also acknowledged that it was founded "after a good deal of consultation with him" (*Siddhanta Deepika,* June 1897, 22).

12. It was republished later as "Some Milestones in the History of Tamil Literature or the Age of Tirujnanasambhanda."

13. The complex genealogy of Nallaswami Pillai's revivalist efforts is captured in a passage he wrote a few years after founding his journal:

The nature of our work and its scope and latitude may be summed up in the brief epigram, "Siddhantam matter in the Siddhantham manner for the Siddhantins." . . . If this feverish wish of ours be realized, and our journal be instrumental in doing ever so little to rouse the dormant minds to their sense of duty and make them feel the benevolent duty of Saivism in the Universe, and the dethroning of the devil (Pasa) by the love of God (Patignana) then and not till then we will boldly be able to assert that we have in a measure achieved that task we originally imposed on ourselves through our desire to serve, aye, if need be, to be crucified for Saivism, Amen! (Balasubramaniam 1965, 38–39)

14. Although Nayakar played a central role in the revival of Saiva Siddhanta in South India, he has received little scholarly attention. For an extended treatment of Nayakar's role see Ravindiran Vaitheespara 1999.

Decentering the "Middle Kingdom": The Problem of China in Korean Nationalist Thought, 1895–1910

Andre Schmid

In the fifteen years between the Treaty of Shimonoseki (1895) and the annexation of Korea into the Japanese empire (1910), the pace of Korea's integration into the world system accelerated dramatically. Much research has focused on how Korean elites, both inside and outside the state, sought to negotiate the terms of the nation's incorporation into this system. Concentrating largely on the various nationalist reform efforts, these works have shown how elites sought to strengthen and enrich the nation by reproducing the supposedly universal criteria of "civilization and enlightenment"—whether legal reform or the cutting of topknots, changes in political and military institutions, the installation of urban sewage systems, or the building of new schools.

These desiderata of "civilization" were not the only universal features of the nation, however. Though not so overtly heralded by nationalist reformers, so, too, was national particularity. For in the nationalist discourse of a world system populated by nations the very act of possessing uniqueness was universalized: every nation was to have a unique character. Korea's coerced incorporation into the world system stimulated various groups not only to pursue the new criteria of "civilization" but also to articulate within the universal form of the nation just what it was that made this particular nation Korean. Issues of identity were just as much a part of the same historical process of globalization as was the growing role of international trade in the domestic economy.

As part of this impulse to identify the nation, representations of China played a significant function. This in itself was nothing new. Throughout the more than five hundred years of the Chosŏn dynasty (1392–1910), the *yangban* elites had always positioned their nation vis-à-vis its continental neighbor. As the common name "Eastern Kingdom" (*Tongguk*) suggests, China functioned as the core—the "Middle Kingdom"—of a transnational cultural realm within which these elites participated. Yet, as this name also implies, Korea was outside this "Middle"—to the "East"—and China often served as the dominant other against which these elites distinguished what made their country different. In this way, Chosŏn elites developed a two-tiered sense of identity as members of a larger transnational realm but with a distinct sense of separateness articulated through the national unit (*guk*). In the years leading up to 1895, and particularly after the Sino-Japanese War, a thorough reappraisal of the central function of China in defining the nation was launched as Koreans became increasingly engaged with Western forms of knowledge. In short, the reconstruction of Korean identity in a new world system was accompanied by a reinvention of China—a process I refer to as the decentering of the Middle Kingdom.

The struggle of non-Western intellectuals to negotiate the at times divergent impulses of a nationalism that seemingly required modernization at the expense of traditions while urging pride in those very traditions that ostensibly impeded progress toward the modern has been a topic of much analysis. In Korea, although a sketch of the different strategies on how to deal with these issues would show a spectrum of responses similar to those of its East Asian neighbors—ranging from the iconoclast through the gradual reformer to the preservationist—there existed a very different dynamic from the experience of China. For according to the nationalizing logic of the late nineteenth and early twentieth centuries the full panoply of beliefs, practices, and symbols that centuries of scholars had shared as part of their participation in the transnational cultural realm of East Asia could be redefined as Chinese. Deemed as particular to China, these could now be rejected as alien to Korea. In newly established nationalist presses, leading writers averred that for Korea to attain national independence, Koreans must rediscover their unique identity by discarding cultural accretions from China. Underlying these explicit calls lay a number of assumptions about the relationship among culture, knowledge, and the nation. In particular, the new emphasis on the recovery of a pure and authentic culture depended on an overly simplified juxtaposition of Korean versus Chinese in which both national categories were presented as historically immutable and uncontested. But, as this essay argues, when various nationalists sought to implement specific reforms, the ways in which Chinese culture was invoked or, just as significantly, not invoked often ran counter to the assumptions behind calls for the recovery of a pure culture. Issues as diverse as writing systems, the institutions surrounding the monarchy, the adoption of a national flag, and one newspaper's conception of the use of classical historical references demonstrate that the legacies of the East Asian world order were not so easily subli-mated into the nationalist ideals of the new world system.

Demoting China

In the first clause of the Treaty of Shimonoseki, signed in 1895 by the Qing and Meiji empires to conclude their recent war, Qing officials recognized the absolute sovereignty of Korea for the first time. In the years leading up to this treaty, a number of prominent Koreans—most notably the leaders of the 1884 coup d'état—had called for an end to the tributary relationship, yet it was only with this treaty that practices impinging on Korean sovereignty were to be once and for all abandoned. So ended the centuries-long tributary relationship.

Over the following fifteen years, a newly established nationalist press explored the consequences of these changes for Korea. The earliest, the *Tongnip sinmun* (Independent, 1896–98), founded by Sŏ Chaep'il, a naturalized Ameri-can who had returned to Korea after an eleven-year absence, caused quite a stir among the official elite with its aggressive editorials calling for sweeping reform (Chandra 1988; Sin Yongha 1975). The *Hwangsŏng sinmun* (Capital Gazette, 1898–1910), established by a number of more moderate reformers who had received classical educations within the country, combined its calls for change with attention to the many past practices that its founders believed could still serve nationalist ends (Yi Kwangnin 1989, 155–95). The *Cheguk sinmun* (Imper-ial Post, 1898–1910), unlike the *Hwangsŏng sinmun* which targeted elites, was aimed at promoting self-strengthening reform among the noneducated popu-lation (Ch'oe Kiyŏng 1991, 11–65). Though the editorial staffs of all three papers differed on many issues, all agreed that China's military loss to Japan was sym-bolic of the defeat of "old knowledge" (*guhak*) by "new knowledge" (*sinhak*)—that is, the "Western learning" upon which Japan had based the reform pro-grams that had enabled its victory.

This conclusion reflected a shift in the definition of "civilization" away from one hegemonic system with its geographical locus in China toward another, centered on the West. For the editor of the *Hwangsŏng sinmun*, this amounted to an outright reversal: "In the past, what one said was right today is felt to be wrong; and what in the past was felt to be wrong, today is under-stood to be right" (29 July 1899). Following this new definition of "civilization," the relationship between previous understandings of the universal and the particular began to shift. And as Koreans sought to assert their status as a sov-ereign nation China was correspondingly demoted, stripped of its formerly privileged position.

An editorial in the 5 June 1899 edition of the daily newspaper *Tongnip sinmun* addressed the changes that followed the adoption of Western norms of "civilization." Remarking that Koreans had lived in "one corner of the Eastern Sea" for thousands of years without knowing anything about the world, the editor continued:

> The only thing [Koreans] knew was to revere China as the central plain (*chungwŏn*), scorn Japan as the country of *wae*, and call all other countries barbarians (*orangk'ae*). Now, for more than ten years, our doors have been open and we have welcomed guests coming from all places. With our ears we can hear and with our eyes we can see the customs and laws of Western countries. We can now generally judge which countries are the civilized ones and which countries are the barbarous ones.

If Korean editorial writers could "now generally judge" the civilized from the barbarous, many busied themselves with drawing up taxonomies of the world's nations according to these standards.

In the most common formulation of the hierarchies of "civilization," countries were ranked in three groups: the civilized, the semicivilized, and the barbarous (Yu Kilchun 1895, 375–84; *Tongnip sinmun*, 26 January 1897). With few exceptions, China fell into the middle rank—a group that according to Yu Kilchun, one of the earliest proponents of "civilization," consisted of countries that were content with small accomplishments, had no long-range plans, and did not commit themselves to the various forms of enlightenment (1895, 377). But in the everyday writings of newspapers and journals, China's ostensible middling rank was for the most part ignored. The former Middle Kingdom's "civilized" features were forgotten as its barbarous aspects were highlighted, bemoaned, and invoked as a warning. China became the most familiar image of a nation lacking "civilization." Such representations unfolded over the course of entire editorials, as writers, wielding multiple examples and emotive exclamations, explored the reasons for China's condition.

Accounts of the hurly-burly of Chinese politics at the turn of the century were explained in terms of "civilization"—or, more strictly speaking, the lack thereof. One newspaper, in a year-end summary for 1897, bluntly stated that all China had done during the preceding twelve months was give up territory and rights to others, making no progress toward "civilization" (*Tongnip sinmun*, 28 December 1897). Few events captured as much attention as the Boxer Rebellion. The *Hwangsŏng sinmun* informed readers of the increasingly tense situation in northern China with a steady stream of reports and frequent editorial comments. By the time foreign troops were heading for Beijing, the editors were already sounding the alarm. Ever since the Hundred-Day reform of 1898, they explained, the obstinacy and stubbornness of the court had further hardened while barbarism (*ya*) and ignorance had intensified (21 June 1900). Xenophobia had become prevalent, they pointed out (30 June 1900). There were no talented or knowledgeable officials; all were conservative, interested in imitating the past, and unwilling to pursue reforms. The editors even cited the licentious behavior of the empress dowager in her Xi'an refuge following the defeat of the Boxers as further evidence of China's plight (17 May 1901). At the height of the rebellion, the editors became so distraught over the possibility that the Boxers might spill over the Yalu into Korea that they published a special editorial—on the front page rather than in its usual position on the second page—calling for extraordinary border preparations (25 June 1900). China's turmoil, they feared, could extend to Korea.

More pervasive than such extended commentaries, however, were the brief mentions of China—often no more than one line—on matters that ostensibly had no direct bearing on China but provided an example of what became of nations that did not engage in the "civilizing" process. The corrupt nature of Chinese law (*Hwangsŏng sinmun*, 12 September 1898) and its inhumane penal institutions (*Tongnip sinmun*, 25 August 1897) were cited as frequently as its dirty streets and hospitals (*Hwangsŏng sinmun*, 9 October 1899). Nor did writers refrain from assailing the Chinese national character, charging the people with being lazy and claiming that "idleness has become a custom" (*Hwangsŏng sinmun*, 13 May 1899).

Reports of Chinatowns both abroad and at home reinforced such representations. This topic was a special favorite of the editorial staff of the *Tongnip sinmun*, whose chief editor, Sŏ Chaep'il, had studied in Philadelphia, where he was undoubtedly exposed to American anti-Chinese writings. One early editorial berated the Chinese who had emigrated to the United States. Even though these immigrants now lived in a "civilized" nation, it declared, they are unable to reform their "savage" customs (21 May 1896). On the issue of Chinese immigrants in Korea, the editor was even less restrained. The Chinese in Korea, the editor charged, made the already dirty streets even more filthy and introduced the people to opium. "There are not even the slightest benefits that accrue in their coming to Korea," he continued, "only many harms." Comparing the Chinese merchants to leeches, the editor lambasted them for merely making profits for themselves without engaging in "civilizing" enterprises. "We don't want such people coming to Korea," he stated.

To be sure, writers differed in their representations of China as barbarous. But in a press that, despite divergent political stances, uniformly defined its mandate as enlightening the people, these differences were for the most part a matter of tone. The *Tongnip sinmun*, one of the most zealous advocates of "civilization," treated China with scorn, calling it "the laughing stock of the world" (20 June 1896). In contrast, the editors of the *Hwangsŏng sinmun* wrote of China with an empathy that reflected a consciousness of ancient bonds and possibly shared fates. "We are extremely worried for China," they frequently told their readers (6 August 1900). A more ambivalent note was struck by the editors of a primary school reader, who followed a statement that China is the object of the "world's ridicule and humiliation" with the simple conclusion: "How pitiable. How laughable" (*Kungmin sohak tokpon* 1895, 25). Whatever the tone, "civilization" and China were inextricably linked in the pages of nationalist publications during these years. Like its counterpart in Meiji Japan (Keene 1971; Tanaka 1993), "civilization" intruded on all matters Chinese and China was regularly invoked as an exemplar of barbarity.[1] If the Treaty of Shimonoseki had disengaged Korea from the ritual-political structures of tribute, the representations of China as barbarous marked Korea's participation in the new ideologies of the world system in which China played not a central but a peripheral role. Such a shift became integral to the rearticulation of Korean identity outside the bounds of the East Asian regional order.

Authentic Culture, Pure Identities

Literature from the field of postcolonial studies has highlighted the process by which nationalist movements have produced and articulated national difference.[2] As part of their critiques of nationalist narratives, these studies have properly cast doubt on the tendency to frame expressions of identity as projects of recovery through which essentialized national cultures are retrieved intact from the precolonial past. Instead, as Homi Bhabha has proposed, projects of recovery are actually creative, leading to the development of hybrid cultures (1994a). In Korea, explicit calls for resurrecting a lost, authentic culture first emerged in the nationalist presses between 1895 and 1910. Unlike in the colonial states of the West, which have provided the bulk of the material for postcolonial studies, in Korea the culture targeted for resistance, even expurgation, was not that of the immediate colonizing power, whether the West or Japan, but that of its neighbor, China.

The hybrid cultural offspring of globalization are generally seen as combinations of indigenous and imperial cultures. But in Korea hybridization did not follow the arrival of imperialism, for by the time Western culture arrived a process of hybridization had already been under way for centuries within the transnational realm of East Asia. For Korean nationalists at the end of the nineteenth century, the task of recovery was one of breaking up this hybrid into what were viewed as its component "national" parts. Former representations of national particularity came to be reconstituted in relation to the new conception of universal "civilization," while the former universals, rooted in a now largely discredited Confucian epistemology, came to be particularized, more often than not, as "Chinese." National meanings—whether Korean or Chinese—were imposed on common beliefs, symbols, and practices that previously had maintained few connections with the nation. As nationalist reformers sought to assert the purely Korean, practices that had earlier been shared without any privileging of geographical origins were sifted to determine just what could be categorized anew as foreign so as to separate them from the "Korean." Geographical origins came to be privileged such that the nationality of cultural forms was inscribable almost wholly by means of its spatial source. If a manufactured good could be identified by its "nation of origin," so, too, could a cultural practice. Consequently, a crucial component of the reconstruction of Korean national identity in these years was the attendant reinvention of the category "Chinese." The Korean vocabulary of authenticity—national essence (*kuksu*), ethnic nation (*minjok*), and national soul (*kukhon*)—gained much of its meaning in contradistinction to China. Just what it was that marked this particular nation as "Korean" was to be juxtaposed to just what is was that made their neighboring nation "Chinese."

For these reasons, in a period when the most immediate threats to Korean sovereignty came from Japan and Russia, Korean writers turned their attention to historical China. Independence in the contemporary world system came to be contrasted with what was increasingly decried as a past Korean dependence on, and even a slavish mentality toward, China. This juxtaposition between future and past, sovereignty and servility, independence and dependence served writers well in their calls for a cathartic elimination of Chinese cultural forms from the peninsula. Only by reestablishing cultural purity, it was argued, could true independence be attained.[3]

To this end, the historical figure Ŭlchi Mundŏk, "the single greatest person in 4,000 years of Korean history" according to one scribe, was prominently resurrected in the pages of the press (Yi Kich'an [1908] 1997, 259). More than a millennium earlier, in 612 A.D., Ŭlchi had led a smaller Koguryŏ contingent against the more than 300,000 troops of Sui Yangdi's invading army. With a number of ingenious stratagems and some ferocious fighting, Ŭlchi did more than just emerge victorious. He handily routed the emperor's army, leaving only 2,100 of the bedraggled imperial troops to scramble back to the haven of Sui territory. Despite this achievement, Ŭlchi's triumphs had been treated only scantily in prenationalist histories. But writers at the turn of the twentieth century, eager to find heroes to inspire younger generations, discovered in Ŭlchi a figure who at once reflected a lost tradition of military greatness and displayed a tenacious spirit of independence vis-à-vis China. No reader of newspapers, journals, or textbooks in these years could miss the extensive pieces detailing the life and accomplishments of this Koguryŏ general. Statues were raised in his honor in front of schools (Hwang Hyŏn 1971, 534), and his name appeared in patriotic poetry (*TaeHan maeil sinbo*, 22 September 1909).

In his introduction to one of the more lengthy biographies of Ŭlchi, the historian and editorialist Sin Ch'aeho recounted his epiphany-like reaction to learning about the Koguryŏ general. Prior to hearing about Ŭlchi's deeds, Sin had assumed that the history of Korea's foreign relations was merely one of endless foreign invasions, where a single word from China would be received by a cowering court—a situation, Sin wrote, that had led him to believe that the natural character of the nation was "inferior and weak." When he read about Ŭlchi, however, his

> spirit surged and his boldness leaped. Raising my face to Heaven I shouted, "This! This is the nature of our nation! It is thus! Nothing in either the past or the present rivals such a great figure and such great deeds. This is how strong and brave is the nature of our nation! [1908] 1997, 2)

The hope of the likes of Sin and others, of course, was that such historical biographies, at a time when the peninsula was besieged by external powers, would provide a paragon of the selfless patriot fighting against the odds to protect the nation. Learning about these battles, another author pointed out, would "summon up a second Ŭlchi Mundŏk" (An Ch'angho [1908] 1997, 266).

Yet Ŭlchi also represented for many writers a time when Koreans were truly Korean, unsullied by contact with a debilitating Chinese culture. As the author of the preface to Sin's biography noted:

> Ever since Chinese culture entered our country, our people have all burned with the fever of revering the foreign and have stubbornly clung to the sickness of degrading oneself. Consequently, even in their dreams they did not think of great heroes such as Ŭlchi Mundŏk. (Yi Kich'an [1908] 1997, 257–58)

Ŭlchi's defiance of China, both as a warrior who had repelled Chinese attacks and as someone who had avoided the Confucian training of later generations, symbolized a glorious instance in the national past. Ŭlchi's very surname served as evidence of that purely Korean past for which they were searching. Yu

Kilchun lamented that ancient surnames such as Ŭlchi had disappeared, replaced with Chinese-style names because Koreans had become addicted to Chinese characters as though they were opium (Yu Kilchun 1908, 2). Elevating the very name of Ŭlchi thus became at once a means of exalting a lost indigenous Korea and a call for the purging of Chinese influence, both political and cultural.

Such calls for the recovery of an unadulterated Koreanness rested on an assumption that there existed a simple, natural separation between the cultural forms that had originated on the continent and those rooted in the peninsula despite centuries of exchange, appropriation, and interaction. Just as an archaeologist could dig up lost relics of the past, national character could be unearthed from the sands of time. As though culture was as objective as shards of pottery, it could be sought, retrieved, and restored—in short, returned to an untainted, original state. The myriad traditions, practices, and symbols inherited by Koreans from their predecessors could be winnowed and the cultural forms newly identified as "Chinese" separated and cast aside so as to reveal an obscured but ever-present "Korean" essence.

More than any other issue, reform of the system of writing best fit these assumptions. The transition from the use of characters to the phonetic alphabet is a well-known story that unfolded over several centuries. What is of concern here is the active promotion of the phonetic alphabet as a *national* script (*kungmun*) in place of characters during the 1895–1910 period. From the inception of the alphabet at the behest of King Sejong in 1443 until the late nineteenth century, this system to "Teach the People the Correct Sounds" (*hunmin chŏngŭm*), as it was first called, had yet to gain as its main attribute a connection with the nation. Rather, scholars underscored its relation to knowledge. And on the basis of this relation, the educated elite rejected King Sejong's invention. Scholars such as Ch'oe Malli vociferously attacked the new alphabet, arguing that knowledge and characters were inextricably linked. As the classics were written in characters and deemed to be the source of all truth, abandoning the character was tantamount to losing access to this knowledge. In a long memorial presented in 1444, Ch'oe argued that the new writing system would undermine learning and harm the order of the world. The people, he cried,

> would not know the writings of the sages and worthies, "they won't study, their faces will be to the wall." They will be blind with respect to right and wrong in the Pattern of things. . . . The Culture of the Right, which our country has amassed and accumulated, will gradually come to being swept from the earth. (Ledyard 1966, 106)

For Ch'oe, there was little use for the alphabet, as he asked, "Why should we change from a long used, uncorrupted script and separately create mean, vulgar, profitless graphs?" (Ledyard 1966, 106). In Ch'oe's memorial, neither the character nor the new alphabet was identified primarily through an association with one nation or another, as is so easily assumed today. Instead, the nature of each writing system was determined by its link to knowledge, one offering access, the other precluding it. Thus, for Ch'oe and successive generations of Chosŏn dynasty scholars, the characters could literally be deemed *chinmun,* the "true script," as only they provided access to truth, while King Sejong's alphabet, which could make no special claim on knowledge, could be ignored, dismissed as nothing more than *ŏnmun,* the "vulgar script."

As new systems of knowledge entered Korea along with the guns and products of the imperialist powers, the privileged relationship between knowledge and the character came to be increasingly challenged. What Ch'oe had called the "Culture of the Right" was less frequently invoked as it came to be gradually supplanted by new definitions of "civilization." A new knowledge was promoted, one to which access was no longer monopolized by the character but was attainable through any writing system, whether English, Japanese—or King Sejong's alphabet. This reconfiguration of the relationship between the written word and knowledge enabled the full nationalization of both scripts. Korean writers began to tout King Sejong's alphabet as the only *Korean* writing system. What for more than five hundred years had been known as "vulgar writing" was transformed into "national writing" (*kungmun*).

In creating these national meanings, writers commonly naturalized the link between nation and writing. Chu Sigyŏng, a prominent linguist, used this linkage to legitimize Korea's claim to independence as natural:

> On this planet, land is naturally divided and groups of people (*hanttŏlgi injŏng*) living in these areas make and use a language appropriate to the local sounds prevalent in this clime. Moreover, they make a script that fits the sounds of their language. In this way, the existence of a special language and script in one nation is certainly a sign that this country is naturally a self-governing nation (*chajuguk*). (Chu 1907, 32)

So, too, could this link be universalized. As the editors of the *Hwangsŏng sinmun* opined, "In all the nations under Heaven, there are none that do not have their own national language and national script" (7 September 1906). Here, in a classic formulation of a deterministic criterion for defining a nation, language in both its oral and written forms served to lay claim to the right to national independence.

By naturalizing the link between the written word and nation, writers simultaneously undermined the claim of the character to national transcendence. The character, formerly considered a truth script for all, now came to be identified fully as the *Chinese* character. Writers, for the first time since the character had been introduced centuries ago, highlighted its Chineseness. As one commentator felt the need to note: "Chinese writing is the national language of the land of China" (Yi Chŏng'il 1908, 12). Writers downgraded the status of the "true writing" to that of the national script of just another foreign country. As another reformer explained: "The national writing is our nation's writing. Chinese writing is the writing of China" (Yi Sŭnggyo 1908, 20). This rejection of the character as Chinese and alien was most manifest symbolically in the numerous demands for the physical relocation of its place of teaching. As many reformers argued, the character should no longer be part of the national curriculum and should only be taught side by side with English and Japanese in foreign-language schools (*Hwangsŏng sinmun*, 28 September 1898; Yi Pogyŏng 1908, 18).

Writers promoted the national script not only as something to be used but also as an object worthy of reverence. If not so venerated, one writer feared, the situation would be like people who "did not respect their own parents and only loved other people" (Yi Pongun 1985, preface). Chu Sigyŏng beseeched his compatriots to love their language and writing system (1907, 34), while Sin Ch'aeho challenged the nationality of any Korean who did not, asking: "Today, if there are still those who scorn the national script more than Chinese writing, can we still call them Korean?" (1908).

Clearly, for Sin the answer was no. Yet, in possibly the only piece published in these years that called for the retention of the character, at least one person refrained from such a judgment. This person was a relatively unknown teacher, Yŏ Kyuhyang, who, in contributing an article to the conservative reform journal *Taedong hakhoe wŏlbo* (Monthly of the Great Eastern Educational Association), adopted the nationalizing logic of the advocates of writing reform (1908). But for Yŏ this logic could be wielded equally effectively to defend the character. His defense rested on the dismissal of his opponents' assertion that the character had "invaded" the peninsula from abroad and then been adopted by Koreans. Instead, he contended that the character had always existed in Korea. "For four thousand years, since Tan'gŭn and Kija first established the country, we Koreans have been using the character." Here Yŏ invoked the same logic as the character's detractors. He did not revert to the old arguments about the special relationship between the character and knowledge, nor did he claim any special transnational status for the character. Rather, he creatively claimed that with its putative origins in Korea the character was Korean, not foreign, and as a Korean writing system, he insinuated, it deserved to be preserved, not purged. Yŏ's piece, despite its very different agenda, shows how deeply the logic of nationalizing culture had penetrated intellectual circles by the early twentieth century. The style of argument leveled against King Sejong's alphabet nearly five hundred years before by the likes of Ch'oe Malli had little constituency among conservative nationalists. Even the embattled defenders of the character sought to frame their arguments in terms of nation and geographic origins. This style of counterargument, sharing as it did the same assumptions about writing and nation, had little chance of stemming the increasingly widespread and ideological use of the alphabet. Out of a neglected linguistic invention, advocates of the formerly "vulgar writing" succeeded in creating one of the leading icons of the nationalist movement.

The call by nationalists to rediscover the indigenous and discard the Chinese was most successfully realized in the writing reform movement. It was in this area that assumptions about national culture most neatly matched the objects of reform. As a new symbol of Koreanness and a reform that manifested the principles of cultural retrieval, the alphabet emerged as one of the most celebrated issues of the period—which, in turn, served to reinforce the wider calls for authenticity and seemingly to substantiate the assumptions about national culture. But not all reform efforts included a pair of cultural objects that could be so neatly inscribed with contrasting national origins. Indeed, as the impulse to nationalize culture was carried into other areas, a number of ambiguities and difficulties appeared, for despite the rhetoric not all cultural forms could be so smoothly instilled with clear-cut national meanings.

From King to Emperor

The months following the conclusion of the Sino-Japanese War in 1895 proved to be the nadir of the political fortunes of the Korean royal house. Early on the morning of 8 October, a group of Japanese ruffians under the direction of the newly appointed Japanese minister to Korea invaded the royal palace, where they assassinated Queen Min, compounding the horror of their deeds by burning her corpse in a garden at the back of the grounds. In fear for his own safety, King Kojong smuggled himself in his consort's palanquin out of the palace to the safety of the Russian legation, where, despite the pleas of his officials and those of the Independence Club, he remained ensconced for eleven months. With the prestige of the royal house seriously damaged by this series of events, the court initiated a series of efforts to reverse the monarchy's fortunes and reestablish the dignity and power of the throne. It was to be a "restoration" (*chunghŭng*)—an expression with a long history among the beleaguered courts of East Asia. This restoration was similar in intent to what Benedict Anderson has called "official nationalism," only here the court was following on the heels of the already burgeoning nationalist movement, hoping to harness the agitation for independence to its own purpose of reasserting the centrality of the throne (Anderson 1991, 83–111). Initially, efforts focused on the vestiges of the tributary relationship that still adhered to the royal institution. Even as King Kojong resided in the Russian legation changes were made: adherence to Qing taboo characters was terminated; an independent year title, *Kŏnyang*, was adopted in 1896; and ancient monuments such as the "Welcoming Imperial Grace Gate" (*Yŏngŭnmun*), where Chinese imperial envoys to Seoul had been greeted for nearly five hundred years, were razed (Hwang Hyŏn 1971, 171). Yet the most powerful symbol of Korea's former subordinate status rested in the king himself. As long as King Kojong maintained the royal title—a title that in the ritual language of tribute was beneath that of emperor—a suggestion of subordination lingered. Court officials moved to eliminate any such implication with a number of changes centering on Kojong's form of address, changes that were marked by a panoply of exhaustive rituals based on classical precedents but instilled with new meaning.

The first steps were taken as early as July 1894, when it was announced that the King's conventional form of address would be raised one level from "sovereign" (*kunju*) to "great sovereign" (*taegunju*). In subsequent months, further elevations were made, as the king came to be referred to as "royal highness" (*chusang chŏnha*) and then in 1896 as "great imperial highness" (*taegun chup'aeha*)—each change a significant rise in ritual language. With Kojong out of the Russian compound, the final stage in this process was set to begin. In October of 1897, a memorial requesting a change in royal status was submitted. A flurry of activity followed, as officials and rural scholars rushed to present petitions beseeching the king to abandon the royal title. For three consecutive days, Kojong's top officials knelt in the palace courtyard for four hours each day, according to protocol submitting nine separate requests. Kojong declined all supplications—except, of course, the last (Hwang Hyŏn 1971, 168).

Even before the king assented, construction had begun on the Ring Hill Altar (*Wŏn'gudan*), suggesting that the publicly humble Kojong was privately not so modest (Yi Kuyŏng 1985). Quickly constructed for his coronation, the Ring Hill was designed along the lines of Beijing's Altar of Heaven, with three terraces separated from one another by nine steps. After the appropriate sacrifices to Heaven in the early morning of 12 October 1897, Kojong doffed the royal red robes and donned the dragon yellow robes of emperors (Hwang Hyŏn

1971, 215–17). King Kojong had become Emperor Kojong. Using ancient rituals to support modern concepts, the reinvention of the throne signified that the source of Korean sovereignty rested unambiguously within the peninsula. In his first edict as emperor, Kojong reversed a five-century-old tradition, announcing:

> The foundation of independence has been created and the rights of sovereignty exercised. The officials and people, soldiers and merchants have called out in one voice, requesting in tens of petitions that We should assume the title of Emperor. We refused them numerous times, but there was no way to end their requests. Thus, on the seventeenth day of the ninth month of this year, We informed and sacrificed to Heaven and Earth on the south of White Hill and ascended the Imperial Throne. Establishing the name of the realm as Great Han (*Taehan*), We called this year the first year of Kwangmu. (Hwang Hyŏn 1971, 218; Yun Ch'iho 1897, 385)

Not only had the king become emperor, but the Kingdom of Chosŏn had become the Empire of the Great Han. In 1394, the two-year-old dynasty had chosen two potential names for itself: Chosŏn, the name of an early kingdom in northern Korea, which in 108 B.C. had been defeated by the Chinese Han dynasty; and Hwanyŏng, an old name for the Hamgyŏng area, where the founder of the dynasty had been born. Presented to the Beijing court for approval, the Ming emperor had picked the former. But by the late 1890s the origins of the dynastic name—a name that had been unchallenged for five hundred years—came to be seen in terms of new concepts of sovereignty. Now associated with the disdained politics of tribute, Chosŏn was abandoned in favor of Han, a term traceable to ancient kingdoms in the southern half of the peninsula—an area, most significantly, that had never been invaded by China. With its connotations of independence, the tradition of the ancient Han kingdom was claimed for the new emperor and his empire.

Throughout this process of reinventing the Korean royal house, a wide-ranging arsenal of imperial symbols and rituals was invoked. Ostensibly employed in a conventional fashion, this mixture of symbols in fact functioned in imaginative ways. Citations from the *Book of Rites*, the time-honored precedents of the Three Emperors and Five Kings, the constant appearance of the sacred number nine (nine requests, nine steps), the use of criminal amnesties, appeals to the benevolent care of Heaven—all these were venerable symbols embedded in the traditions of the East Asian regional order, symbols known by all educated Koreans and regularly used in court debates and official documents. Yet in the last years of the dynasty these traditions were wielded untraditionally. Reinvented to serve the new purpose of independence, they maintained their external form yet embodied fresh meanings.

Central to this reinvention was a reformulation of the concept of emperor. One Heaven, One Emperor had been the accepted order until Kojong donned the imperial robes. Only one man, the Son of Heaven, could sacrifice directly to Heaven, yet by mounting the Ring Hill and undertaking the rituals of supplication Kojong rejected the exclusivity of Sinocentric definitions. His coronation as emperor marked a rupture with traditional protocols, challenging the solitary legitimacy of Beijing's own claimant to imperial status. It was this deliberate violation that paradoxically infused fresh meaning into the hoary symbols. The reinvention of the royal house offered a new definition of an independent nation with the emperor as its symbolic center, or, in the words of Kojong, as "the foundation of independence."

At one level, the reinvention of the royal throne functioned, as did writing reform, to decenter the Middle Kingdom. The rituals created a metonymic symbol for the nation: just as Kojong could now claim equal status to his Beijing counterpart, so could the Great Han empire claim equality with the Qing. When in 1898 a Chinese plenipotentiary arrived in Seoul to seek a commercial treaty, he carried a letter that began "The Great Emperor of Great Qing respectfully greets the Great Emperor of Great Korea," marking the first communication between the two sovereigns as equals (Hwang Hyŏn 1971, 232–33).

Yet there was also a very different dynamic in this reinvention. Unlike writing reform, where two divergent systems could be sharply juxtaposed—one "ours," the other "theirs"—court officials did not attempt to attribute any inherent nationness to the rituals themselves. Instead, meaning was interpreted solely in terms of their function. This meaning—independence as signified through the willful violation of received protocols—nevertheless was derived from the still resonant potency of traditional East Asian symbolic orders. The sacrificial altar, the color of the robes, and the supplicative actions of the officials—all were symbols that under other circumstances could have been inscribed with Chinese meanings and, according to the logic of the nationalizing of culture, rejected as other. But such meanings were not invoked by the court. Instead, its political needs and motivations took precedence. In seeking to reassert its own power and prestige, these symbols and rituals proved useful to the court because they linked throne, nation, and independence, making each essential to the others. In a period when various social groups were participating in a contested process of reconstructing national identity, the court used the imperial rituals and symbols in an attempt to position the emperor at the center of newly emerging visions of an independent Korea.

As with many public rituals, however, the emperor and his officials could not monopolize the meaning of the throne's reinvention. Individuals outside the court had strong reservations, not so much about the crown's new enthusiasm for independence as about the means by which the court pursued the goal. Yun Ch'iho, a prominent journalist, upon hearing about the plans to elevate the king's status wrote in his diary on 27 May 1897: "I wonder which of the many asses in the government has put this piteous notion into the royal head?" (Yun 1971). Later, in the more public forum of a missionary-run publication, Yun showed a more diplomatic side. He gently ridiculed the behavior of officials and the conduct of various rituals, dismissing the memorials of the officials as reflecting the "ancient classic style of China, full of obscure allusions and bombastic phrases" (1897, 387). In the official *Tongnip sinmun* editorial on these changes, to which as an editorialist Yun may have contributed, an even more optimistic stance was assumed. In particular, the piece focused on the court officials, who, it noted, had until very recently always looked to China. That even these men now worked for independence was a "sign that Chosŏn is gradually becoming an independent nation" (1 October 1897). But such compliments were tempered with the editors' resentment of the tendency to reduce independence to titular matters. Regardless of whether a nation was "an empire or a kingdom," they insisted that the level of enlightenment was what determined a nation's status. Willing to accept a symbolic end to royal subordinance, the editors of the *Tongnip sinmun* were less eager to endorse the court's plan to make the throne the "foundation of independence."

The delicate position of promoting the king as a symbol of patriotic loyalty while hesitating to embrace the court's own efforts to repackage the royal institution is manifest in the *Hwangsŏng sinmun*'s response to a Chinese newspaper's account of these events. According to the Korean newspaper, its Chinese counterpart, the *Wanguo gongbao*, had described the ritual using the terminology "to claim the throne" (Korean *ch'ingche*, Chinese *chengdi*) as opposed to "ascending the throne" (Korean *chŭkwi*, Chinese *jiwei*). The former term in conventional ritual language implied illegitimate usurpation of the imperial mantle while the latter signaled the legitimate mounting of the throne by the individual holding the Mandate of Heaven. By choosing to describe the ceremony as Kojong "claiming the throne," the Chinese paper in effect rejected the legitimacy of the action. The editors of the *Hwangsŏng sinmun* barely restrained their ridicule: "we laugh" at the Chinese scribes for such "self-adulation and for still being mired in the corrupt theories of Song Confucians" (21 September 1898). Yet these so-called corrupt theories were the very theories invoked by the court in the imperial rituals. What the Chinese editors interpreted as illegitimate was precisely the violation of established norms that the court deliberately manipulated to symbolize the independence of the nation through the throne. The interpretation of these rituals depended on the same assumptions, but could lead to very different conclusions.

Though chary of criticizing an institution that they, too, wished to promote as a symbol of patriotism, the editors of the *Hwangsŏng sinmun* had no reason to restrain themselves from scoffing at the *Wanguo gongbao*. To mock their use of these theories was to level an indirect critique at the court's methods of restoration. The *Hwangsŏng sinmun* editors sought to separate the choice of the imperial title from these theories. As they asked, "don't they know that every sovereign nation has the right to establish its own titles as it so desires" (21 September 1898)? The choice of title was reduced to little more than a perquisite of sovereignty. The editorial exemplified the transitional character of this period. Written in classical Chinese without the use of Korean (perhaps for the benefit of the writers at the *Wanguo gongbao*), the piece was based on a grasp of the intended implications of the Chinese newspaper's manipulation of these terms. Yet the editorial's objection, unlike the court's rituals, worked from outside Confucian legitimacy theory, denying its relevance. For the editors of the *Hwangsŏng sinmun,* the court's reinvention of the throne, stripped of its rituals and symbols, could mean independence, but it was an independence defined according to international conventions of sovereignty.

The divergent interpretations of these rituals reflected conflicting views on the status of the sovereign in a reformed nation. Nationalist reformers, eager to present themselves as the champions of enlightenment and national progress, were less than enthusiastic about the attempts of the court to use what they perceived as outdated rituals and symbols to reassert its own power. Moreover, any reassertion of the throne had implications for the self-perceived role of reformers as the rightful leaders of "enlightened" society. This conflict over who best represented and spoke for the nation eventually came to a head. By November 1898, these contending visions spilled into the streets of Seoul. Rumors—possibly planted by its detractors at court—suggesting that the Independence Club harbored plans to establish a republic began to circulate around the capital. This provided top officials with an opportunity to crack down on an organization that through its newspapers and street demonstrations had repeatedly—and in the eyes of these officials presumptuously—criticized government policy. In one of the more renowned incidents of the period, these officials unleashed the hooligans of the Peddlar's Guild, who attacked club members participating in a large demonstration on the central street of Seoul. By December, the court had officially banned the club (Chandra 1988, 204–8; Sin Yongha 1975, 550–76).

A National Flag

The ways in which the shared traditions of the East Asian regional order were variously employed can also be observed in the symbol par excellence of the nation at the turn of the century, the national flag. The dual function of the flag is best reflected in one of the recurrent images, both visual and rhetorical, of this period: the Korean flag fluttering in a line of the world's many national flags. Flying as one among equals, the flag represented the sovereignty of Korea in a world populated with nations, and at the same time the arrangement of design and color exhibited national uniqueness within a single standard format.

The nationalist press deliberately cultivated the association of flag and nation. The editors of the *Tongnip sinmun* complained that "when they [the people] see the national flag, they do not have reverent and loving thoughts" (22 September 1896) and devoted much space to increasing its profile. Writers urged their compatriots to "bring glory to the national flag" (*Hwangsŏng sinmun*, 25 November 1904), sing patriotic songs to it, and consider it more important than their own lives (*Tongnip sinmun*, 22 September 1896). Schoolchildren were inculcated with romantic feelings for the flag, "as the light of the sun shines onto the national flag and the national flag flutters in the wind, the entire sky is filled with a feeling of fortune" (Ministry of Education 1907, 57). Through such efforts, the flag emerged as a constant feature in the social life of the nationalist movement, appearing on newspaper mastheads and school textbooks, hoisted nationwide on the occasion of the imperial birthday, and even included prominently on the packaging of "Key" brand cigarettes.

What is of interest in the promotion and use of the Korean flag is the silence surrounding the origins, not of the flag design itself but of its constituent parts. The design used in this period—and still used in the Republic of Korea today—was arguably first proposed by the official Pak Yŏnghyo in 1882. According to Pak's own account, he had decided on the basic design of the flag prior to his departure on a mission as envoy to Japan. Making a few alterations during his voyage to Tokyo, Pak later sent a copy to Seoul. Before receiving official approval of the design, Pak began flying it over his residence in Japan. The following year, in 1883, King Kojong approved Pak's design, officially proclaiming it the national Korean flag (Yi Sŏngŭn 1959). In this design, nationality was asserted through a blue and red symbol known as the *t'aegŭk* on a white background, flanked by four sets of trigrams, one in each corner. Such venerable symbols, with their associations with classical texts, laid claim to an ancient cultural past for the nation, muting the significance of the flag's recent invention. As such, the *t'aegŭk* flag combined both new and ancient, universal and

Korean. Both the *t'aegŭk* and the trigrams had been used in Korea for a variety of purposes for centuries. The former has been generally associated with neo-Confucian debates ever since its use by the Song scholar Zhou Dunyi (1017–73) in his metaphysical works. On the peninsula, the *t'aegŭk* was employed at a folk level in tombs, temples, and even medical texts. The trigrams, also associated with metaphysical debates and the *Book of Changes* (*Yijing*), were at a popular level used for fortune-telling.

The use of these symbols reflects much more than just the limits of the impulse to decenter the Middle Kingdom. It demonstrates the indeterminacy of the national categories upon which the move to nationalize cultures rested. Texts like the *Book of Changes* and the forms of knowledge from which the *t'aegŭk* and trigrams were derived were precisely the types of texts and knowledge that newspapers such as the *Tongnip sinmun* castigated for stifling Korean creativity and leading the nation into its precarious political situation. Observing the situation in China, the editors noted that tens of thousands of scholars had mastered the Four Books and Three Classics, yet "this knowledge is not in the slightest helpful; on the contrary, because they have this knowledge they are dying like a sick body." The editors urged their readers to heed this evidence as a warning, asking, "What use does learning this knowledge have for protecting the country?" (13 January 1898). More simply put, they advised their readers to "forget the Four Books" (27 July 1898). In the eyes of these editors, such books could be derogatorily dismissed as nothing more than "Chinese knowledge" (1 March 1899). But when it came to the *t'aegŭk* and the trigrams, the association of these symbols with the very forms of knowledge and texts decried as both useless and Chinese was overlooked by the same editors. Instead, in this particular context—stitched together on a white background—the symbols took on the most national of meanings. The *Tongnip sinmun,* by placing the flag's image on its front page and calling for its wider use, helped make the national flag one of the most prominent icons of the nationalist movement.

The design and use of the national flag reveals the more complicated nature of creating national meanings than is suggested by calls for cultural retrieval based on a dichotomy between Chinese and Korean. If the characters and texts that constituted these forms of knowledge could be instilled with Chinese meanings, so, too, could derivatives of the same forms of knowledge such as the *t'aegŭk* and trigrams be used to establish purely Korean meanings in the specific context of a national flag. Both outcomes were a part of the same process—a nationalizing process that was less an epiphany of national consciousness in which an inherent Chineseness or Koreanness was recognized than an effort to instill nationality into texts and symbols that until very recently had been considered universal.

Korea in the East

Similar dilemmas appeared in the *Hwangsŏng sinmun*'s efforts to negotiate the at times divergent aims of decentering China while at the same time arguing for a non-Western "civilization" in the East. More skeptical of the West and advocating a more moderate reform program than their colleagues at the *Tongnip sinmun*, the editors of the *Hwangsŏng sinmun* like Namgong Ŏk and Chang Chiyŏn were more ambivalent toward China. Eager to decenter China in support of Korean national independence, they also wrote of a shared Eastern (*tongyang*) heritage still relevant to the new international environment. By drawing attention to the commonalities of the three countries of the East, the paper's articulation of a regional identity muted the decentering impulse to locate the indigenous in contrast to China, resulting in a number of ambiguities in the representation of the East and China.

The early issues of the *Hwangsŏng sinmun* expended much effort in explicating to its readers the rather nebulous definitions that had been offered for "civilization." While the editors accepted the claim that "civilization" was indeed a universal term, they rejected any suggestion that the West maintained a monopoly over "civilization." Using one of their favorite literary conventions, a conversation between a foreigner and a Korean, the editors had a compatriot admonish a foreigner for daring to suggest that Korea was incapable of becoming "civilized." For what reason, he asked, do you think that only the West can become enlightened (*kyemyŏng*)? "I have heard that soon you will be returning home. Tell the people of the West on my behalf," he sternly instructed, "that Korea too . . . will soon head in a progressive direction" (30 May 1899).

This was not just a question of the Korean ability to imitate the West. The editors of the *Hwangsŏng sinmun* sought to dispossess the West of any proprietary rights to "civilization" by discovering evidence of it in the Korean and Eastern pasts. In so doing, the editors of the *Hwangsŏng sinmun* remolded inherited narratives based on Confucian historical conventions to fit this new conceptual framework such that both Korean and Chinese history could be wielded as evidence of an enlightened age outside the West. In another editorial in the conversational style, this time taking place between two Koreans, one figure begins with the comment that enlightenment had come to mean little more than imitating the West. He asks whether there had been enlightenment in the East; to which his interlocutor curtly responds "How could there not have been?" before detailing in the remainder of the piece the many accomplishments of the classical sages. Now the sages—Fuxi, Shennong, Yu, Yao, the duke of Zhou, and Confucius—were dressed up as exemplars not of Confucian morality and governance but of "civilization," with their deeds described in the vocabulary of enlightenment (23 September 1898).

The use of Confucian precedents, refurbished to meet the demands of a new discourse, was a common strategy, as can be seen in the frequent use of venerable terms like *kyŏngmul*, the "investigation of things." With its locus classicus in the opening section of one of the Four Books, the *Daxue, kyŏngmul* came to be equated with the principle of enlightenment—a principle, they strove to show, that had existed in the past as well as the present and in the East as well as the West. Our ancestors discovered fire by *kyŏngmul*, they noted, and the same principle had led to much later inventions such as the railroad in the West. The end products may have been different, but the principle was the same (3 April 1899). The "investigation of things" was deemed little different from "research" (*yŏn'gu*), the term used to describe Western science (29 January 1899). Again, different expressions were used but the principle was the same.

The editors moved beyond terminological equivalence to draw comparisons between past Eastern practices and current Western ones, working to downplay differences and arguing that a common principle of enlightenment was at work, regardless of time or place. Contrasting the methods employed during the Three Dynasties to train and recruit students for government service with those of the contemporary West, the editors found similarities. "For the most part," they concluded with an affirmation of the universal, the ways of the West are "similar to the ways (*pŏmyu*) of the Three Dynasties" (27 October 1898). Another piece on the role of trust between the officials and the people concluded that governance rested on the same principle. "The Way of governing during the reigns of Yao and Shun and during the Three Dynasties was truly nothing more than trust. Today the fundamental technique of making governance by the powers also is nothing more than this trust. How could it be that there would be two Ways of governing the base?" (3 April 1903).

That examples from the classical period would be deemed relevant to contemporary Korea reflects the educational roots of the editorial staff in Confucian learning and their commitment to its continued relevance at the turn of the century. Both Eastern and Korean citations, in the view of these editors, were of the same lineage—one that was to be fleshed out in these years through a regional identity with what they called the "East" (*tongyang*). To be sure, not all examples were derived from Confucian classics. Korean cases were just as frequently cited, be it King Sejong's invention of the alphabet or the construction of Yi Sunsin's armor-clad naval ships, which defeated the Japanese at the end of the sixteenth century (28 April 1899). Also high on the list were Korean ceramics and the world's first movable-print typefaces (25 April 1900) together with various achievements in agriculture and the establishment of school systems (9–12 December 1902).

These uses of the Korean and Eastern pasts functioned to sever the concept of "civilization" from the West, making it a principle of history that belonged just as much to Korea and the East. This was the universal history of the West (Duara 1995), but it was no longer relentlessly unilinear and progressive because the editors of the *Hwangsŏng sinmun*, in a style reminiscent of Confucian historiographical concepts of time, underscored an earlier, rosier period when the organizing principle of history—enlightenment—had been more fully realized in Korea and the East. In so doing, however, the editors of the *Hwangsŏng sinmun* reinterpreted the Korean and Eastern pasts in light of this new concept. This version was a usable past, one that served to universalize enlightenment; yet it was the concept of enlightenment itself that, when cast over that past, determined what was usable. Received narratives of ancient Korea and the East were recast accordingly and achievements that could be lauded as enlightened were highlighted, while formerly acclaimed accomplishments, unable to fit within the parameters of the concept, were relegated to an unusable past. This reinterpretation of history produced a selective past, the process of selection infused with Korean derivatives of an originally Euro-American notion of enlightenment. In so doing, the process of appropriation delocalized the particularity of the Korean and Eastern experience, incorporating both as two more cases in the overarching narrative of progressive history.

Over the years of *Hwangsŏng sinmun*'s publication, as the calls for the recovery of an authentic Korean culture crescendoed, appeals to the Confucian classics and their historical analogies seem to have become increasingly problematic for the editors. In part, this was because they finally heeded their own requests for greater attention to Korean history. To their compatriots who had "abandoned their own and were enamored with others," they issued a warning, for this was tantamount to "failing to convey the genealogy of your own household while learning the pedigree of another home" (19 May 1899). Though such criticisms were directed at those readers who continued this practice from the position of one already aware of the problem, the editors of the *Hwangsŏng sinmun* need have looked no further than their own editorials on the East as evidence of the problem they cited. Gradually and without fanfare, however, such citations decreased in frequency.

At the same time as this decline, more attention was paid to the work of late Chosŏn reformist thinkers. Invoked as examples of past enlightened practices, these thinkers supplanted the sages but still functioned as evidence of a non-Western "civilized" past. Untainted by any association with China, they were at once enlightened *and* Korean. The eighteenth-century scholar Chŏng

Yagyong (1762–1836) in particular attracted the editors' attention. Chŏng's works on economics were seen as sufficiently relevant to the times to be abstracted and reprinted verbatim in place of editorials (4 August 1899). In 1903, when his works were published for the first time, the *Hwangsŏng sinmun* welcomed the event as an opportunity to learn about reform initiatives in the Korean past. Too many people, it decried, are absorbed in either the writings of the Zhou dynasty or Western political and economic tracts, ignoring the writings on Korean institutions and customs (19 May 1903). Seeing themselves as the intellectual descendants of these men, the editors of the *Hwangsŏng sinmun* devoted much space to promoting them, writing a number of editorials on late Chosŏn dynasty figures like Pak Ch'iwŏn (29 June 1901) and Yi Ik (25–26 June 1903).

This shift toward indigenous historical figures became especially pronounced after 1905 once the Japanese had stripped Korea of its sovereignty. With Japan occupying their own country, it became increasingly untenable to appeal to notions of a cultural East let alone use such a regional identity to advocate a united resistance to the West. Not surprisingly, virulent attacks were leveled against such proposals (Sin Ch'aeho 1909). In place of the sages, a boom in writing about the mythical progenitor of the Korean race, Tan'gŭn, arose in the diverse publications of the period, including the *Hwangsŏng sinmun*. One editorial noted that all civilized nations cherish their founders and only barbarians forget them (21 April 1909). To ensure such memories, the newspaper regularly cited Tan'gŭn's achievements, devoted entire editorials to commemorating his birthday (21 November 1909), and recounted the "sagely history of our race's divine founder" (27 April 1910). In so doing, the editors participated in a societywide rethinking of the Korean nation, where ethnicity, defined through the neologism *minjok* and marked by Tan'gun as progenitor, was positioned as more fundamental than the state (Schmid 1997). In such a conception of the ethnic nation, China played no role in defining Korean identity. It was the ultimate step in decentering the Middle Kingdom.

Nevertheless, Tan'gŭn's ascendance did not signal the complete disappearance of the sages from the pages of the *Hwangsŏng sinmun*. For in the last few years of its publication, under the leadership of Pak Ŭnsik, such citations, though fewer in number, were still made as part of a movement to promote a reformed Confucianism as a personal and public moral guide. In the rhetoric typical of many earlier Confucian reform efforts, this style of Confucianism would maintain its original spirit while discarding the corrupt practices that had developed over the course of the Chosŏn dynasty (3 June 1909; 9 November 1909). Mixing references to the sages with accounts of famous peninsular scholars, the editors were silent on the issue of the national origins of Confucianism. Again, this was a deliberate silence. Not defined as either Korean or Chinese, this brand of Confucianism was simply promoted as a set of values beneficial to the political and social conditions of Korea.

In their writings on reform Confucianism, the editors were grappling with the dilemma of fitting the rich traditions of the East Asian regional order into two mutually exclusive categories: Korean and Chinese. Short of deeming all practices that had first arisen on the continent, even if observed more faithfully in Korea and employed without regard to nationness for centuries, to be "Chinese," Korean intellectuals were forced to negotiate a delicate balance between the impulse of nationalizing culture and the incorporation into their own vision of national heritage those cultural forms that the logic of that same nationalizing impulse problematized as Chinese. Such attempts, while always exposing these advocates to accusations of insufficient national consciousness, became one more mode of reappraising the shared traditions of the East Asian regional order.

Conclusion

In their reconstruction of national identity, Korean nationalists used a number of others, against which they fashioned a new understanding of "Koreanness." China was only one of these. But in a transitional period when Korea was moving beyond the Sinocentric East Asian world order into the larger world system and when the definition of universal knowledge was shifting from Confucian forms to those of the West, representations of China were crucial to the process. Reformers sought to consider anew just what "belonged" to China and what "belonged" to Korea. The decentering of the Middle Kingdom was much more than the rejection of "things Chinese" in favor of "things Korean"; indeed, the very categories of Korean and Chinese came to be defined anew in these years as Korean intellectuals gradually sought to divide and nationalize inherited cultural forms—a task that was not as straightforward as the calls for cultural recovery implied.

This urge to separate and impose national meanings on shared East Asian cultural practices should hardly be surprising to readers of English-language materials on Korea, for this approach has an equally long history in Western studies of Korea. From pioneering missionary writings by the likes of Homer Hulbert ([1905] 1962) and James Scarth Gale (Rutt 1972) to the dominant postwar interpretations of East Asia by Fairbank, Reischauer, and Craig (1968) a main narrative thread in Korean histories has been a recounting of the interaction between what is retrospectively viewed as indigenous Korean culture versus imported Chinese culture. Yet these works neglect to problematize the national categories and extend them back over centuries of history, employing a view of culture—both reified and nationalized—that would have been quite familiar to Korean nationalist writers at the turn of the century. That much postwar Western academic writing, despite skeptically treating many Korean nationalist claims, has such fundamental assumptions in common with Korean intellectuals from the period between 1895 and 1910 perhaps best shows that both are the product of the same nationalist discourse rooted in the nation-state regime of the world system. In this sense, the reconstruction of Korean identity, including the underlying shifts in assumptions about culture, knowledge, and the nation, can be seen not only as part of the struggle for national sovereignty but also as a product of the peninsula's deepening integration into the world system and its ideologies.

NOTES

My thanks to Prof. Martina Deuchler for her helpful comments on an earlier version of this essay.

1. The relationship between Japanese and Korean newspapers and nationalist discourse is examined in detail in my *Korea Between Empires: Nation and Identity in East Asia, 1895–1919* (forthcoming).

2. For one useful survey of this literature, see Ashcroft, Griffiths, and Tiffin 1989.

3. It was only in the colonial period that the expression *sadaejuŭi*—sometimes translated as "toadyism"—came to be a standard expression for this critique. For a treatment of *sadaejuŭi* in Korean history and politics, see Robinson 1989.

Two Kinds of Nation, What Kind of State?

R. Bin Wong

The twentieth-century world has been a world of nationalisms. For all our late-twentieth-century awareness of global capitalism, transnationalism, and regional political orders, "nations" and their "nationalisms" remain basic, if problematic, constructions for personal identity, social structures, and political systems. China represents an unusual, if not unique, case of an agrarian empire that has made the transition to a twentieth-century nation. Some agrarian empires, like the Mughal and Safavid, never made it to the twentieth century. Others, like the Ottoman and Austro-Hungarian, were torn apart by groups making claims for their social and cultural distinctiveness and consequent rights to political self-determination. Russia, the one other example of an agrarian empire that was transformed into a twentieth-century nation without the experience of Western colonial rule, has of late become vulnerable to ethnic conflict and competing notions of nationhood within its own (much smaller) territory. As the twentieth century closes, China is the only pre-twentieth-century agrarian empire to have sustained its political cohesiveness to the end of the twentieth century and to have become and remained both a nation and a state.[1]

How do we account for the creation of China's twentieth-century nation in relation to its earlier basis as an agrarian empire? We do not want to accept as natural and necessary the creation of a Chinese "nation" in the twentieth century. The common narrative of modern history, which is centered on the forging of a "nation," cannot be accepted as obvious in China's case or any other.[2] Since the "nation" that was constructed in twentieth-century China was neither natural nor necessary, we must explore how it was in fact constructed.

Approaches to the study of nations and nationalism differ with respect to whether or not they view these as recent phenomena or not. One position argues that nations and nationalisms are eighteenth- and nineteenth-century constructions made possible by the twin processes of state-making and the formation of industrial capitalism, which unfolded in conjunction with the international political order that resulted from these processes in Europe; a variant of this position locates the beginnings of nations a bit earlier, in the time when print media emerged to facilitate the sharing of ideas (Anderson 1991; Gellner 1983). But many nations claim far longer histories as identifiable peoples. A second position recognizes this fact and accepts the idea that nations can have long histories as long as groups of people have been able to label themselves in ways distinct from others. This approach stresses such practices as language, cuisine, and customs as markers of difference (Breuilly 1982; Smith 1986). Working within the second approach, one can identify many groups of people that at some earlier point in time existed as "nations" but not all of which have survived as nations into the twentieth century. Then there are groups whose social and political identities do not stretch back into the deep mists of time but came into being within the past three centuries. The dramatically different spatial scales of territory, different demographic scales, and varying markers of distinctiveness that characterize human groups make it difficult to argue conclusively that one approach to nations and nationalisms works better than the other to explain the construction of nations in the twentieth century. Each more successfully accounts for some features of certain cases than the other.

Twentieth-century Chinese nationalism can be seen from both positions as a long-standing cultural construction that predates European state-making and as the specific product of nineteenth- and twentieth-century interactions with Western powers. In this essay, I will sketch two types of twentieth-century Chinese nationalism, each related to one of the basic perspectives on nations and nationalism. The question I will pose is how the two types relate to each other and to processes of state-building.

The Imperial Legacy: Culture and Politics

To understand what ideological and institutional resources officials, intellectuals, elites, and common people had to work with to create a Chinese "nation" in the twentieth century, we have to begin in late imperial times, roughly during the Ming (1368–1644) and Qing (1644–1911) dynasties. The empire included various non-Han peoples, but it was also Chinese in terms of the state's cultural expectations of the vast majority of its subjects. These expectations defined

China's civilizing project of late imperial times to create social order and political integration.

The process of establishing order and fostering integration within the national territory is most exposed in the frontier regions, where it could not be assumed but had to be introduced or imposed. In logic, the civilizing mission reaching into the Ming and Qing empires' expanding border regions and among non-Han peoples was an extension of a general imperial project with precedents dating back to the beginnings of imperial history and in particular to the neo-Confucian commitment since the Song dynasty to "order the world" (*jingshi*). The state sponsored military settlement and encouraged civilian migrations to northwest and southwest border areas, where migrants would reproduce their sedentary ways of agriculture as the basis for establishing a Chinese way of life. Where indigenous non-Han peoples lived within areas under effective Han control, the government recognized that ordering the world brought them more firmly under imperial rule when Chinese language and customs were adopted.[3] The great investment of time, organizational energy, and fiscal resources to create schools and granaries in southwest China offers an eighteenth-century example of this logic. In this region, charity schools (*yixue*) were established with the explicit goal of educating minority peoples in proper Confucian principles. While serving as governor in Yunnan, Chen Hongmou spearheaded the founding of 650 charity schools, ordering local officials to implement his instructions to establish these institutions (Rowe 1994). Through repeated questioning of his subordinate officials, Chen made them increasingly uneasy about their failure to establish these educational institutions. Whenever possible Chen sought land endowments for charity schools so that they would have a secure source of funding. Elite efforts complemented the official effort to establish charity schools through financial contributions as well as gifts of land.

The program of sinicization of non-Han people was not limited to ideological persuasion. Officials also labored to create a system of granaries to meet the subsistence needs of native peoples and Han immigrants. Chen Hongmou played a key role in stimulating the expansion of community granaries (*shecang*) by establishing granaries and stocking them with grain from official reserves (James Lee 1991, 441). Awareness and acceptance of different culinary habits among non-Han peoples prompted Yunnan governor Liu Zao in 1758 to note:

The non-Han like to eat secondary grains (*zaliang*). . . . And yet most of the grain currently in storage is husked and unhusked rice. The grain we

loan and sell during the spring and summer goes against non-Han tastes.
... Eleven administrative districts ... are presently proposing that, according to local conditions, all or part of their stores be kept in buckwheat.
They should be authorized to restock in buckwheat when replacing
annual disbursements (461).

Bringing native peoples the benefits of imperial rule thus included both efforts
to socialize them into accepting Chinese cultural practices and an attempt to
acknowledge differences, like those of preferred grains, while pursuing the
larger project of promoting social order.

Under Manchu rule, the construction of Chinese identity was a complex
project because the Manchus also strove to maintain their non-Han identity
and those of other northern peoples. They envisioned the Qing empire as a
political system composed of different peoples; within this system, they generally applied principles of cultural sinicization to peoples south of the Great
Wall but not north of it. Across the larger empire, the Qing emperor presented
himself variously as a Buddhist king, a central Asian khan, and a patron of the
Dalai Lama. But within China proper he acted as a Confucian emperor. The
multiple dimensions of Manchu rule across the Qing empire have led several
scholars recently to underscore the importance of Manchus as non-Chinese to
the construction of the last Chinese empire (Rawski 1996). But these features of
Manchu rule should not blind us to recognizing the great diversity even within
China proper. The state's goal of creating order across this diversity was to be
met by defining the acceptable boundaries of cultural and religious difference.
Manchu rulers, as Ping-ti Ho (1998) has recently reminded us, continued a
process of interaction among non-Han and Han peoples, a key component of
which was a dynamic of sinicization. The Confucian-inspired project of identifying practices that were deemed foundational for proper personal behavior
and social order was imposed on a society in which popular beliefs ranged far
beyond the dimensions of a Confucian template. Yet, whatever its limitations,
the state's drive to control cultural practices contributed to the definition of a
Chinese identity. The Manchu state had at its disposal a repertoire of strategies
for creating social cohesion developed by earlier rulers that far exceeded what
European rulers of multilingual empires could even imagine. A late imperial
fusion of culture and politics was thus part of the basic construction of state-
society relations as China headed into the twentieth century. The state played
an explicit role in promoting this identity, especially in periods of official
activism (both local and central) and in frontier areas where Han Chinese
sometimes came into contact with people with differing customs.

The cultural construction of Chinese identity in Qing times matters not only if we are to understand what late imperial state efforts were about but also if we are to comprehend the nature of twentieth-century Chinese nationalism. This relevance is often obscured by influential assertions about modern state-making and nationalism. Ernest Gellner, in his *Nations and Nationalisms,* presents a picture of what he calls "agro-literate polities" that seems virtually anti-thetical to China, the world's largest such polity. For Gellner, the fusion of culture and polity is the essence of modern nationalism and only occurs when industrialization begins to transform agrarian societies. In agro-literate societies, he claims, "almost everything militates against the definition of political units in terms of cultural boundaries" (1983, 11). Gellner argues forcefully for what many other scholars also believe, namely, that so-called premodern states were unable to exercise much cultural influence over their subject populations. In many historical cases, this is no doubt true.[4] There are, as Gellner argues, cases of sophisticated agrarian societies that seek to differentiate people in groups or castes—witness South Asia. Culture divides horizontally and vertically in a manner that precludes its playing a role as an integrative force. As Gellner reads his evidence, politics and culture do not become fused in agrarian societies.

In a similar vein, John Hall has remarked, in marking off the distinctive notion of nationalism: "There have always, of course, been distinctive cultures, and particular upper classes have had some sense of shared ethnic solidarity. But the power of the nationalist idea—that people should share a culture and be ruled only by someone co-cultural with themselves—seems historically novel" (1993, 3). Historically specific, yes; but limited to the modern world and first taking place in Europe, no. In early modern Europe, Christianity came to play a key role in defining what it meant culturally to be European, and a partial parallel with Confucianism's role in China is obvious. But it is the divergence between the two cases that I wish to underscore here. Christianity transcends the political boundaries of European states while Confucianism fuses the cultural and political into a single, though complex, compound. The legitimacy of Manchu rule within China proper depended crucially upon both the Manchu emperors and their mostly Han officials pursuing a Confucian agenda of rule. Were we to grant the premise that the fusion of politics and culture is a unique feature of modern nationalism, we would face the awkward dilemma of treating imperial Chinese state-making strategies as "modern." The Chinese state and the society's elite shared a common neo-Confucian agenda for creating public order both before and after the Manchu conquest. Peasants were members of the same neo-Confucian cultural order even if this Confucian structure did not embrace and domesticate all popular beliefs.[5] The cultural sense of "Chineseness" that was created in late imperial times and the intimate relationship between this construction and political action were severely challenged by the collapse of the Qing empire. The ending of a particularly strong connection between culture and politics made uncertain the bases upon which social cohesion and political order would be built.

The Republic Experience: The Problem of Unity

State-building in the twentieth century took place on three different levels— national, provincial, and county—with relations among them uncertain. At the national level, officials succeeded in creating new bureaucracies to manage various financial matters, including the salt administration, maritime customs, and foreign relations. These activities were quite separate from provincial-level competition among contending military leaders. The competition was only partially constrained by political unification in 1927 when the Nationalists won recognition for their government from provincial leaders, who in some cases remained in power within their provinces. Finally, county-level expansion of taxation and the increasingly formal roles of elites within the administration took place both as part of and in reaction to the political changes taking place at higher levels. Amid the uncertainties surrounding state-building in the postimperial period, two plausible scenarios did not develop.

Given the far weaker lines of control between central and provincial levels of government than had existed in the late imperial period, one possibility was a federal structure with a union of provinces each handling its internal affairs and a central government charged with foreign relations (see Duara 1995). Provincial governments had acted independently of each other and of the center to some degree since 1912. What distinguished the Beijing-based government from these provincial governments until 1927 was more its dealings with foreigners than any domestic span of control. Provincial governments made de facto claims for their autonomy from the center with respect to finances and personnel, but little effort went toward the formation of a federal structure of government. To form a federal system of government would have required an agreement to divide powers and responsibilities among levels of government. This arrangement would have represented a fundamental administrative change, since the late imperial Chinese state had been a unitary entity in which the central government assigned responsibilities to bureaucrats at different levels of administration without compromising central government authority; in the late imperial state, most officials serving in counties, provinces, and the capital were responsible for the same basic functions. There was a hierarchy of authority but no division of powers. While no central state enjoyed the ability to act as a unitary center of political authority throughout the country between

1912 and 1927, the logic of bureaucratic administration remained that of a unitary state overseeing as much of the former empire as was feasible. Federal systems usually emerge as a way to coordinate the authority of previously more autonomous and institutionally powerful bodies. The postimperial Chinese situation was not one in which provincial-level power holders held institutionalized authority with which the center could then negotiate and bargain.

A second plausible scenario would have been for the military competition among regional power holders to have led to the formation of a system of competing states within China. Alternatively, the civilian leaders struggling to form new institutions of civilian rule could have aimed to forge "independent" provinces. Provinces did in fact declare their independence three times between 1911 and 1916, but in each case they were declaring independence from a particular central government as a form of protest against its actions, not as the prelude to the creation of institutionally autonomous positions. Perhaps the major reason that fully autonomous provinces did not develop rests with the difficulties faced by military men and provincial elites, not so much in creating new armies and assemblies but in integrating these institutions with older forms of bureaucratic rule and transforming state institutions to give either military or representative institutions a larger role. In addition, however, it mattered that no smaller groups within China could create a notion of "nation" to displace China as "nation." No provincial-level process of state-building could introduce a process of political engagement to persuade people that they belonged to an identifiable group with a particular history and a consequent right to their own political system. The success of the late imperial state's construction of a Chinese identity meant that the formation of alternative identities around which to mobilize people in opposition to other Chinese was difficult to imagine. Neither independence nor federalism could make sense in a political situation in which people failed to forge politically significant identities able to displace the notions of Chinese identity created and reproduced in late imperial times.[6]

A third scenario for state-building, and the one that did develop, rested on a postimperial Chinese nationalism that celebrated unity, but a nationalism clearly different from the Qing empire's construction of cultural unity. Areas beyond China proper, to which the eighteenth- and nineteenth-century government had not applied a program of cultural sinicization, became increasingly separated from both the Chinese state and nation, despite the new state's anticipation of ruling the territories and population of the Qing empire. With its establishment in 1912, the Republic of China promptly declared its authority over the "five peoples" of the former Manchu state—Manchus, Hans, Mongols, Muslims, and Tibetans. The first president of the Republic, Yuan Shikai, proclaimed that Mongolia, Xinjiang, and Tibet would be treated administratively as provinces. Ironically, given the central government's uneven control over provinces, one might view Republican control over these three areas as simply the endpoint of the limited territorial integration that the central government was not able to exert. But with the cultural resources to forge claims of national identities distinct from the Chinese, Mongolians in Outer Mongolia won political independence from the Republic of China, and Tibetans in central and western parts of the area populated by Tibetan people achieved de facto political independence.

Within China proper, the kind of nationalism that developed in postimperial times was only partially based upon the politically promoted cultural norms and sensibilities of late imperial times. The construction of a Chinese cultural identity helps to explain the absence in the twentieth century of regional "nationalisms" to compete with Chinese nationalism. But the late imperial cultural construction of Chinese identity was in many ways a weak one. It was not the basis upon which people conventionally conceived of themselves or acted. Most people's senses of personal identity were tied to far smaller groups based on territory or kinship. Their sense of common national identity would have to come from elsewhere.

Two Kinds of Nation

The constructions of a twentieth-century Chinese nation and nationalism were very much specific to the new context of competition and conflict with foreign powers, such that the new nation differed in important ways from the earlier cultural construction of Chinese identity. The notion of "nation" that developed in the late-nineteenth and early-twentieth centuries in reaction to confrontations with Western powers was at least as much a "racial" notion as it was a cultural one. It was put together out of materials introduced from Western discourses about races and nations. In a world of Social Darwinism in which the Chinese nation was struggling to avoid what looked like extinction, only a strong and fit Chinese nation would survive the threats of Western and Japanese power. An identity that was forged in the Chinese state's relations with foreign governments represented a kind of nationalism distinct from the previous cultural construction of a Chinese identity. It began to take form in the second and third decades of the century, when urban Chinese criticized their government's agreement to contract forced loans with Japan and then to acquiesce in the treatment of China by Western powers following World War I. Elites conceived of their country's situation in "national" terms because of the system of states in which China henceforth had to act. The demands and anxieties of the country's situation spurred both them and the common people in China's cities to demonstrate against a government they feared would not represent the "nation's" interests effectively. Opinions voiced in the press at that time helped to shape the sentiments around which elites and common urban people mobilized for mass boycotts and demonstrations.

This kind of nationalism was certainly a twentieth-century phenomenon and generally fits within the genre of nationalism conceived of as a recent historical phenomenon shaped by ideas and information that print media disseminated. But the Gellner-Hall theory of nations and nationalisms doesn't describe, let alone explain, China's evolution as a nation in the postimperial period. When, according to Gellner and Hall, we enter a time in which there can be Chinese nationalism, we do not in fact witness the political creation of a common culture spanning elite and commoner. The linkage of politics and culture had already occurred under the late imperial state. Instead, a widening gap opened between the Western-influenced culture of a rising urban elite and the imperial culture of the still largely rural masses. The state proved unable to play much of a role in constructing the nation for several decades. As elites increasingly faced problems and posed solutions drawn at least in part from Western influences, their cultural distance from popular sensibilities grew. The twentieth-century notions of "national" crisis that urban elites recognized were not shared by China's peasant masses in the early decades of the century.

The new nationalism that developed in Chinese cities was part of a larger set of differences that defined a growing cultural gap between cities and the countryside. It became part of the May Fourth (1919) cultural iconoclasm that rejected much of late imperial China's culture, the very Confucian precepts that formed the basis of China's politically constructed cultural identity. Thus, this new nationalism directly challenged earlier forms of Chinese identity. It was clearly a product of recent contacts with Westerners and thus not a phenomenon indigenous to Chinese society. The nationalism of the May Fourth era pitted largely urban Chinese against the dangers and challenges they perceived as emanating from Westerners and the Japanese, fusing state capacity and social prosperity. According to this vision, the Chinese state was principally that state facing these foreign threats, and Chinese society was largely the urban society troubled by foreign threats. In the background remained the challenge of ruling rural China, the China in which identity remained defined largely in the cultural terms the late imperial state had worked to shape. Although peasants did engage in antiforeign protests against missionaries and some took advantage of economic ties to international markets, rural China's problems and possibilities remained largely rooted in the soil. Some rural issues, such as opium cultivation and consumption, were created by foreign contacts, but most were structurally and cognitively the same as those of a century or two earlier: hopes for more land or a good marriage for a son or daughter. Through their struggles with subsistence and family, rural Chinese strove to live the Confucian ideal of family and society, which was an ideal that urban Chinese took as their target of critique and rejection.

Allowing that there were two kinds of nationalism in China during the 1920s and 1930s, how were they to be brought together and their points of contradiction resolved? The contradictions were serious. The partisans of urban nationalism saw the practices and beliefs making up rural Chinese identity as having little, if any, place in the construction of a "modern" Chinese nation. For their part, rural Chinese had little use or taste for the anxieties and desires of urban reformers. The question of what kind of Chinese nation would be formed in the twentieth century was further complicated because the new sense of Chinese identity was not limited to Chinese living in Chinese cities but extended to those who had migrated abroad as merchants, miners, coolies, and farmers. These people formed the target group for Sun Yatsen's appeals for funds in the late Qing to foment political change in the migrants' homeland. Their diasporic movements were part of what created the new Chinese nation.

What kind of synthesis could be built from the two basic types of nationalism, one culturally based and spanning rural China, the other politically motivated by contacts with foreign powers and including Chinese living in cities and abroad? The synthesis imagined by elites rested upon a vision of uniting the country under a strong state in order to save it from foreign dangers. In *The Principle of Nationalism,* Sun Yatsen wrote:

> An easy and successful way to bring about the unity of a large group is to build upon the foundation of small united groups, and the small units we can build upon in China are the clan groups and also the family groups. The "native place" sentiment of the Chinese is very deep-rooted too; it is especially easy to unite those who are from the same province, prefecture or village. As I see it, if we take these two fine sentiments as a foundation, it will be easy to bring together the people of the whole country. (N.d., 43)

Sun Yatsen's logic for building modern Chinese nationalism posits building blocks of identity. He starts with the smallest block, family groups, on which he places larger lineage groups; on these groups he then balances ever larger blocks based on territorial identity, village, prefecture, and province. The crowning piece is the nation. But this inverted pyramid seems very unstable. Could nationalism really be built out of kin and smaller territorial sentiments? Nationalism is not in fact easily built out of small rural identities. The shared sensibilities that the late imperial state did so much to promote were not adequate to mobilize large numbers of rural people to oppose some outside threat; their similarities did not create commitments to sacrifice for each other unless the outside threat became visibly a local problem.

Late imperial Chinese identity did not create this kind of "nationalism," even if this identity helped to preclude much imagining of alternative bases of nationalism within China proper. Late imperial efforts had already created what Benedict Anderson refers to as "anonymous solidarity" among people of different provinces, making it both less likely and less necessary to create a similar kind of identification among people of the same province. Sun's image of mobilizing people based on small-scale local loyalties had an empirical base in his travels outside China; he was perhaps ever hopeful, or even misguided, in anticipating the power of these institutions and sentiments to create a sense of "nation" within China. The Chinese "nation" he observed overseas in the United States and Canada was formed in distinction from, and even in opposition to, the larger host society. The "national" consciousness he found in the small groups of Chinese residents abroad would be difficult to develop within China, where small groups of Chinese would not immediately confront others who were not Chinese. Building a nationalism on native place sentiments in rural China therefore seemed an unlikely project. But this does not mean that no small-scale groups could be the basis for articulating nationalist sentiments. Native place ties could indeed matter crucially, as they did in the urban-based project of constructing nationalism, as Bryna Goodman's study of native place ties in Shanghai between the 1850s and 1937 shows. There people linked with others from their home districts into a new kind of native place organization to promote the community-transcending goal of a "nation." The rhetoric of the 1930s explicitly stressed the formation of the nation out of progressively larger groups. As the Shanghai educational reformer Huang Yuanpei wrote in 1933:

> How should we save China? Many people have ideas, all of which require one thing: People must abandon their selfish individualism and begin to form small groups. Then they should knit together small groups into large groups and unite large groups into one great national group. When the entire country becomes one group, the mass foundation for the nation will be established, the nation will be strong and long-lived. (cited in Goodman 1995, 300–301)

When Huang and others built their national project from groups with urban social bases, they appear to have succeeded. Whether protesting the accidental killing of a Ningbo native by a Russian sailor or organizing the anti-American boycott of 1905, native place organizations were the units responsible for civic action in Shanghai. Issues of nation were represented by local urban groups, whose bases of mobilization linked Shanghai to other areas transcending the immediate community.

The "nation" was an abstraction, but it was concretized on different spatial scales. National salvation was to be achieved through the efforts of officials and people working in particular parts of China. Although elites that were motivated to save the "nation" lacked an institutionalized structure spanning the entire country, they could do so on more modest spatial scales. This sense of "nation" meant that state-building efforts at provincial levels were not immediately and necessarily seen as contributing to the goal of independent provinces, though some people harbored such aspirations. Instead, provincial-level state-building was often thought to serve a "national" purpose. The image of the "nation" thus became a focus for state-building efforts that spanned the distinct scales of local, provincial, and central government without actually connecting them institutionally. With linguistic differences so marked that Mandarin and Cantonese were pronounced as differently as English and Dutch, and with local religious customs and a distinctive culinary tradition, Guangdong had the potential to separate from Beijing, yet the assertion of an independent political identity by the Cantonese or any other provincial group never displaced preoccupations with "national" identity.

Before 1937, therefore, the project of saving the nation was very much an urban-based project led by a mix of political, social, and economic elites whose efforts were articulated by intellectuals, most of whom accepted the May Fourth distinction between a backward, rural China mired in Confucian traditions and a progressive, Western-influenced, urban China leading the country in its battle to achieve survival. The war with Japan (1937–45) changed the spatial dimensions of Chinese nationalism by making resistance to the Japanese an immediate issue to people in both cities and the countryside. Questioned and qualified in many ways since its publication in 1962, Chalmers Johnson's thesis that the Communist Party mobilized peasants around a core of national resistance to Japanese aggression is relevant because it alerts us to the Communists' success in representing the nation; not all peasants may have conceived of their struggle as a national effort, but at a minimum we can recognize that peasants were mobilized successfully by Communists who for their part claimed to represent the interests of the peasants as those of the Chinese nation. Moreover, the nation the Communists represented was principally that of a backward and isolated rural China, not of the economically more advanced urban world. Their Chinese "nation" would later expand to embrace urban China as well, as the Communists moved from participating in victory over the Japanese to defeating the Nationalists and establishing the People's Republic in 1949.

After its success in 1949, the Communist party-state developed and implemented policies to define, monitor, and control belief and behavior. While these policies obviously differed in substance and technique from the kind of Confucian agenda pursued by the late imperial state, their logic of creating normative ideals places the Communist effort in a line of descent from late imperial political efforts at constructing Chinese identity. Clearly, other influences have been blended into the bloodline, but the link to the past remains.[7]

At the same time, the Communist party-state has been able to claim to speak for the Chinese nation on the strength of having fended off foreigners and reestablished territorial security and integrity. But defending the integrity of territory does not create a substantive meaning for Chinese nationalism once the territory is not under significant threat. The problematic legacy of May Fourth iconoclasm, of which Marxism is a part, features an ambivalent, if not completely antagonistic, attitude toward China's Confucian past. The state is thus in a difficult position as it tries to represent two kinds of nationalism. From an urban perspective, it is vulnerable to the political critique of representing an agrarian bureaucratic past and therefore unable to lead the nation into the twenty-first century. This argument was an implicit component of the widely celebrated and criticized *River Elegy* television series of 1988. This extremely popular six-part program aired twice, once in June and again in August. It proclaimed the death of traditional Chinese civilization, part of which it suggested was an authoritarian state. The symbol of China's traditional culture is the yellow soil of the agrarian past; the symbol of China's future is the blue ocean connecting China to a vast world beyond its borders. One key consequence of the assertion that traditional culture was moribund was China's lack of a "national" tradition or cultural identity appropriate for China's future. If the *River Elegy* producers are correct, the "nation" can no longer play the role of history's subject. History may no longer need rescuing from the nation, but the future may demand a new subject. To displace a nation rooted in the soil with one floating on the seas creates a precarious situation in which the reality represented by the symbol of the blue sea lacks certainty. These expressions of unease over China's future do not create or resolve the problem of what the "nation" will mean and what its relationship to the state will become, but they do give voice to the difficulties.

In recent years, some intellectuals have carried forward this critique of the state and nationalism by arguing that the nation's dynamism and future lie not with the traditions of a bureaucratic and landlocked north leading an anti-imperialist struggle but with those of an innovative maritime south long in favor of contacts with foreign countries. This southern nationalism celebrates China's tradition of overseas contact, its commercial dynamism and social openness, as distinct from the bureaucratic and imperial north absorbed in the politics of a land empire (Friedman 1994). Significantly, this critique does not promote the independence of a Cantonese or Fukienese identity as the foundation of a separate "nation."[8] It does not challenge the spatial scale of China as a nation but instead the state's ability to represent the nation; rejecting Beijing's nationalism leads to a spatial decentering of nationalism to the south. While it is a challenge to state-constructed notions of nationalism, the southern variant often still affirms China as an integral unit. This southward recentering of the Chinese nation shares in, and can be seen as a response to, the *River Elegy* critique of the Chinese cultural past, a critique that targets those elements composing the common cultural construction of Chinese identity. By diverting the center of national tradition to the maritime south, critics are inventing an alternative lineage for the Chinese nation and a subject for a future still to be mapped across the deep blue seas.

Even as political critiques of the bureaucratic state tradition and its role in defining Chinese cultural identity are made, alternatives do not forsake all notions of a Chinese nation. Instead they attempt to free the concept of nation from the state's control. Though all these inventions of national tradition and identity create imagined connections, the persistence of a tension and uncertainty over what kind of Chinese nation will be constructed and the role of the state in its construction suggest at the very least that Chinese nationalism continues to be a live issue at the end of the twentieth century and as well that the nation itself is a reality. The Chinese empire did not disintegrate into competing groups of ethnic nationalities, as has happened in other agrarian empires, in part because the late imperial state's cultural construction of Chinese identity reduced the likelihood of mobilizing people in rural areas around competing identities and in part because the foreign challenges to China motivated urban Chinese to face a common set of difficulties separate from rural concerns. The cultural construction of Chinese identity closed off the federalist scenario and helped to block provincial-level "nationalisms" but without providing a strong base for a day-to-day commitment to China at the grass roots. Urban Chinese bent upon "modernizing" their society were so critical of rural conditions, as urban elites throughout postcolonial Asia have been, that it was difficult for them to imagine the rural Chinese identity as offering much positive potential for building a new nation. No wonder the Communist party-state's effort since 1949 to manage these two kinds of nationalism, but especially to promote the rural kind, has proven difficult. How these nationalisms combine or fall apart will determine what kind of nation China becomes in the next several decades.

NOTES

I thank my colleague Kenneth Pomeranz for his suggestions and comments on an earlier draft of this essay.

1. Large agrarian countries in South and Southeast Asia that were ruled by Western colonial powers did not have systems that we conventionally consider to be forms of agrarian empire. The processes of their twentieth-century narratives of nationalism are intimately enmeshed with their colonial experiences, which sets them off from the agrarian empires considered in this paragraph.

2. Prasenjit Duara (1995) rightly warns us against just such a danger. His own strategy for rejecting a simple teleology of modern Chinese history with the forging of a national subject as its centerpiece has two basic components. First, he shows how many leading Chinese intellectuals since the 1890s have made the Chinese "nation" the central character in their narratives in order to address the internal and external crises confronting them. Second, he sketches alternatives to a nation-centered history of modern China, looking at topics like *fengjian*, a kind of local rule, and provincial federalism, to identify what the narrative of nation-making suppresses as a means of exploring alternative possibilities in China's modern history.

3. On northern border development, see Yuan 1991. On the northwest, see Wang Xilong 1990; and Wang Zhizhong and Wei Liying 1989. On the southwest, see James Lee 1982.

4. To suggest a contrary case, Islamic culture is dotted with states making strong claims for cultural orthodoxy. If neither China nor the Islamic world fits the model, it can hardly be as general as Gellner claims.

5. My argument is not that elites and common people agreed upon all cultural matters. Indeed, the gap between them began opening in the eighteenth century when stricter Confucian control over popular practices was first attempted. What matters for the present argument is that officials, elites, and common people shared a cultural universe in which expectations of proper and desirable behavior spanned both groups.

6. The fates of these areas is enmeshed in complex international politics. The construction of ethnic nationalisms began for some of these groups during this period; for example, the Turkic Muslims became Uyghurs in the early 1920s. For a succinct account of the fortunes of the peoples in these areas in the postimperial period, see Fletcher 1979, 41–51.

7. An argument about the late imperial state's strategies of social control and their relationship with post-1949 strategies of rule is made in Wong 1997, 105–22, 190–202.

8. Duara (1995) sees the Cantonese effort as a "provincial narrative of nationalism." What needs further emphasis is that the Cantonese do not choose to *separate* themselves from northerners and create a distinct "nation," but rather they aim to *displace* northern definitions of a Chinese "nation," invoking the maritime tradition to represent China more generally.

Chen Gongbo and the Construction of a Modern Nation in 1930s China

Margherita Zanasi

"What is nationalism? In simple words, it is realizing the unity of the national economy" (Chen Gongbo 1934c, 191). With these words, Chen Gongbo, minister of industry of the Chinese Nationalist Government from January 1932 to December 1935 and prominent leader within the left wing of the Nationalist Party or Guomindang (GMD), summed up the main rationale underlying his plan for economic nation building. Only by developing a nationally integrated economic structure could China become a "modern nation" (*jindaishi guojia*) and successfully fulfill its "nationalist mission of equality and freedom" among the world powers, finally bringing to an end almost a century of imperialist penetration (Chen Gongbo 1936, 7). With this statement, Chen offered an economic answer to the questions that characterized the debate on nation building in 1930s China: what is a modern nation and how to transform China into one?

After the demise of the imperial system in 1911 and two decades of protracted civil war, it was only with the establishment of the Nationalist Government in Nanjing (1927) that most Guomindang leaders felt that the moment for the long-postponed "reconstruction" (*jianshe*) of China into a modern nation had finally arrived. In this atmosphere of high expectations, however, it soon became evident that even among the members of the GMD there was no consensus on what a modern nation was or what reforms were needed for China. It also became evident that this long-awaited opportunity was being spoiled by Japan's attempt to draw China into its colonial empire. Nation-building and resistance to Japan thus became one and the same issue in Guomindang thinking, monopolizing the lively debate on the future of the nation that filled journals and newspapers in the interwar years. Most Chinese officials and intellectuals, cut off from administrative policy-making and implementation channels, were forced to confine their contribution to purely theoretical statements. Chen Gongbo, however, participated in this debate from a more enviable position. As the minister of industry, he was able to implement reforms aimed at the realization of his ideas. In 1933, he announced a four-year industrial plan that closely reflected his vision of a modern Chinese nation. The plan found its closest realization in the work of the Cotton Control Commission (Mianye tongzhi weiyuanhui, CCC), which serves here as a case study.

It is not just because Chen's ideas found their way to practical realization that this essay focuses on Chen Gongbo's reforms. An analysis of the development of Chen's vision of a modern Chinese nation-state and how this vision was realized in the work of the CCC is essential for better understanding the origins of concepts of state and nation that were to become hegemonic in China for decades to come. Chen's reforms offered a crucial contribution to the construction of a national identity that came to underpin the Chinese nation-state from the 1930s through the Maoist years. As Chen's reforms illustrate, this identity was built on a variety of ideas of both global and local origin. Chinese nationalism in the 1930s came to combine a late-nineteenth-century self-strengthening conceptualization of national power as bolstering the foundation of the country (*guoben*) with new global conceptions of the nation and nation-building. Chen believed that China's crisis vis-à-vis foreign imperialism, especially the crescendo of Japanese aggression, was rooted in the weakening of China's foundation. But how he came to define this foundation and what he believed to be the right cure to bring about its regeneration deeply differed from the ideas and practices of previous Chinese officials. By the 1930s, an economic dimension of Chinese nationalism had risen to unprecedented prominence. Inspired by Marxist-Leninist economic determinism and popular social Darwinist theories, many Chinese intellectuals and officials came to identify the nation with its economic structure. They perceived the nation as developing along a predetermined path of economic-political evolution that reached its highest level with the formation of the industrial nation. Chen Gongbo, like many of his contemporaries, thus reached the conclusion that the essence of modern nationhood rested on the establishment of a unified/centralized industrial structure. This led him to attempt the transformation of the Chinese economy from what he considered "feudal" (agricultural, locally bounded, and "backward") to "national" (industrial, integrated at the national level, and "advanced").

In addition to this unprecedented stress on the economy, Chen's reform plan introduced new trends emerging in the interwar period, such as state leadership over the economy—what Mussolini called *dirigismo economico* (economic dirigism) and Chen Gongbo dubbed *tongzhi jingj* (controlled economy)—autarky, and a corporatist organization of the state. For Chen, the modern nation was essentially based on a nationally integrated and autarkic industrial structure. Centralization, social and economic unity, government intervention at all levels of the economy, and the mass mobilization of all national, and nationalist, economic forces (*minzu jingji*) were the fundamental characteristics of his vision.

I translate the Chinese term used by Chen in his writings, *zizu zhengce,* (literally, "the policy of self-sufficiency") with the term *autarky* because he specifically refers to economic policies adopted in Europe at the end of World War I (Chen Gongbo 1934c, 190), thus expressing a conscious participation in that particular trend. The interwar idea of autarky is generally described as aimed at establishing a self-sufficient and independent national economy. In reality, it differed from simple economic self-sufficiency due to its radical nationalist and political connotations. In the interwar years, autarky emerged as a distinctive model of economic development and political organization based on corporatism, mass mobilization, and nationalism. An autarkic economy came to be perceived as necessary for the survival of a nation, thus imposing extreme nationalist goals for industrial development. The conception and practice of autarky also came to change the idea of the role of the state in the economy. Unable to rely on imports and exports, the government of an autarkic country is forced to take action in support of its industry, which suddenly has to rely almost exclusively on domestic markets and supplies of raw materials. The government thus needs to decide which industries are crucial to the country's strength (generally basic food staples such as grains and war-oriented industrial production) and how to promote them regardless of supply and production costs. Autarky thus undermines all of the basic assumptions of a liberal economy, above all its ability to regulate itself if allowed to freely respond to the "natural" laws of the market. In an autarkic regime, the state needs to rely on such nonliberal strategies as direct intervention and the mobilization of all the economic forces of the country in order to develop an industrial system that runs against the country's current market and production structure. It is primarily for this reason that autarkic policies are often combined with attempts to set up a corporate state, a political organization perceived at the time as the most efficient tool for mass mobilization.[1]

A corporatist system is characterized by the presence, at the national level, of a single representative organization for each industry or economic group, be it workers, businessmen, or farmers. These national organizations are recognized and legitimated by the government, with which they are, at least in theory, in a relationship of equal partnership. Corporate organizations are entrusted by the government with carrying out or facilitating the implementation of state policies. The state, for its part, posing as the supreme arbiter or mediator between the parts involved in the corporation, helps organize the relationships between them in its capacity as "the guardian of the common good, of a national interest that supersedes the parochial interests of each sector" (Unger and Chan 1995). The corporate model was largely applied by many conservative governments in the interwar period—most notably the fascist regime in Italy—as a means of overcoming the idea of class struggle and harnessing all economic groups to pursue a single national objective. Under the banner of nationalism and national interests, they promoted social unity vis-à-vis a real or imagined threat against the nation.[2] It was in this spirit that Chen Gongbo attempted the reorganization of China's economy into a corporate structure in order to provide the state with an effective tool for intervention at all levels of the economy.

If Chen's autarkic and corporatist plan illustrates, on the one hand, the unprecedented integration of China's political life in current global trends, it does not, on the other, imply a passive reaction to changes imposed upon it by the surrounding environment or a mere attempt to imitate alien models. Chen's conceptualization of autarky and corporatism was peculiar to the Chinese experience—as were the attempts to create a centralized nation by other Chinese leaders from Guomindang leader Jiang Jieshi (Chiang Kaishek) to Mao Zedong. Chen certainly admired Mussolini's achievements in this regard—at least until Italy joined the German-Japanese alliance, a move that revealed the different nation-building postures of the two governments, the Italian being aggressive and the Chinese contingently defensive.[3] But Chen did not perceive himself as a follower of the Italian *duce* and never expressly referred to his own policies as fascist. Rather, he saw himself as participating in a global political and economic trend at a time when fascist-style policies were becoming subtly pervasive all over the world (Thompson 1991). In this context, trying to determine whether Chen Gongbo was fascist, or whether fascism was a strictly unexportable Italian phenomenon, is not a fruitful exercise. What is important to understand is that, together with many other Chinese officials and intellectuals, Chen participated in and experimented with new and widely subscribed political and economic models. He shared with other leaders around the world a feeling that their countries were under attack from economic imperialism and needed to resort to autarky in order to survive; that in this predicament national interests came before class interests; that liberalism and liberal capitalism were responsible for the tragedy of the Great War and the Great Depression; and, finally, that the world was inexorably heading toward new forms of "nonliberal," highly centralized, economic and political organization—all contributing to the formation of a discourse on the new Chinese nation that lasted until the 1970s.

Since the time of Chen Gongbo, Chinese have often been called upon to pool their efforts and follow state leadership for the fulfillment of the nationalist goal of economic development. Only recently has that idea come to be challenged. Although leaders may still debate nation building as their primary goal and deem economic development as crucial for strengthening China, perceptions of the nature of nation building and development have changed. These changes involve most obviously the abandonment of the Maoist model and the consequent relaxation of state control, but they also include a different idea of the Chinese nation that reaches beyond the debate on the development of the communist state. The idea that Chinese nationalism finds its highest expression in "realizing the unity of the national economy"—an idea that had characterized the nation-building efforts of both the GMD and the Chinese Communist Party—is now openly challenged, and economic decentralization has replaced the urge for unity. The liberalization of the Chinese economy appears presently to be the key to growth. At the same time, economic confrontation with foreign powers, which played such an important role in the thought of both Chen Gongbo and Mao Zedong, has given way to a return to the global market. These recent trends call for a redefinition of the Chinese nation in terms no longer characterized by centralization or unity. While most pessimists among China's observers and analysts interpret this development as a sign of the disintegration of the Chinese nation (Goodman and Segal 1994), the current phase appears as a new effort to redefine it by abandoning the tenets of the 1930s to 1970s discourse on state and nation, thus reclaiming local autonomy, allowing private business to lead economic growth, and actively engaging in the global economy.

The Nation as an Economic Unit

By the 1930s, Japan's aggression and the question of how to deal with it had come to constitute the central issue in China's political life. Japan's attempt to draw China into its economic sphere of influence appeared to most Chinese to prove the veracity of Marxist-Leninist theories of imperialism and social Darwinist ideas, leading them to believe that the extinction of the Chinese race was inexorably approaching. Such a widely shared sense of urgency spurred a more markedly nationalist reelaboration of the revolutionary programs of both the GMD at large and the Chinese Communist Party (CCP), which shifted their focus from the realization of the Sun Yatsen's principle of "people's livelihood" (*minsheng zhuyi*) in the case of the GMD or, in the case of the CCP, the realization of a socialist society, to finding a solution to the national question. The principle of "people's livelihood" was forgotten outright by the Nationalists while the realization of socialism was temporarily postponed with the program of New Democracy of Mao Zedong. Class and social issues had succumbed to the call for social unity in the interest of national salvation.

By the early 1930s national unity had also come to constitute the core of the political platform of the GMD Left, which, under the leadership of Wang Jingwei, remained the last bulwark of Marxism within the party. It was on this point that Wang entered a new cabinet in coalition with Jiang Jieshi in January 1932. Agreed upon after long negotiations by Wang and Jiang, the political platform of the new cabinet, *annei rangwai* (pacify the domestic front while resisting foreign aggression), stressed above all the need for national unity against the Japanese assault and proposed economic nation building as the solution to China's international and domestic problems. In this sense, it was a direct expression of the GMD Left's approach to the national crisis and marked Wang's temporary political victory over Jiang Jieshi. Jiang had wanted to postpone direct military confrontation with Japan in order to focus on the military unification of the country—meaning, first of all, the elimination of the Communists in Jiangxi—at the expense of economic and political reform. Wang, on the other hand, maintained that military action against either the Communists or the Japanese was destined to fail if it were not accompanied by reforms targeted at strengthening the foundations of the country. Finding his position weakened by a protracted political crisis and renewed military pressure from Japan in the northeast, Jiang was forced to compromise with his rival, Wang, who had succeeded in gathering under his leadership those groups within the GMD that opposed Jiang's military authoritarianism and wanted to regain control over both the party and the government in favor of a civilian leadership. In the new political formation, Wang attempted to confine Jiang to the military sphere and to counterbalance his influence in the higher echelons of party and government organizations with a new infusion of members loyal to his own cause (Zanasi 1997; So 1991; Luo 1952; Coble 1991; Zhang and Shen 1987).

While negotiating with Jiang in Shanghai, Wang repeatedly advocated "national reconstruction" (*jianshe*) as the solution to both of China's problems—internationally, Japan's aggression and, domestically, political disunity. "My position toward the solution of the present situation is not similar to those who want to use military force," he declared in a Shanghai newspaper in October 1931. "I believe that only with reconstruction is it possible to unify [the country]" (*Shenbao*, 22 October 1931, 13). Two days later, he discussed the two slogans that underpinned his political position, "use reconstruction to save the country" and "use balanced powers to save public politics." The rationale behind these slogans was that China needed first to unify by means of reform. Only then would it be able to resist Japan ("using reconstruction to save the country"). Unification, on the other hand, could be achieved only by finding a balance between local and central power ("using balanced powers to save public politics").⁴ Wang aimed this slogan at curbing the power of local militarists and strengthening that of the center, thus presenting unity/centralization as the essence of national reconstruction.

The theoretical justification of the *annei rangwai* policy rested on the self-strengthening image of *guoben* ("foundation of the country") China, like a plant, needed to be cured at its roots for a lasting and effective recovery. Adapting the logic of traditional Chinese medicine, Wang presented his policy as dealing with China's problems at the root (*zhiben*) rather than curing only its superficial symptoms, as he characterized Jiang's military approach. The latter strategy, he argued, would lead the patient (China) to sure disaster. Wang's holistic self-strengthening conception of China's current crisis—identified as the weakening of the national foundation—was combined with a social Darwinist reading of China's historical development and a Marxist-Leninist view of imperialism. The Chinese people, Wang wrote, like "all nationalities (*minzu*) aspire to be unified and have a consciousness of their manifest destiny for unification" (Wang Jingwei 1931). Only economic reconstruction would realize this aspiration and put an end to a long period of troubles and foreign intrusion, begun when the Chinese fell under Manchu domination—a view that Wang was enunciating as early as 1905. Popular social Darwinist theories thus met, in Wang's thought, with ethnic nationalism, giving birth to the idea of the right to self-determination of the Chinese people. Wang's conception of national unity was intimately intertwined with that of its independence, as the two basic conditions of nationhood. National unification and resistance to imperialism were, for Wang, one and the same goal in the Chinese national revolution and required more than a strong army for their fulfillment. In his interpretation of the dynamics of the current international system, industrialized nations exploited the markets and resources of the unindustrialized, creating a complex network of power relations in which countries were connected at their domestic core rather than just at their borders. In this situation, China needed to mobilize the totality of its resources in its struggle to preserve its independence. "In order to repel imperialism, we cannot use only the military. We have to focus all our energies—military, political, diplomatic, industrial, and economic—on the anti-imperialist struggle." Reforms and diplomatic action were thus the basic policies of Wang's *annei rangwai,* assuming that a combination of the two was the only effective solution through which China could "repel imperialism . . . [and] become a free and equal nation" (1935a, 291).

It was on this general framework of *annei rangwai* that Chen Gongbo developed his project for economic nation building. In keeping again with social Darwinist and Marxist-Leninist themes, Chen represented history as a process in which nationalities (*minzu*) progressed up an evolutionary ladder. Some had fallen behind in the evolutionary competition in which only the most advanced could achieve the status of "nation." If China wanted to catch up, Chen concluded, it needed to transform itself from a "backward" nationality into a "nation" (1928b, 1934b). But Chen's idea of historical evolution and nations was more firmly inspired by Marxist-Leninist theories of economic determinism than was Wang's. Chen explicitly identified the economic structure as the foundation of a country and therefore as the main motor of the evolutionary process of a nationality. In his conception of historical evolution, each of the three main stages of political organization that characterized the evolution of a people—tribal, feudal, and national—rested on a different stage of economic development: agricultural, commercial, and industrial, respectively. China could achieve nationhood only by overcoming its regionally based economy, which preserved a "feudal" economic and political mode: "If [China's] feudal economy does not break down one day, China will never be able to become a modern-style nation-state (*jindaishi de guojia*)" (1936, 7). Accordingly, the unification of China as a modern nation was to be achieved by reorganizing the industrial sector on a large and centralized scale, overcoming its current provincial boundaries.

Taking Wang Jingwei's concern for national unity one step further, Chen enclosed it in a more economically deterministic framework. Even after he left the CCP and joined the GMD, Chen had continued to advocate the use of Marxist methodologies in the interpretation of Chinese history: "Regardless of what point of view [one approaches history] from, there is no way to escape economic relationships . . . [for] a political system is a reflection of its economy" (1928b, 2–4). Chen therefore advocated "economic" unification as the most effective way to achieve national unity:

> Only the economy constitutes the foundation of unification. During the last twenty years of domestic chaos, [we] have repeatedly tried [to achieve unification] through political [or military] means. However, in spite of the fact that the central government [nominally] rules over the entire country, today people are still debating why China cannot be unified.

From this we can see that the claim of unification is only superficial. I personally wonder why center and provinces appear to have no relationship at all. The simple answer is that there are very few economic contacts [between the two]. (1936, 7)

Chen criticized all centrifugal regionalist tendencies on the grounds that they kept the initiative for economic reform decentralized at the local level. For this reason, he rejected federalism. Like most Nationalists and Marxists, he perceived federalism as divisive and thus a manifestation of "backward" feudalism. As the Marxist Zhang Tingfei summed it up: "Only that which unifies is progressive; division means reaction" (As quoted in Fitzgerald 1996, 156). Such a stress on national unity, in reality, testifies to a Nationalist identification of nation with state and, in turn, of state with party, confusing unity with centralization and centralization with the leadership of the party throughout the entire country. The 1930s debate on federalism was above all a debate on the role of state, party, and social groups in the country's political and economic life. Most supporters of federalism perceived it as a system of political decentralization that would ensure the participation of elites in local government. "Guangdong to Guangdong people," advocated the warlord of Guangdong, Chen Jiongming, who inspired Zhang Tingfei's remarks on division and reaction (Fitzgerald 1996; Duara 1995). Chen Jiongming's advocacy of provincial self-government implied a conception of a "modern" Chinese state that was diametrically opposed to Chen Gongbo's. Chen held fast to the idea that "a nation cannot be divided. If it is, it does not constitute a nation anymore" (1934c, 190).

Fighting Colonization: Industrialization and the Development of a National Economy

Moving away from a localized economy was, for Chen, the first thing that the Chinese people had to do in order to become a nation and "keep up with the development of the human enterprise (*renlei shiye*)." It was a matter not just of national pride but of national survival. By projecting China to the forefront of the "progressive" nations, they would finally be able to resist "the threat coming from other countries" (1935b, 168). In other words, only by becoming a nation could China avoid colonization, since a modern nation could not be colonized. It was only those countries that failed to achieve nationhood that fell prey to imperialist powers. However, Chen warned, national unity was the first, but not the only, requisite for nation building. Two other characteristics distinguished modern nations, industrialization and the development of a national and "nationalist" economy (*minzu jingji*). It was the failure to fulfill these conditions for nationhood that was causing China to suffer the current process of colonization.

Analyzing the international situation, Chen Gongbo identified two groups of nations. On one side, he placed the world powers, which based their strength on a strong system of industrial production characterized by low levels of imports and high levels of exports. On the other side were the victims of the world powers' expansionist drives, colonized countries that had basically agricultural economies and weak systems of industrial production characterized by low levels of exports and high levels of imports. From this perspective, Chen warned, China was destined to become a colony unless it abandoned its traditional policy of giving priority to agriculture and began focusing its energies on industry. "A nation based on agriculture not only will experience a constant decline of its economy, but also will easily turn into a colony," he wrote. "Nations with a peasant population of under 5 per cent are all rich and powerful countries. Those with a peasant population of over 55 per cent are all poor." He closed his argument with the example of "colonies such as Egypt and India [which] all have [a peasant population of] over 60 per cent" (1935b, 169).[5]

The idea that China's colonial destiny was linked to its agricultural economy was not unique to Chen Gongbo's thought. It was shared by many Chinese officials and intellectuals, and it was also reflected in the Japanese policy "ruralize China, industrialize Japan," which destined China to serve as both a reservoir of raw materials and a market for growing Japanese industry (Wang Shuhuai 1984, 714). This policy struck many Chinese as an uncanny confirmation of the Marxist-Leninist theory of imperialism and fed the Chinese interpretation of their country as colonial or "semicolonial." Japan was forcing China to remain rural, and, in a vicious circle, it was the rural nature of China that attracted and allowed Japan's colonizing effort. China was turning into the rural periphery that made the growth of the industrial-metropole, Japan, possible.

The extent to which certain sectors of the Chinese economy were being inexorably drawn into the sphere of Japan's economic influence and the perception of China as a victim of imperialism had an important impact on nation-building reforms (Duus et al. 1989). In this context, the assertion of China's semicolonial status appears to be more than an overused, meaningless refrain of Communist rhetoric. It played, in fact, an important role in formulating the concept of what was called "the national economy" (*minzu jingji*)— the national and "nationalist" part of the Chinese economy that did not cooperate with imperialist forces—as the central actor of the Chinese national revolution. It was this sector of the economy that Chen identified as the revolutionary force in China. This idea was later adopted by Mao Zedong as an element of his New Democracy. Mao regarded the mobilization of a revolutionary alliance of all national economic forces as only a temporary stage in the longer process of realizing a socialist society in China; for Chen Gongbo, it constituted instead the core of his theory of the establishment of a corporate state. This important difference between Chen and Mao cannot obscure, however, the facts that the two leaders accommodated nationalist goals in their class-based revolutionary projects and that the category of "national economy" loomed large over both.

This nationalist-economic interpretation of the Chinese revolution had its roots in the political debate that flared up within the Nationalist Party following the 1927 split with the CCP.[6] At that time, members of the GMD Left experienced a profound identity crisis, which set off a heated debate among its leaders on the political nature of the GMD and its role in the Chinese revolution (Hoston 1994). Chen Gongbo participated in the debate with a series of influential articles in which he attempted to preserve the revolutionary spirit of the GMD Left while maintaining his distance from the Communists.[7] In his articles, Chen accused conservative groups within the GMD of having sacrificed class-struggle ideals and mass-organization activities in favor of overall nationalist goals. Taking a position against these new developments, Chen asserted that class struggle in China did exist, although not to the extent or in the manner maintained by the Communists. According to Chen, class struggle in China was not of the sort described by "scientific Marxism" because capitalism had not yet developed sufficiently to create the conditions for a systematic confrontation between workers and capital. In China, there was only a "random" class struggle between individuals. On this basis, Chen criticized the CCP for insisting that China was primarily feudal, as this position implied the priority of a social over a national revolution. For Chen, instead, China was primarily semicolonial because obstacles to industrial development did not lie in the semifeudal forces of the countryside but in imperialism. Feudalism, he argued, no longer existed in China. Only "feudal forces" survived, and these were being manipulated by imperialism for its own gain (1928c, 8; see also Hoston 1994, 298; and Tao 1930). Chen thus sought to strike a balance between the total negation of class struggle among conservative GMD groups and the Communist subordination of the national question to class struggle. His analysis linked imperialism to a random class struggle in China and advocated tighter government control on the means of production in order to prevent the future development of the bourgeoisie, that would ultimately lead to the widening of class struggle in its "scientific form." While for Mao's New Democracy the feudal and bourgeois classses used imperialism to strengthen its position, for Chen it was imperialism that used random, unorganized feudal elements as its pawns.

As a consequence, Chen perceived the Chinese revolution not as targeted against the capitalist class, which did not exist in China as such, but against imperialism and those bourgeois who cooperated with it. Chen thus shaped an idea that would play an important role in Chinese politics for decades to come, the notion of "national economy" (*minzu jingji*). It was this idea that he used to distinguish the revolutionary forces within Chinese society rather than using the concept of class. Chen divided economic forces into two groups: one that supported foreign imperialism and one that did not. This division also applied to the high bourgeoisie. Because the "national (*minzu*) bourgeoisie" opposed imperialism, it participated in the national revolution and should be part of the GMD class base. Those groups in the high bourgeoisie that collaborated with imperialism hindered the revolution. Because their interests were tied up with those of the imperialist powers and ran against the nationalist goals of the GMD, they should not be included in the GMD class base (Chen 1928a; Dirlik 1975). A Chinese cotton mill owner would be included among the ranks of the national bourgeoisie or not depending on whether he collaborated with Japanese bankers or entrepreneurs. If he did not, Chen considered him as contributing to the development of a national economy and thus to China's nation building. If he did collaborate, Chen perceived him as undermining China's reconstruction and labeled him counterrevolutionary. According to Chen, therefore, the building of Chinese capital, be it state or private, always carried nationalist significance as long as it was "national" in its ownership and goals (1928a). This constituted a major point of disagreement with Jiang Jieshi and other conservative leaders of the GMD, who argued that the party represented the whole of China. This was not possible, Chen argued, because the interests of certain groups were too intertwined with those of foreign imperialism to coincide with the goals of the nationalist revolution. The national unity Chen advocated needed qualification. It was a "nationalist" unity and excluded non-"nationalist" elements. It also needed to be economically independent and be committed to the industrialization of the country. Only by fulfilling these three requirements—unity, industrialization, and independence, all three summed up in the term *minzu jingji*—would China be able to achieve nationhood.

Chen's career as a whole exemplifies China's participation in the global political and economic trends of the interwar period. His passage from the left to the right of the political spectrum uncannily resembles that of many contemporary leftist radical leaders in Europe (such as the Italian *duce*, Benito Mussolini), who under the pressure of nationalism abandoned the idea of class struggle and aligned themselves with national-socialist movements (De Felice 1956; Sternhell 1987). In this respect, Chen's political journey illustrates the development of nonliberal alternatives to Marxism-Leninism in Asia to adapt to the needs of local nationalist movements.

The idea of the nation as an independent, nationalist, economic unit was crucial for shaping Chen's autarkic plan, signaling a large stride away from a vision of China integrated in a system of free international exchange, which had characterized earlier self-strengthening economic reform programs.

Facing Imperialism: From Mercantilism to Autarky

In the decades from the 1870s to the 1930s, Chinese officials adopted a variety of strategies for overcoming the national crisis initiated by imperialist aggression. Their efforts included a military strand, which survived in the person of Jiang Jieshi and was both promoted and strengthened through the Northern Expedition (1926–28). A different strand was based on the idea of the economy as China's national foundation (*guoben*). This focus on the economy, inherited by Chen, was carried over into the twentieth century by such late Qing officials as Zheng Guanying (1842–1922). Zheng, a Western-trained Shanghainese comprador and a protégé of Li Hongzhang, shifted the attention from the military to the economy as the source of a country's strength. In the early twentieth century, he argued, China faced a new state of affairs because it had found itself suddenly integrated into a system characterized by international exchange and commerce. Each country in this system focused mainly on gaining profits, based its power on trade, and used its army only for protection. In such a situation, Zheng asked: "If we want to restrain the West by self-strengthening, is there anything better than promoting [international] trade?" (quoted in Zhong 1992, 32; see also Chen Yutang 1993).

Zheng's idea that China could resist imperialism only by engaging in a "trade war" with the West (Zhong 1992) was shared by many local officials and members of the elite, who, in the absence of an effective central government, were taking the initiative for reforms. Kenneth Pomeranz's characterization of early-twentieth-century officials in Shandong as pursuing economic growth "because it will help preserve China's independence, not because it will promote individual welfare" can safely be extended to officials of other Chinese provinces (1993, 47). The reforms they carried out aimed at achieving a variety of nationalist goals such as reclaiming foreign concessions. The most prominent aspect of these regional economic reforms, however, was that they promoted export-oriented manufacturing in an attempt to readdress China's unfavorable balance of trade, a mercantilist strategy and vision of what constituted a strong economic system. For this reason, they tended to strengthen the links between one particular locality and the international market rather than ties with other Chinese regions. In this respect, although already closely related to anti-imperialist goals, they were hardly nationalist in the sense later constructed by Chen Gongbo. They tended to be provincial- or county-based, creating a high level of economic fragmentation both among localities and between locality and center while projecting export-related areas into the international economy, competing directly against industrialized countries. Competition at such a level with the imperialist powers, however, soon proved to be impossible because of the latter's superior industrial and commercial structure and, not least, because China was not allowed to enter the international arena on an equal footing since it had lost control over its tariffs and tax administration in the late nineteenth century.

The first change in this mercantilist and local approach emerged with Sun Yatsen's critique of the free international exchange system, which he denounced as a tool used by strong economies to dominate weaker ones. This idea undermined mercantilist theories, such as Zheng Guanying's "trade war," reversing the idea that China's national interests were best served through full participation in the international market. It was only in the 1930s, however, that anti-international market policies were actually applied, experiencing their full development in Chen Gongbo's plan for autarky.

By the time Chen Gongbo became minister of industry, mercantilism had given way to Marxism-Leninism and the new ideas of mass mobilization and autarky to which the international economy was increasingly subject. At the same time, the target of self-strengthening reforms had also changed, for China was now facing the unprecedented threat of outright colonization by Japan, which went well beyond previous infringements of its sovereignty by Western powers. This change in the nature of imperialism was perceived as the crescendo of late-nineteenth-century foreign imperialism and the natural conclusion of nearly a century of domestic disintegration, which was inexorably leading to the end of China as an independent political and ethnic entity (Pusey 1982). Such ideas, while allowing for the continuity of a general self-strengthening narrative, implied at the same time its transformation. Japan's aggression reflected a new kind of autarkic imperialism, which emerged worldwide in the interwar years. Japan's attempts at outright colonization and the deliberate exploitation of China's primary resources were unlike anything China had experienced. Chinese leaders identified more closely with problems of colonial dependency and clearly sensed that the nature of interwar imperialism was moved by more authoritarian forces than earlier imperialism had been. This new experience served to strengthen the Marxist-Leninist understanding of colonialism among Chinese officials and intellectuals, who also projected it back to explain the pre-1930s period. The idea of a "semicolonial" China, which played such a large role in Communist nationalist propaganda and historiography, was not just an empty rhetorical device. In the 1930s, it constituted an important conceptual category in the Chinese discourse on nationalism and reconstruction, effectively influencing economic reforms and leading to a series of attempts at autarky (under Chen Gongbo) and later self-sufficiency (under Mao Zedong).

In Chen's vision, 1930s China was surrounded by a new world divided into autarkic economies. It was to meet the needs of an autarkic economy that industrialized nations attempted to control or colonize agricultural countries and areas rich in raw materials. This was the case with Japan and China. The Chinese economy became increasingly intertwined with that of its neighbor, shrinking the national economy (*minzu jingji*) and coming to depend on Japan. Chen demonstrated China's dependency by showing its unfavorable balance of trade, which was characterized by dropping exports and rising imports. This sign of China's low level of industrial production was in turn a negative effect of imperialism on its productive system. Because China had lost the power to protect itself, it was forced to let foreigners extract its resources and dump their excess production on its market, as Japan was doing with cotton yarn, for example (Chen 1935b). This situation made it impossible for China to industrialize, trapping it in its agrarian economic mode. Above all, it forced China to concentrate its imports on daily necessities, which were creating a dangerous dependency on foreign countries. According to Chen's data, China spent more than 736,509,911 custom taels buying oil, cotton, rice, cereals, and wood. Such economic dependency on foreign sources for "clothes, food, shelter, and consumption (*yi shi zhu yong*)," he warned, jeopardized China's survival. "How can a nationality sustain itself in such a situation?" (1933c, 160). With this formula, Chen adroitly modernized Sun Yatsen's image of the four basic economic needs of the people—*yi* (clothing), *shi* (food), *zhu* (shelter), and *xing* (transportation)—by replacing transportation with *yong* (consumption) (Sun 1953). By echoing Sun's four economic functions, Chen could claim his legacy, a useful credential for political legitimacy in twentieth-century Chinese politics.

Chen strengthened his argument by asserting that national reconstruction would not be possible if these four crucial aspects of the people's livelihood (*minsheng zhuyi*) were in the hands of foreigners. At the same time, by identifying them as the economic foundations (*guoben*) of the Chinese nation he could evoke the powerful image of national disaster. According to a popular image of the Mandate of Heaven, when the *guoben* was shaken, the entire country must experience a period of misery and destruction. Chen's suggestion that China had already reached the point of losing control over the four basic needs—its foundation—leaving them in the hands of foreigners, effectively conveyed the idea of China's extreme weakness and of the urgency of the national question. Traditional images encountered an analysis of China's new situation as well as new myths and theories emerging globally in the wake of World War I.

To observers around the world, World War I appeared to have taught a fundamental lesson: national power rested in a country's ability to control the production of basic agricultural staples and industrial raw materials so that a nation could keep its productive apparatus working and feed its population in times of war and peace.[8] According to Chen, it was the wartime shortage of these products that determined the outcome of a war. In spite of its powerful offensive apparatus, Germany had been defeated because it did not have enough grain and raw materials (1935a). Chen's perception was not much different here from that of Hitler, who devoted his career to making sure that Germany conquered its "vital space" by ensuring, through military conquest, direct control of neighboring areas rich in raw materials. The emergence of autarkic empires in the postwar period testifies to the universality of this economic-political myth (Polanyi 1944). Chen noted these changes and in 1935 pointed out that after the war the governments of many European countries had moved to apply autarkic policies:

> During the European war, defeated Germany as well as the victorious powers all deeply felt the lack of raw materials. It is for this reason that after the war they all sought national autarky. . . . This so-called national autarky means that regardless of whether in war or in peace, none of the goods needed must be sought abroad. (1934c, 193)

From this point of view, China was in an extremely weak situation:

> China does not have an industrial production worth mentioning. Although it is nominally an agricultural country . . . imported grains constitute one fourth of [domestic consumption]. China has historically relied on silk and tea for its exports, but in the last ten years silk and tea are insignificant fractions of foreign trade. China is threatened by foreign countries but it does not have any defense worth talking about. It has not even started a defense industry. No doubt this is not enough to rank as a modern nation, but we cannot even discuss conditions for survival. (1934c, 190)

China's economic dependency became a direct threat to its survival and a clear sign that the crisis was at the country's doorstep (1935a, 1936). "Let's close our eyes and think: were something to happen to China, isn't it the case that we would have no alternative but to wait for death?" (1936, 173–74; see also 1935a). "With such economic drawbacks, we don't cry for protectionism, but raw material self-sufficiency is our least expectation (1936, 42–43).

Autarky appeared to be the first step on the path of nation building because it allowed China's national economy to regain control over daily-need products as well as over raw materials. It would boost domestic industry, thus strengthening the country and avoiding the slide into colonization. In Chen's estimation, it was the task of the government to place itself at the head of all national productive forces and lead them in their fight against dependency.

Having defined the goals of its economic nation-building program, the first action of the new *annei rangwei* cabinet was the establishment of a Ministry of Industry in 1932, which, under the leadership of Chen Gongbo, was intended to be a crucial element in the establishment of a nationally integrated and independent industrial structure. It rested on Chen, however, to devise a practical realization of the complex conception of nation that had inspired the *annei rangwai* program.

Chen proceeded to organize the mobilization of all "producers" in support of his plan. Combining socialist-style mass mobilization with a radical defensive nationalism, he envisioned the creation of a corporate state that would bring together all of China's producers for the establishment of a *minzu* economy. His plan provided for the creation of six state corporatist organizations: the Agriculture Control Commission (Nongye tongzhi weiyuanhui), the Industrial Control Commission (Gongye tongzhi weiyuanhui), the Commerce Control Commission (Shangye tongzhi weiyuanhui), the Transportation Control Commission (Yunshu tongzhi weiyuanhui), the Banking and Insurance Control Commission (Yinhang ji baoxian tongzhi weiyuanhui), and the Labor Control Commission (Laogong tongzhi weiyuanhui) (Chen 1933b). These commissions were to act as the government's supervisory economic agencies and the channels for the mobilization of all producers for the economic building of the country.

Mass Mobilization and the Corporatist Organization of the State

Although Chen Gongbo never directly identified his reforms with corporatism, his project for the reorganization of the economic administration of the government had a decisive corporatist character. Each control commission was designed to be the only association of a particular sector or industry at the national level, bringing together the effort of all groups involved, from peasants to workers, industrialists, bankers, merchants, experts, and representatives of units within the state's economic administration. The theory underpinning his corporatist program rested on a combination of two ideas: economic control (*tongzhi jingji*) in the form of direct intervention of the government in the economy, and cooperation (*hezuo*), both between the government and private entrepreneurs and among social groups, especially labor and capital. The cooperation (*hezuo*) of all economic forces was to be the vehicle by which the government could assert economic control (*tongzhi jingji*) and thereby reorganize the economy along national, autarkic, and industrial lines.

The corporatist character of the reforms sponsored by Chen was already discernible in the official plan for reconstruction presented by Wang Jingwei on behalf of the GMD Left in his 1930 "Proposal for Economic and Financial Policies" (Wang Jingwei 1930). Here Wang argued that a coordinated effort of all groups in society with the government was necessary for the success of reconstruction. "The entire populace, from the highest to the lowest, must co-operate in attempting to realize the national economic policy," he pleaded. "It is essential that different factors in production should learn to understand one another" (118). Wang thus advocated social and political solidarity as a precondition for implementing a unified national policy that would be decided centrally and considered binding on all sectors nationwide. The ambiguity of the line that divided conscripted enrollment and mass mobilization, which is intrinsic in most corporatist organizations, was very much present in Wang's program.[9] Class solidarity, implied in the idea of economic cooperation, (*hezuo*) and socialist-style mass mobilization were bound together to form a system of joint party and mass control over the government, which added a revolutionary and fascist edge to the plan: "In order to prevent reconstruction from transforming itself into a tool of imperialism or bureaucratic capitalism we must (1) train the masses to rise and really participate in the government, and (2) unify the party so that it can really lead the masses and check on the government" (Wang Jingwei 1935b, 277).

While at the Ministry of Industry, Chen further articulated Wang's general call for a national joint economic effort in the more specific terms of class solidarity, calling for the coming together of labor and capital. Chen recognized that solidarity would be difficult to achieve: "China's labor force and capital are not easily brought together. [Under such circumstances,] the idea of mobilizing the entire country is just an idle dream" (1936, 8). The goal for both Chen and Wang was to replace class division with mobilization, which would lead China to develop into a nation of "producers" rather than social classes. The government's role would be to influence the nature of industrial development in such a way that social conflict would be eliminated. The government would be forced to allow a certain degree of initiative to private businessmen, due to its chronic shortage of resources, and private business would inevitably thrive, but capital would not be permitted to develop an organized, Western-style bourgeois class. Chen argued that the Western bourgeoisie based its power on the monopoly of economic production, transportation, foreign trade, land, and other resources. These circumstances would never develop in China because of the GMD's policy of state capitalism, its tax strategies, and its monopoly over foreign trade. At the same time, the growth of a state economy would prevent the rise of class differences and inequalities. The majority of the working class would ultimately work in the state economy; class distinctions would disappear as everyone became a "producer in society." The petite bourgeoisie would also gradually become a "producer" as the state took control of increasingly larger spheres of the economy. The entire process designed by Chen was thus intended to lead to the ultimate reconciliation of class interests, a goal that characterized most contemporary corporatist nation-building projects (Chen 1928a).

In China, the idea of a nation of producers was popular in diverse political circles. The leaders of the Fujian federalist movement, for example, advocated the establishment of a federal system kept together by only one common principle, "political power for the producing masses." Having formed a "producer party" (*shengchandang*), they adopted as one of their slogans "Establish a Government of the Producing People!" (Fitzgerald 1996; Duara 1995). The idea was also part of the Blue Shirts' program, which stated as its goal the transformation of each individual into a producer (Eastman 1990, 82, 130–31). Corporatist trends were thus much in the air in 1930s China, although the corporatist projects that reached the realization stage proved to be very diverse in nature. Jiang Jieshi's post-1935 plan of corporatism excluded private entrepreneurs from real participation in policy-making and closely resembled the conscription of private economic groups (Kasza 1995). Chen Gongbo, on the other hand, considered the participation of private entrepreneurs crucial for the success of the plan, not only because they had the capital the government needed desperately but also because they were still participating in the economy and therefore working for the national revolution. As he argued: "Productive factors (*shengchanzhe*) still are productive factors and [policies that do not respect them] will not only harm the tool of [national] production but also obstruct its vitality" (1933b, 178). Their participation as active members of China's corporatist organization was thus essential to the expansion of its national economy and its struggle against imperialism.

Chen's ambitious corporatist plan never assumed the ample scope for which he had hoped. While at the Ministry of Industry, he encountered severe financial limitations, political opposition from Jiang Jieshi, and the marked reluctance of private entrepreneurs to cooperate (Chen Gongbo 1936; Wang Shuhuai 1984). Unable to reorganize the entire administration, Chen focused on the basic industrial and agricultural products that were crucial to meeting China's daily needs, giving priority to those that had fallen under Japanese control such as oil, cotton, cereals, and wood (Chen 1933b). The agency through which he acted was the National Economic Council (Quanguo jingji weiyuanhui, NEC). The NEC was founded and directed by Song Ziwen (T. V. Soong), the minister of finance. Song was closely tied to the powerful Zhejiang-Jiangsu cotton mill owners, who had on earlier occasions resisted cooperation with Chen Gongbo but were now eager to participate in the NEC under Song's protective umbrella. Chen believed that the NEC was the last hope for China because it was the only administrative agency of the government endowed with independent funding, escaping the quagmire of the GMD factions' scramble over already scarce government resources.[10] Furthermore, the NEC was empowered with the function of coordinating the various agencies of the government's economic administration at the central and local levels, thus enjoying a nationwide reach far superior to that of the Ministry of Industry. When Chen was appointed minister, he became a member of the Standing Committee of the NEC, heavily influencing it with his autarkic plan.[11] Within the NEC, Song and Chen established, in addition to the Cotton Control Commission in 1933, the Silk Improvement Commission (Cansi gailiang weiyuanhui) in 1934 and the Industrial Cooperation Commission (Hezuo shiye weiyuanui) in 1935, chaired by Chen himself. Of these, the CCC was the most successful.

The Cotton Control Commission

The CCC was the most complete realization of Chen's economic nation-building plan in both its goals and its administrative structure. The CCC's main goal was an autarkic development of the Chinese national (*minzu*) cotton industry in order to break its dependency on Japan. Its organization was clearly corporatist, devised to mobilize all groups involved in cotton production from peasants to cotton mill owners, industrial workers, bankers involved in financing the cotton industry, and agriculturalists engaged in cotton improvement experimentation. The cooperative (*hezuo*) structure was finally intended to be a channel for top-down, far-reaching, government intervention. In this way, the CCC realized both basic principles of Chen's idea of corporatism.

While the interests of workers and peasants were underrepresented, as generally happened in corporatist states of that period, private business played an important role in the highest decision-making body of the CCC, reflecting the original idea of Chen Gongbo and Song Ziwen of making private entrepreneurs and capital a vital pattern of the CCC's nation-building efforts. Chen Guangfu, the general manager of the Shanghai Commercial and Savings Bank, became the chairman of the CCC. Chen Guangfu, who was close to Song Ziwen, had long been involved in joint state-private projects sponsored by Song. His bank had been connected with the cotton industry since its early days, pioneering in industrial and marketing loans. Private business and state interests were jointly represented also in the Standing Committee, which was composed of mill owners, bankers, and expert agriculturists as well as representatives of the government tax administration.[12]

The cotton industry was well suited for Chen's nationalist plan. Traditionally, it was China's strongest industry and export leader, but by 1933 it had grown increasingly dependent on Japanese business. Japanese cotton yarn poured into the Chinese market, while Japanese mills in China, which could rely on large amounts of capital and strong organization back home, waged unfair competition against domestic products. Driven out of business, Chinese mills were little by little falling under the control of Japanese capital. The cotton industry also appeared crucial for China's autarkic industrialization and for strengthening the country's foundation because, as Chen pointed out, in times of peace it fulfilled one of the four basic economic functions, the *yi* (clothing) function, while in wartime it supplied military uniforms and bandages, assuming a defensive function (1933c). According to his calculations, China had to import almost 50 percent of the cotton it consumed (1936). These ideas underpinned the 1934 CCC plan, as indicated in its opening statement: "Our country is vast in territory and rich in resources. The areas fit for growing cotton are vast. However, domestic production of raw cotton does not meet demand. Its quality is not fit to be used. Consequently the annual value of imports of foreign raw cotton, yarn, and cloth is huge. This seriously damages the foundation of the country (*guoben*)."[13]

Because, the CCC's plan identified the inadequacy of domestic agricultural supplies of raw cotton as the most crucial reason for the weakness, and consequent dependency, of the industry, its primary goal was solving problems at the agricultural production level. Indeed, the agricultural crisis that swept the countryside—due to unfavorable weather conditions, protracted warfare, and scarcity of capital in the rural areas—led to declining output and, together with the disruption in the transportation system, seriously compromised the consistency of supplies of raw cotton to coastal mills. It was not, however, just a matter of quantity and consistency, as Chen Gongbo and the CCC's plan pointed out, but also one of quality. One of the major problems of cotton manufacturing was that domestic yarn could not be used with modern textile machines because it was too short. Cotton mills were thus trapped in a vicious circle. They could not afford to buy foreign raw materials because they were too expensive, especially after the rise in the price of silver following the 1934 American Silver Purchase Act. Forced to rely on low-quality domestic supplies, they consequently produced low-quality goods that were not competitive on foreign markets and were easily outsold by Japanese cotton imports at home. On the other hand, upgrading the equipment in Chinese mills was not an easy matter because new machines had to be imported at extremely high prices. Once in place, they could not be used since domestic low-count yarn was too short and the foreign variety was too expensive. Based on this analysis, the CCC's 1934 plan focused on both expanding domestic production of raw cotton and improving its quality so as to start fulfilling the first prerequisite for the modernization of the industry.[14]

Although the CCC also planned—and carried out—intervention in the industrial production of cotton goods, it was forced initially to concentrate its energies on rural areas because its autarkic goal depended on the development of the hinterland and rural areas into reliable reservoirs of raw materials and markets for industrial goods. This initial stress on agriculture, however, should not obscure the fact that the CCC's ultimate goal was industrial development and harnessing rural resources to it. The overall industrial priority was exemplified by the fact that the main office of the CCC was in Shanghai, where it was directed by Shanghai bankers and industrialists. It was this body that decided the general guidelines for the commission's intervention in agriculture. Once decided upon, these policies were implemented throughout the entire cycle of the industry. Such far-reaching implementation was made possible by the centralized corporatist structure of the CCC, which worked as a channel for the mobilization of all economic groups.

The CCC's corporatist structure was organized roughly as a three-layer pyramid. The central policy-making agency, the highest level of the network, was the Standing Committee, located in Shanghai. At the next level were a series of experimental stations and research bureaus, which carried out experiments related to increasing and improving cotton production—through seed amelioration, innovative growing technologies, fertilizers, antipest devices, and industrial machinery innovation—following the directives of the Standing Committee. Successfully developed techniques were then spread to the grassroots production level by organizing rural communities of peasants into cooperative societies (*hezuoshe*) under the leadership of the CCC's specialized personnel. These societies formed the bottom layer of the structure. Conceptually they were integrated in the corporation because they shared its cooperation principle—*hezuo*, being part of the Chinese term for cooperative society (*hezuoshe*)—and were the vehicle for "economic control" (*tongzhi jingji*). Cooperative societies thus created a powerful weapon for centralizing and far-reaching top-down economic reforms. It was the network of societies that allowed strategies and policies decided upon in Shanghai by the Standing Committee to become part of an integrated plan for national development implemented at the grassroots level.[15]

Cooperative societies were popular in China in the 1920s and 1930s, mushrooming all over the country under the sponsorship of numerous foreign and Chinese organizations. Filling a vacuum created by a weak central government, these groups, often working in cooperation with provincial reconstruction bureaus (*jiansheting*), used cooperative societies for locally circumscribed economic improvement experiments. However, as pointed out earlier, because they planned from a provincial perspective, their work tended to deepen local economic autonomy rather than promote nationally integrated economic growth. Their reforms often conflicted or directly competed with similar programs in neighboring provinces, creating deeper fragmentation than already existed. The NEC and CCC instead used cooperative societies in a revolutionary way, as a tool for creating a nationwide centralized network for intervention in the economy. Their cooperative structure aimed at effectively overcoming the current fragmentation in the reform initiative by breaking down regionalism and integrating local production of cotton within a centralized plan. In the CCC's plan, cooperative societies were organized either directly by CCC personnel or by local reconstruction bureaus and other existing local agencies under the close supervision of the CCC, thus bringing coordination and centralization to the reform process and linking rural villages and local reconstruction agencies to a new administrative center in Shanghai.[16]

The national scope of the CCC's cooperative network was, together with a shift from mercantilism to autarky, the most innovative aspect of its work. Its national scope allowed it to achieve results that had eluded previous reform attempts, as was the case with the rise in cotton quality triggered by the CCC. The introduction of new, improved cotton seeds had proved particularly difficult in locally based experiments elsewhere because the fields sown with new cotton varieties were located too close to old, low-quality fields. This situation inevitably led to crossbreeding and the quick deterioration of the newly imported varieties. The CCC was able to avoid this problem by relying on its nationwide network and selecting Shaanxi and other northwestern provinces as the place to locate experimental fields, well away from areas where old vari-

eties were grown. In cooperation with local reconstruction bureaus, it organized experimental stations, cooperative societies, and marketing facilities
aimed at promoting the delivery of the improved raw cotton to mills in coastal
areas.[17]

Its Shaanxi experiment exemplifies the CCC's use of cooperative societies
as a tool for national economic integration based primarily on reorienting the
industrial sector toward the hinterland and away from foreign markets and
Japanese influence. The CCC used cooperatives in a variety of strategies aimed
at bridging the coastal and rural economies. In addition to interprovincial marketing, as in the case of the sale of Shaanxi cotton to coastal mills, the CCC
established a network of credit societies, which made agricultural credit sponsored by urban coastal banks available in rural areas. The CCC's credit system
was intended to break local moneylending patterns in the countryside, creating
a link between urban and rural finance. This strategy had a double goal. On the
one hand, it intended to direct urban capital into productive investments,
enticing it away from unproductive speculations in the stock exchange and
government bonds. This was an initial success because participating in the
NEC's rural finance program represented a new avenue of investment for
urban banks—an especially welcome opportunity after the collapse of the
Shanghai real estate market in the early 1930s. A new infusion of much-needed
capital in rural areas would also bring to an end the chronic capital shortage
that prevented peasants from adopting technological innovations. In this way,
the CCC intended to stimulate capital accumulation in the countryside and
trigger an increase in agricultural production. According to members of the
CCC Standing Committee, improvements in the economic condition of the
peasants, triggered by urban investment, would ultimately lead to improvements in their livelihood and expansion of their purchasing power. The cotton
industry would then be able to rely on a domestic market that could absorb the
expansion of the coastal cotton-manufacturing industry, freeing it from
reliance on exports, which were inevitably declining following the transformation of the international market from a system of free exchange to one of closed
autarkic units.

According to the CCC's plan, this remapping of the economy would allow
Chinese cotton mills to rely on a steady supply of domestic raw cotton and on
a healthy domestic market without having to look outward to the international
market. And, because the improvement of raw cotton would occur within the
framework of the CCC corporatist organization, which controlled the growth
and marketing of cotton, it was the Chinese national economy, not Japanese
industry, that would benefit from the new and improved varieties of raw materials.

The CCC corporatist organization, in fact, included only China's national (*minzu*) economic forces in its nation-building project because it was the *minzu* economy, according to its leaders, that constituted the foundation (*guoben*) of the new nation. The CCC represented a promising beginning in the realization of such a plan. Unfortunately, it soon became evident that the weakness of Chen's political position in Nanjing constituted an insurmountable barrier to its full execution.

The Limits of Economic Nationalism

In March 1935, Chen attempted to take his reform project a step further. In cooperation with Song Ziwen, he called a National Cooperation Conference, jointly sponsored by the NEC and the Ministry of Industry. The conference drafted guidelines for the implementation of the newly promulgated National Cooperation Law, which brought the management of cooperative societies under provincial government administration. The law attempted finally to put an end to the fragmentation of the cooperative movement by subordinating to the provincial government, and through the provincial government to the central administration, the myriad private and county-level experiments with cooperative societies. In connection with the promulgation of the law, the Ministry of Industry promptly created an Industrial Department of Cooperation. Soon after, on 1 October 1935, the NEC formed a Cooperation Commission, chaired by Chen Gongbo, which was entrusted with the coordination of the movement at the national level.[18]

This new step toward centralization was soon thwarted by the political marginalization of the GMD Left within the Wang-Jiang coalition, which began late in 1935. At that time, the composition of the administration, which in 1932 had largely favored Wang Jingwei and Chen Gongbo, was gradually changing. Jiang Jieshi was in fact easing Chen's allies out of crucial positions, replacing them with party members loyal to himself. Chen's political demise came with the end of the coalition in December 1935 when Wang left China and took shelter in Europe after a failed attempt on his life. Having regained control of the government, Jiang gradually centralized the administration under his control and abolished all the organizations that were the expression of other GMD groups. In the process, Chen's control commissions were closed and all their resources transferred to the newly inaugurated Natural Resources Commission, an offspring of the Planning Agency of the military, under Jiang's direct control.

By 1936, a disappointed and bitter Chen realized that the central part of his nation-building plan had failed. His economic control reforms were not generating national political and economic centralization; rather, it appeared that centralization was prerequisite for the successful implementation of the reforms. The problem originated in the discrepancy between the nature of Chen's nation-building project and the reality of his political power. Reflecting the GMD's general political orientation, Chen's nation-building project was at its core a state-building enterprise in which a political group identified itself with the state. Such a project implied the consolidation of one political group in Nanjing and the establishment of a centralized state under its control. Only then could national reforms be implemented, bringing consistency and unity, first of all, to the Nanjing administration, which had been parceled off among GMD groups pursuing conflicting reform agendas. Without unity in Nanjing, the economic nation could not be built. It was, in fact, the lack of sustained central authority that constituted the most formidable obstacle to Chen's plan. Provincial interests and the resistance of local elites to government intervention, although posing serious challenges to the CCC, would not have constituted insurmountable obstacles were they not accompanied by the lack of political unity in the government leadership. Centralizing reform needed unified leadership to support implementation, and this was not forthcoming.

Entangled in factional struggles, the government never officially adopted a policy of economic control because every faction feared that it would not be able to control the central administrative apparatus and thus would be cut off from government resources. This anxiety was the main reason why Jiang Jieshi continued to fiercely oppose administrative centralization until December 1935, when Wang retired abroad and Jiang's leadership became unchallenged. Only then did Jiang begin the process of centralizing the Nanjing regime.

Eager to take over the CCC's network of cooperative societies for the purpose of gaining political control over the rural areas, Jiang worked actively to undermine the development of the CCC cooperative society system and sponsored a competitive organization for rural credit that gradually cut off from the rural areas private banks linked to the CCC. Between July 1934 and June 1935, the Shanghai Commercial and Savings Bank lent more than $2 million to 125 cooperative societies in seven provinces where the CCC was most active. Meanwhile, the Bank of China nearly quadrupled its percentage of loans made to agriculture during 1933–35 (Ting 1936). By 1937, however, banking institutions under the direct control of Jiang Jieshi, above all the Farmer's Bank, had gradually cut off private businesses from rural credit. Chen Lifu, Jiang Jieshi's secretary and a leader of the Farmers' Bank, clearly expressed to Chen Guangfu his views on the matter, arguing that the management of cooperative societies was not their concern, for it fell within the scope of government intervention. "You cannot do this; this is our job" were his exact words according to Chen Guangfu's recollection.[19] What Chen Lifu meant was that the organization of cooperative societies could not be a channel for the expansion of private business. Rather, its purpose was the political and military control of rural areas. The latter was the path followed by the cooperative organization developed under Jiang's control in Jiangxi (Zhang Li 1981). Jiang Jieshi and Chen Lifu thus reversed one of the basic aspects of the CCC's reforms—the involvement of Shanghai private business as an equal partner in its corporatist-reformist enterprise.

The GMD's failure to establish control over recalcitrant provinces added to the general political fragmentation of the country, creating new opportunities for the unexpected development of the increasingly popular policy of economic control. Indeed, in the late 1930s, economic control was being used by provincial governments to consolidate their local power against the centralizing spirit originally envisioned by Chen. In 1936, he denounced this development and called for its postponement. (Chen 1936, 57). Chen's remarks were accurate insofar as economic control policies were used locally to fend off Nanjing's attempts at political centralization, for in the 1930s some provincial governments adopted full-fledged economic control programs aimed at supporting local power bases against Nanjing's attempt at political and economic centralization. This was especially the case in Guangdong, the heart of the Chinese federalist movement and a core of political opposition to Nanjing, which in 1934 adopted a four-year plan for economic development centered on the policy of economic control.

Guangdong was simply one of many cases in which the CCC found it impossible to effectively penetrate the local economy where the interests of local militarists or elites were counter to its own. Where elites were strongly organized, the CCC attempts to control rural credit and marketing were especially unwelcome, as they deprived moneylenders, landlords, and merchants of some of their most profitable activities. In other areas, where local elites where economically weakened, the intervention of the CCC presented new opportunities for income and were thus more favorably accepted (Pomeranz 1993). Above all, it was its political connections with local authorities that determined the success of the CCC in each area. In Shaanxi, for example, where it enjoyed close ties with the head of the local Reconstruction Bureau, the CCC was able to establish a large network of cooperative societies and significantly enlarge and improve the local production of raw cotton.[20]

The main goals of the CCC's plan, national economic and political unification, thus eluded Chen Gongbo. Because of its inability to penetrate local pockets of power and because central bodies of the administration remained loyal to other GMD factions, the CCC was unable to achieve a real national scope. The CCC, however, showed potential for centralizing economic development and integrating the hinterland/rural and coastal/industrial economies by linking the areas it was able to access with the Shanghai industrial economy. Above all, the CCC marked the first attempt to empower the Chinese state with the abilities and functions later fully developed by the Communists. The state envisioned by Chen in his economic nation-building plan was highly centralized, able to extend its intervention to the grassroots level, and capable of achieving nationwide mobilization of the economy. Such a statist conception of the modern Chinese nation—based on its masses of producers engaged in a joint effort for the industrialization of the country under the leadership of the government—was growing popular in China in the 1930s. In spite of important differences, it ran through both the Nationalist and the Communist nation-building projects, building on the common ground of the worldwide crisis of liberalism that characterized the interwar years (Sternhell 1986). The CCP and GMD leaders thus shared perceptions of the state and mass mobilization.

They also held in common other concepts of the Chinese nation that emerged from the encounter of a local self-strengthening tradition with new global trends in economic and political thought and imperialist practices. Under the pressure of Japan's aggression and an increasingly radical Chinese nationalism, many leaders came to formulate revolutionary plans based on the idea of China's national economic forces (*minzu jingji*) and their struggle against Japanese economic imperialism. Such a concept was at the core of not just Chen's corporatist reforms but of Mao Zedong's winning strategy of a broad national alliance across shared nationalist interests. His "On New Democracy" marked a momentary shift of priority in the CCP's political program from class to nationalist struggle. Echoing Chen Gongbo, Mao declared that Japan's imperialism aimed at transforming China into a colony. Under this circumstance, the nationalist (*minzu*) part of the capitalist class had seen its business decline under Japanese pressure. For this reason, the "nationalist" (*minzu*) capitalists were temporarily sharing the revolutionary goals of the peasants and workers and could be admitted to the CCP's revolutionary New Democracy alliance of all *minzu* groups (Mao [1940] 1967). The concept of the national economy (*minzu jingji*), as part of the Marxist-Leninist anti-imperialist struggle against Japan, allowed Mao to take over the GMD idea of a national revolution and extend the CCP revolutionary leadership to include the majority of the Chinese. Unlike Chen Gongbo and Wang Jingwei, however, Mao never stopped reminding his followers that the large *minzu* alliance against imperialism constituted only one phase of the Chinese revolution. The interests of the bourgeoisie would once again differ from those of peasants and workers after the China's victory in its nationalist revolution. At that point, they would become the natural enemies of the second phase of the Chinese revolution, the socialist revolution. It was on this fundamental point that Mao and Chen disagreed. Chen believed that a capitalist class did not yet exist in China due to the lack of significant industrial development. For this reason, bureaucratic capitalist organization of the economy under the guidance of the government would be sufficient to prevent its development in the future. Mao, on the other hand, argued that a Chinese industrial bourgeoisie had already developed. Once it had succeeded in its nationalist revolution China would need to move on to a socialist one. In spite of these differences, however, Mao and Chen clearly built their visions of a new China on the conceptual category of a national economy and its resistance to Japanese imperialism. Such commonality in Chen's and Mao's views should not obscure crucial political differences between the two, but it does reveal that both leaders shared some of the basic themes of a wider discourse on nation building that extended across the Nationalist and Communist camps.

Conclusion

Chen's corporatist and autarkic plan for economic nation building highlights the main themes of a Chinese prewar discourse on nation building that grew out of the encounter of China's self-strengthening tradition with new, global, political, and economic developments. The persistence of self-strengthening motives and imagery into the 1930s does not imply immutability in Chinese political and economic thought. On the contrary, it was often the case that, borrowing the words of Joseph Levenson (1965, xxviii), the "vocabulary and syntax may remain the same . . . but the statement changes in meaning as its world changes." Chen's idea of economic nation building, although drawing upon much of the conceptualization and imagery of the self-strengthening tradition and answering the same question of how to strengthen China's *guoben* against imperialism, was in fact a long way from Zheng Guanying's mercantilism, having adjusted to a global economic, political, and intellectual environment that was different from what Zheng faced at the turn of the century.

Whereas his predecessors had followed a mercantilist approach, Chen subscribed to theories of dependency and autarky. This change was spurred by the pressure of Japan's aggression and the rise on the international scene of autarkic empires, which in their search for direct control over industrial raw materials and markets appeared to confirm the worst scenario of social Darwinist and Marxist-Leninist interpretations of a global struggle for economic survival among nations. At the same time, mercantilist policies became unavailable to Chinese officials because of the collapse of the international market. To Chen Gongbo, it appeared that China needed to brace itself to face the new situation. He believed that the best solution was the one attempted by most leaders of the world, autarky, which in the Chinese case meant closing its economy to defend its resources and markets from the predatory Japanese empire.

Chen's political career illustrates China's participation in global interwar trends. As was the case with many contemporary European leaders, growing nationalist feelings led him to abandon the Marxist idea of a nation propelled by the dialectical dynamic of class struggle. By the 1930s, Chen had embraced a new image of national progress as engendered by social unity under the umbrella of nationalism, the joint effort of all "producers in the economy." This idea of the nation excluded the Marxist vision of ultimate modernity as internationalism, the alliance of the world proletariat. It instead focused on the rather apocalyptic vision of a nation forced into an extremely defensive position, unable to reach outside its national borders, and deeply entrenched within itself.

Because of his strong nationalist and anti-Japanese feelings, it would have been difficult in the 1920s and 1930s to imagine that Chen Gongbo, the young enthusiastic revolutionary engrossed in anti-imperialist and mass mobilization activities, would end his political career branded as a traitor and collaborator. This was, however, the inglorious and tragic end that awaited him. On 3 June 1946, he was executed by the Nationalists because of his leading position in the government established by Wang Jingwei in Nanjing (1940–45) in cooperation with Japan's occupying forces. The relationship between Chen's prewar economic nationalism and his wartime collaboration was not as contradictory as it appears at first glance. Chen's wartime experience will be the focus of a separate study, in spite of its importance for the understanding and assessment of Chen's political career as a whole.

Chen's economic nation-building plan in the 1930s, built on a new conception of the Chinese nation, was not just a passive reaction to changes imposed upon it by the surrounding environment or a mere attempt to imitate alien models. Rather, it constituted full participation in new global trends. On the one hand, his plan was strikingly similar to those of other countries around the world during the interwar years, including Italy, Spain, and many South American countries. It also possessed, however, distinctive features that made it an original development of current autarkic and corporatist trends. Chen's plan was ultimately shaped by the persistence of the self-strengthening conceptualization of the nationalist question and by a radical but defensive anti-imperialism directed against Japan. This radical nationalism thus combined elements of a preexisting ethnic nationalism and emerging ideas of economic dependency and mass mobilization, generating the new conceptual category of the *minzu* economy that was to play an important role in future Chinese political thought and practice.

NOTES

1. On the development of the idea of autarky and the transformation of the international economy in the 1930s from free exchange to a system of closed autarkic units, bilateral agreements, and exchange monopolies, see Polanyi 1944 and Zani 1988.

2. For an example of a corporatist organization set up by a fascist government during the interwar period, see Perfetti 1991 for a detailed discussion of the Italian House of Fasci and Corporations (*Camera dei Fasci e delle Corporation*).

3. Because of its centralizing nature, Chen's nation-building program left little room for diversity and autonomy. Chen's plan for economic nation building was perceived as aggressive by those who advocated a federalist model for China and those who lived in the border areas.

4. *Shen bao*, 24 October 1931, 13–14. Wang Jingwei advocated Sun Yatsen's idea of "balanced power" (*junquan*), though he gave the formula a different meaning. Sun intended it as a way to divide power equally between center and locality. Wang, however, really intended *junquan* as a means to curb the power of local militarists vis-à-vis the center.

5. See Chen 1935a, 168–71. According to Chen's data, China even lagged behind India and the Soviet Union.

6. In 1927, Jiang Jieshi, who had entered Shanghai at the head of the Nationalist army in the final phase of the GMD Northern Expedition, ended the cooperation between the CCP and the GMD that had been initiated by Sun Yatsen in 1923. On 12 April 1927, without warning, Jiang proclaimed the end of the alliance and proceeded to arrest and execute anyone that his civilian-clothed policemen assumed to be member of the Communist Party.

7. Chen published his articles mainly in his magazine, *Gemin pinglun* (Revolutionary Critic), which he founded in Shanghai after the events of spring 1927, and in *Minzu zazhi* (The Nation). For a detailed discussion of the 1927 debate on mass movements and class between Jiang Jieshi's faction of the GMD and the GMD Left, see Hoston 1994 and Dirlik 1975.

8. Polanyi 1944, 20–21. According to Polanyi, the dissolution of the world economic system—its transformation from a free exchange system to one of autarkic units—had been in progress since 1900 and was responsible for World War I. The outcome of the war and the treaties that followed it, by eliminating German competition, eased the tension only superficially, while the disarmament of the defeated nations forestalled the reemergence of a balance of power.

9. For a discussion of conscripted enrollment and administrative mass organizations, see Kasza 1995.

10. During a trip to Washington, Song had contracted a cotton and wheat loan with the United States Farm Board. The loan granted the Chinese government a credit of U.S.$50 million, four-fifths of which were to be spent on 600,000 bales of American cotton and the remainder on American wheat. The loan was secured on China's customs revenue at 5 percent annual interest to be repaid in three years. The Chinese government was to sell the American cotton and wheat on the domestic market and invest the profits in reconstruction. A clause in the loan document specified that sales and returns were to be managed by the National Economic Council. See China Number Two Historical Archives (NTHA), file 44, Archives of the National Economic Council, minutes of the third meeting of the NEC's Standing Committee; Bush 1982, 213; and Parks 1980, 127.

11. Chen 1936. Chen was eager to work through Song's council for two reasons. He was frustrated with the chronic lack of adequate funding for the Ministry of Industry, which prevented him from successfully implementing the four-year plan he had announced in 1933. In addition, the NEC was intended to be the highest economic planning agency of the government with the task of coordinating economic reforms across the various agencies of the economic administration.

12. NTHA, file 44, Archives of the National Economic Council, Quanguo jingji weiyuanhui chengli jiyao; Zhang and Shen 1987. The Standing Committee of the CCC was composed of Li Shenbo (Dasheng Cotton Mills) and Tang Xinghai, who had sponsored Chen Gongbo's American education; Ye Zhuotang, a banker and a member of the board of directors of the Chinese Merchants Steamship Company; and agriculturist Zuo Bingwen, a pioneer in agricultural extension reforms sponsored jointly by local officials and mill owners of the Zhejiang-Jiangsu area. To safeguard the government's interests, and especially to make sure that the government obtained its share from the development of the industry, the director of the Consolidated Tax Division of the Ministry of Finance, Xie Qi (Xie Zuokai), was also appointed to the Standing Committee. Regular members of the CCC were mill owners Rong Zongjing, Guo Xun, and Nie Lusheng; the general manager of the Bank of China, Zhang Jia'ao (Gongquan); and the director for exports of the Foreign Exchange Office of the Bank of China, Bei Songsun (Zuyi). Other members included agriculturalists Mu Xiangyue and Sun En (Yushu), the latter also serving as the director of the commission's Central Cotton Production Improvement Bureau (Zhongyang mianchan gaijingsuo). The government representatives among the regular members were He Bingxian, director of the International Trade Office of the Ministry of Industry, and Chen Bozhuang, a member of the Legislative Yuan. Following Wang's ideas of party control over the government, the regular membership also included Wu Xingya, a member of the Shanghai branch of the Guomindang and director of the "CC Clique" organization in Shanghai, and Liu Yinfu. Chen Lifu joined the NEC in 1934. Du Yuesheng, leader of the Shanghai-based Green Gang and linked to the Nationalist government since 1927, was also a member. Du had invested some of his ill-gotten capital in the cotton industry, but his presence in the CCC was motivated by the mill owners' need to control labor. Du had a reputation as a labor representative and dispute mediator, and it was most probably in this double capacity that he was appointed to the commission. See NTHA, file 44, Archives of the National Economic Council, "Quanguo jingji weiyuanhui zhiyuanlu" 1937; Zhang and Shen 1987; Bush 1982; and Perry 1993.

13. NTHA, file 44, Archives of the National Economic Council, NEC CCC 1934 annual plan.

14. Ibid.

15. NTHA, file 44, Archives of the National Economic Council, NEC and CCC 1934 general plans.

16. NTHA, file 44, Archives of the National Economic Council. The CCC also planned the rationalization of the entire cycle of the industry (from agricultural production of raw cotton to industrial processing and marketing of the finished manufactured goods) and modernization of industrial manufacturing (by experimenting with improvements in machinery and new industrial management techniques).

17. NTHA, file 44, Archives of the National Economic Council: 1933 CCC plan, Campbell report (title missing) 1935, Campbell "Report on Co-operation in Shensi," June–July 1936; and Bush 1982.

18. NTHA, file 44, Archives of the National Economic Council, minutes of the National Cooperative Conference.

19. Chen Guangfu interview, Columbia University Oral History Project.

20. NTHA, file 44, Archives of the National Economic Council: 1933 CCC plan, Campbell report 1935, Campbell, "Report on Co-operation in Shensi," June–July 1936; and Bush 1982.

Collaborationist Nationalism in Occupied Wartime China

Timothy Brook

If the people do not survive, where is the nation?
—Gu Cheng, Minister of Education, 1939

When the Japanese Army launched its 1937 offensives against China, first at Beijing in July and then at Shanghai in August, its opening task was to overwhelm Chinese military resistance. Once its soldiers had prevailed on the battlefield, however, Japan faced a second and more subtle challenge: what to do with the territories the army had occupied. Several models for an occupation state were available, most of which were ruled out. Japan did not impose a conquest regime over China that gave them direct rule, as such earlier conquerors as the Manchus and the Mongols had done in previous centuries. Japan did not declare the claims of the Chinese nation to be null and void, nor did it cancel Chinese sovereignty over a portion of its territory and detach it for absorption into the Japanese empire, as it had done in Taiwan in 1895. It did not wish to set up a full military administration to manage the occupation, nor did it institute a civil administration, as it had done when it gained possession of Korea in 1895. Instead, the Japanese government chose to deal with the problem of administering occupied territory by authorizing for the rest of China what the army had forced it to accept in Manchuria after 1931: a Chinese regime that was nominally independent but formally committed to collaborating with Japan.

Japan sponsored several collaborationist regimes throughout China during the war. As in Manchuria, none enjoyed jurisdiction over what the Chinese would recognize as an intact national territory. The dismembering of the Chinese nation was not something that the Japanese government either wanted or intended, and at no point during the occupation was the division of China among multiple collaborationist regimes viewed in Tokyo as anything but undesirable, even in the short run. If in the end China was divvied up among competing regimes, as it was, this was not by design but because the Japanese government could not control the process of occupation. And if these regimes resisted being incorporated into a single state body, as indeed they did, it was because Chinese collaborators realized that a Japanese-brokered unification would expose the illegitimacy of their several regimes as well as negate in advance any claim that a national government created by such a merger could make to ruling the Chinese nation for the Chinese nation. In the end, none of the arrangements made to administer occupied China could be sustained after the war ended in 1945, when the Japanese occupation forces were withdrawn and the National Government under Guomindang (Nationalist Party) leader Jiang Jieshi (Chiang Kaishek) was able to return to the capital in Nanjing.

For Minister of Education Gu Cheng, whose rhetorical question graces the head of this essay, as indeed for most Chinese, the issue facing China in the late 1930s was how to survive in the face of potential national extinction. Gu was a minister in the Reformed Government (Weixin zhengfu), the first national regime that Chinese politicians set up in Nanjing under Japanese sponsorship. It was founded in 1938 and lasted for only two years, at which time it was replaced by the regime of the more prestigious Wang Jingwei and his faction of the Guomindang. Early in the war, anti-Guomindang politicians such as Gu Cheng regarded Jiang Jieshi's resistance as foolhardy, driving China toward extinction. From his perspective, collaboration was the only realistic means of ensuring the survival of the nation; resistance threatened to bring about its annihilation. Those, like Gu, who collaborated with Japan invoked the rhetoric of national salvation to justify what they did, not the motives of opportunism and complicity with which the resistance branded them. Collaboration was for them a desperate response to the most severe crisis that the Chinese nation had ever suffered. What they did, in their own eyes, they did for China, not for Japan, despite the apparent loss of sovereignty that this arrangement entailed, because they conceived of that loss as temporary. Their state power proved to be as temporary as the occupation, of course, for those who came in on the coattails of Japan's defeat in 1945 voided the collaborators' claims to have served the national interest.

The victors' dismissal is not sufficient for us to accept this judgment on the collaborators' auto-interpretation as morally vacant and merely self-serving, even if it amounted to little more than that for most of the opportunists who conceived it. The nation was a conceptual category as well as a physical reality for them, as much as it was for their competitors in the resistance, and they felt entitled to invoke the nation just as certainly as the resistance did to enunciate what they thought they were doing. Both sides appealed to nationalism, the one to unify the people to fight against Japan, the other to mobilize them to work with it. Accordingly, I argue in this essay that the collaborators, too, deserve a place in the chaotic history of Chinese nationalism in the twentieth century, however righteously and persuasively they have previously been excluded by both the resistance leaderships, Communist and Nationalist, which have between them controlled the writing of China's wartime experience as a unified history of heroic struggle against Japan. That historiography has conditioned us to regard the collapse of all the various state entities created under the duress of occupation as evidence that the entire process of regime formation and ideological construction during the occupation was bogus. While it may well be true that not all of the collaborator's claims were given, or were even intended to be received, at face value, the regimes that were floated, and those that stayed afloat for several years, invested much effort in propagating an ideology of national service and survival. Even if the Japanese supplied most of the flotation devices for the state bodies that came into being, the Chinese who collaborated with them had to declare their commitment to the existence, independence, and territorial integrity of the nation even when these were most infringed. They claimed, as they had to, that they spoke for the "moral consciousness" of the nation.[1]

Nationalism and Collaboration

Nationalism was the boldest ideological claim that the collaborators made to explain why they were working under Japanese tutelage. Their claim, which I shall refer to in this essay as collaborationist nationalism, represents a coherent ideological position and must be taken seriously if we are to take full account of the history of twentieth-century nationalism. Collaborationist nationalism sounds like an oxymoron, of course. Nationalism is the earnest sentiment that acknowledges the nation as the highest object of personal loyalty. It relies on two premises: that all nations have an equal right to exist (the struggle comes over what is to be designated as a nation) and that no individual can conceive of the right to be independent of nations. Subjectively, this double condition imposes on everyone an identity of national belonging and the expectation of favoring the primacy of his own over all other nations.

At first glance, collaboration appears to be nationalism's opposite. *Collaboration,* in the sense that the term has gathered in European languages since Philippe Pétain declared at Montoire in 1940 that France would "collaborate" with Germany, is taken to indicate a willingness to accede to the demands of a nation other than one's own and to accept infringement of one's national sovereignty to the extent that infringement is regarded as necessary to secure the interests of the occupying power. Collaboration would seem to suspend the hard distinctions of exclusive identity and absolute territorial sovereignty that are so characteristic of nationalism both as political ideology and as personal experience. Nationalism does not compromise, whereas collaboration is invariably seen, and despised, as complete compromise.

Yet collaboration in this twentieth-century sense is constructed entirely in nationalist terms. It speaks in the language of the nation, on behalf of the nation, and in the interests of the nation. Like the nationalist, the collaborator accepts the two premises of nationalism: he does not abandon the nation's absolute claim that it has a right to exist, nor does he accept that a collaborating nation relinquishes its rights over those living within its territory. (I use gendered phrasing consciously here to reflect the historical reality of collaboration in wartime China, which is that it was almost exclusively enacted by men.) What collaborationist nationalism does to make its position of accommodation plausible is to refuse the commonplace distinction between utter compromise and pure resistance. It promotes this refusal by asserting that a collaborative arrangement with another nation, which is invariably expressed as provisional in any case, serves the higher interests of one's own. This assertion is greatly strengthened if it can be nested, as it usually is, within a larger claim repudiating a previous leadership for having acted in such a way as to threaten the nation through its own compromises and mismanagement. Collaboration accordingly pictures itself not as "selling out the nation" (*maiguo*), in the popular Chinese phrase, but as reforming and restoring the nation to an original and purer condition. Politically, therefore, collaborationist nationalism was not a nationalism in isolation but a "competing nationalism" (Bickers and Wasserstrom 1995, 460) mobilized as an ideological counterstroke against what got depicted as an opportunistic regime that had soiled the integrity of the nation.

The nationalist claim of collaborators deserves as much notice as the equally and far more commonly noticed historical fact that collaboration with Japan was rejected by the majority of Chinese at the time it was made. The rejection does not do away with the claim; indeed, those who reject collaboration may be embarrassed by its bold inversion of the conventional appropriation of nationalism by the resistance. That embarrassment exposes the conceptual difficulty attached to nationalism, which is that opposing sides could mobilize the same arguments to construct opposing ideologies. The ambidexterity with which the nation could be invoked on both sides of a violent struggle deserves closer scrutiny than the normalizing ideology of twentieth-century nationalism has generally allowed. Standing as we do in the continuing wake of the high tide of nationalism in this century, we can deepen our understanding of nationalism as a historical problem by examining with greater care the countercurrents flowing within that tide. After all, the difficulty of competing claims can be found elsewhere on this terrain. This difficulty seems to be particularly prominent in Asia, where the locus and identity of the nation have been contentious issues for nation-states emerging as independent entities from imperial status or colonial domination over the past century and a half. The perspective elaborated toward the end of this essay is that collaborationist nationalism in Asia is not simply another instance of nationalism at free play in the political realm but a historically specific form of late colonial ideology that is always bound to declare independence under a condition of dependence. Understanding how collaboration could have been construed as nationalism provides an intriguing opportunity to think about what *nation* meant in Asia at this time and more generally what attachment to a nation consists of and allows.

The Early Formation of Chinese Nationalism

China emerged formally as a postimperial nation-state in 1912 after a century of military, diplomatic, and economic shocks arising from its relations with European nations, although it was not yet clear how great the rupture with its imperial past would become. Under the pressure of these shocks, Chinese politicians and urban intellectuals gradually conceived that it was necessary to recreate China using a portion of the lexicon of the Western nations. The Manchu aristocracy attempted to transform the Qing dynasty from a neo-Confucian polity into a constitutional monarchy and thereby assemble a new "official nation" of China in the wake of the defeat in the war with Japan in 1895 (beginning a half century of Japanese encroachment on Chinese territory) and the destabilized political environment caused by the Boxer Rebellion in 1900. The legitimacy of Manchu rulership depended on sustaining a base broader than narrow Han Chinese ethnic roots, which made the transformation of the Manchu emperor from a *Qing* emperor to a *Chinese* national ruler difficult (cf. Anderson 1991, 83–86). The Manchus were unable to convince provincial and national elites that the constitutional polity they were creating in the opening decade of the twentieth century represented the Chinese nation, and at a moment of poorly managed crisis in the fall of 1911—a brief tumble of events quickly dignified by nationalist discourse as the Republican Revolution—they were obliged to forfeit their rule overnight. A new republic (*minguo*, "nation of the people") replaced the old empire and claimed a sovereignty over the Chinese nation that dynastic rule, tolerant of heterogeneous composition and multiple ethnicity, had never had to consider.

The formation of this new nation took place in the shadow of colonialism. Although China never became a direct colony, other Asian regimes were or had been, and Chinese politicians and intellectuals were intensely aware of the danger of being reduced to colonial status, which threatened the national entity with disappearance into a different type of imperial body. The argument for being a nation rather than a dynasty rested in the first instance on the fearful recognition that European nations impaired the sovereignty of existing regimes when their economic demands were not met. A recharged sovereign state, in the style of Meiji Japan, for example, came to be regarded as essential for fending off colonial incursions. The reformers of 1898 embraced the notion of a Meiji- or Tudor-style constitutional monarchy in the hope of strengthening the nation without rending it, but advocates of republicanism in the next generation, such as Sun Yatsen, found it convenient to exploit the minority ethnic identity of the Manchu house as a reason not just for removing the Manchus but for dismantling the entire structure of monarchical rule. The republicanization of China was thus invested with a mission to save Chinese culture from its Manchu present as well as from its imperial past. Little of this thinking was at the forefront of public discourse when the Qing dynasty collapsed, but it gained ground during the second decade of the twentieth century.

China's apparent inability to secure for itself a coherent national identity induced a widespread crisis of confidence in the early Republic. Nationalist sentiments of different complexions sprang up in the years immediately before and after 1920, usually in relation to Western notions of the nation and its necessity rather than to any historical construction of the Chinese national experience. Every attempt to fashion the Western ideal of the ethnic nation in Chinese dress invoked the concept of *min*, formerly meaning "commoners" but now used to signify all the people of the nation regardless of status or ethnicity. It appeared in the new term for "republic," *minguo* (literally, the nation of the people), and it was the subject of *minquan*, "the right of the people," the first of Sun Yatsen's "Three Principles of the People." Though translated conventionally as "nationalism," *minquan* was intended to connote less a people's ethnic identity as a nation than its political right to resist being colonized. Nationalism as an anticolonial (rather than antidynastic) posture became widely popular during the urban labor unrest of the 1920s. During the Northern Expedition (1926–28), it was fully absorbed into Nationalist/Communist ideology, which attributed China's failure to assume full nationhood to the two Others of the Chinese people, the imperialists and the warlords.

Warlordism was less a problem than a symptom of the difficulty of creating national institutions. That difficulty may more usefully be attributed to the structural challenge of making the transition from dynasty to nation in the absence of a political elite or leading class able to project the necessary authority and legitimacy to take command (or, in the standard Marxist terminology, the absence of a bourgeoisie to lead a bourgeois revolution). Warlords and their political cliques made bids for that authority, and might at times control sufficient resources to assert regional hegemony, but they could not create an indisputable link between themselves and the nation's fate. After 1927, most provincial military governors and their politicians (including Liang Hongzhi, of whom we will hear more) disappeared from public life once Jiang Jieshi forged a successful identification between his military power and the fate of the nation. With that identification, and his claim to the revolutionary mantle of Sun Yatsen, Jiang could transcend the status of regional warlord and proclaim the delayed reunification of the nation in 1928.

Imperialism, flagged in dominant Chinese ideologies as the great obstacle to nation-building, has been dismissed by Western historians as less significant for explaining the "failure" of nation building in the Republican era than internal sources of disunity (Barlow 1993b). Yet the global environment of the colonial period was such that in few places in colonial Asia did unified nation-states emerge before 1945 (Japan was a fortunate early exception). Direct colonialism blocked national self-determination obviously, but so did arm's-length imperialism. By controlling terms of trade and entry into global markets, sponsoring comprador elites, demanding territorial concessions, and dominating the diplomatic practices of international relations, Western actions in Asia limited the likelihood of national elites forming coherent nations that were not in some way hostage to Western economic or political interests. Under the shadow of imperialism, urban Chinese could imagine their nation—and do so in waves of fervent nationalist sentiment in 1919 (the May Fourth Movement) and again in 1925 (the May Thirtieth Movement)—but they could not fully bring that vision to reality. And just when the Nationalists were striving to develop foundations that would set China on the path to nationhood (as described by Margherita Zanasi in this volume), a foreign colonialism of unsurpassed intensity forced on China a new upsurge of nationalist struggle and a new type of nation work.

The Terms of Occupation

Japan's invasion of China in 1937 was not its first. Earlier invasions provided several precedents. When Japan occupied Taiwan under the Treaty of Shimonoseki in 1895, it set up a direct colonial administration there. In Manchuria in 1931–32, it sponsored the formation of an independent state in a region that did not have a tradition of being a discrete national territory. The difference between these regime modes is significant. In 1895, colonial administration was still the standard arrangement through which a colonial power administered occupied territory. By 1932, in the wake of the postwar League of Nations' discourse about the right of nations to self-determination, direct colonial administration was no longer regarded as acceptable. Indeed, Japan created the puppet state of Manchuria (Manchukuo, Ch. Manzhouguo, J. Manshūkoku) in part as a defensive response to censure by the League of Nations. This arrangement was universally recognized as a fiction, but it was an important and necessary fiction nonetheless. Quite apart from its weak attempt to mollify international opinion, it acknowledged that nationalist sentiment mattered and that it had to be tapped or stimulated within the occupied territory and directed away from China toward the new "nation." In contrast to early colonialism, which suspended the nation and banned sentiment in favor of it, late colonialism professed to provide for that sentiment by constructing closely controlled client states. The bid in Manchuria to win the hearts and minds of the local people by granting them national status failed miserably—no heart beat faster when the name Manchuria was spoken, with the possible exception of restored emperor Puyi's—but Japan was obliged to make the attempt if it wished to claim that a "nation" other than Japan or China was present in Manchuria.

Neither 1895 nor 1931 supplied the model for the regimes that the Japanese Army would sponsor in China in the wake of its larger 1937 invasion. At the time of the invasion, the Japanese government had no intention of setting up colonial administrations on the continent, having the sense to recognize that such administrations were not only internationally unacceptable but beyond its capacity to operate. Nor was it bent on setting up more Manchuria-style facades behind which to export capital and labor. Only after surmounting strong resistance in the cabinet in the fall of 1937 were the Japanese expeditionary armies in China given permission to set up regional Chinese-led regimes, and then only as provisional expedients. The North China Area Army (NCAA) founded what it was obliged literally to name the Provisional Government of North China (Huabei linshi zhengfu) in Beijing in December 1937, and the Central China Area Army (CCAA, redesignated the Central China Expeditionary Army [CCEA] in February 1938) brought into being the Reformed Government in Nanjing three months later (Brook 2000).

The avowed purpose of having these regimes in place was to pressure Jiang Jieshi initially to negotiate with Japan and later, when that proved unsuccessful, to relinquish power and dissolve his regime. The aim was not to carve China into colonies, although many, both Chinese and Japanese, feared that the melon, as the saying went, would be carved. During the often intense struggles between the NCAA and the CCEA to control Japan's political and military offensives in China in the spring of 1938, the commander of the China Area

Fleet in Shanghai raised the specter of unwanted outcomes when he telegraphed his vice minister a week before the Reformed Government was inaugurated to warn that the NCAA was bent on turning North China into "a second Manchuria." To do so, as the commander put it, would lead to "calamity." Japan should stick to its goal of destroying the Jiang regime and seeing it replaced with one more amenable to Japan's demands and not embroil itself in more puppet regimes (Usui 1966, 145). This view was widely shared within the Japanese government, which for the most part remained cautious and unenthusiastic about undertaking political experiments of this sort. Despite the sensible caution being urged in some quarters, the Provisional Government and the Reformed Government aspired to be, and projected themselves publicly as being, more than bargaining chips between the Japanese and the Guomindang. The Reformed Government in particular hinged its legitimacy on being able to claim that it, rather than the Guomindang regime, represented the Chinese nation. Nationalism was its refuge.

Nationalism was a sentiment of which Japan had been made intensely aware through the recurring waves of anti-Japanese protests and boycotts in China since the 1890s. Japanese assessments of the strength of that nationalism after Japan had successfully occupied Manchuria varied wildly, however, depending on who was making them and in what context. A Japanese intelligence document prepared and disseminated in Changchun in September 1936 reflects the confidence that some Japanese felt over the relative ease with which they were able to control the northeast. Its author disparages the power of nationalism to shape Chinese politics:

> Most Chinese activists [politicians] are concerned with the fortunes of only themselves or their small group and lack the concepts of "for the nation" or "for the people," and so they become warlords with private armies. They take no responsibility for the survival of the nation or the sufferings of the people. All they understand is preserving the status quo in order to satisfy their grand political and material ambitions: they desire only to protect their power. Those who truly love their country or love the people are extremely few. Most look out only for themselves and ignore their country. (Zhong 1938, 128)

The failure of Chinese leaders to launch any serious challenge to Japan's position in Manchuria is cited as evidence of the weakness of Chinese nationalism. "Chinese people by nature have no time for patriotism and do not understand what a country is," the Japanese author concludes. Accordingly, Japan's strategy for enlarging its influence in China should be to manipulate ambitious politicians in order to suppress the few real nationalists on the political scene. This cynical assessment of Chinese nationalism represented the extreme view of some military analysts, who advocated carving China into several regimes operating under Japanese supervision (134). It was not a view that dominated policy-making in Tokyo, but it was sufficiently influential within some military circles to lead Japan into unanticipated difficulties when it occupied the rest of China.

A contrary assessment of Chinese nationalism may be found in two documents produced by Japanese nonmilitary personnel early in 1938. Their authors saw things differently, though admittedly by then the situation in China had changed. The first, a representative of the Japanese Foreign Affairs Association, went on a fact-finding mission to Manchuria and occupied China in January and February. In his report to the Association in March, he declares that he went with an open mind about Japan's invasion but concludes that Japan's prospects for securing an ideological foothold in China are poor. Chinese at all levels of society—and he emphasizes the extent of solidarity by saying it includes coolies in the street—are strongly anti-Japanese. He observes that this attitude is held consciously by some and blindly by others, but it was universally espoused everywhere he went in urban China (Takagi 1938, 73–75). A concurring assessment comes from an early report on the agricultural economy of central China produced by the Shanghai office of the South Manchurian Railway Company (Mantetsu) in May. This report looks at rural, not urban, Chinese. The author observes that peasants are used to putting up with dynastic change, even when this involves conquest by foreigners, and that they object only when they can no longer secure a livelihood. This should not be interpreted to mean that Japanese control is assured, however. "Semicolonialism," in the Marxist formulation that lingered on in Japanese sinology, had made Chinese society much more complicated than it was when the Manchus took over, and anti-Japanese propaganda had increased the difficulty of imposing Japanese hegemony. The author concludes vaguely by observing that Japan will need to devise intelligent policies that respond to the needs of the peasantry if it hopes to secure their cooperation (Mantetsu 1938, 66). In other words, some measure of nationalist sentiment was in play even in the countryside, where political apathy was assumed to be the norm, and Japan should take that into account in assessing its prospects in China.

Neither report calls this sentiment nationalism, and the Mantetsu report may be accurate in representing anti-Japanese sentiment as inculcated rather than spontaneous. Hatred of an invading military power could be seen—as the Mantetsu authors chose to see it—as a nationalism that is xenophobic (sentiment against) rather than proactive (sentiment in favor) or at most a reactive sort of nationalism that has not yet entered mass subjectivity. Reactive nationalism may nonetheless have provided Chinese peasants with an essential conjunctural bridge from their agrarian indifference to states and their allegiance to the purely local to a late–colonial type of nationalism that blended intense antiforeign sentiment with an imported cosmopolitan ideology of equal states in a community of nations. If so, Japan's invasion charged the political environment of late colonial China (as elsewhere in Asia) with sufficient psychic energy to generate the degree of sentiment needed for twentieth-century Chinese nationalism to attain the potential of mass allegiance. It was no longer simply the thwarted ideal of cosmopolitan intellectuals or the manufactured piety of political opportunists. It now meant something in the sense of promoting tangible political effects.

Back in Tokyo, the Japanese government sought to intercept and redirect the threat of an anti-Japanese political linkage between elites and peoples by creating an official ideology of anticolonial liberation for its new empire in Asia. This ideology was not fully in place when the Japanese Army invaded China in the summer of 1937, but it was quickly assembled as foreign territory came under Japan's control and had to be pacified. This ideology, called the New Order in East Asia, was not a celebration of Japanese imperialism but a declaration of East Asian liberationism. In remarks on Japan's international relations delivered in a speech the prime minister gave in December 1938, when this ideology was first unveiled, Prince Konoe offered the following formulation:

> The age of total imperial hegemony that prevailed in the nineteenth century has already finished its role. The contrary spirit to rebuild the world that is alive today must be to work in the direction of liberating the nations of oppressed peoples and giving full play to the creative power of each. Once it has realized that the old ideology of materialist individualism, along with its transformation, communism, has brought on the crisis in today's world, the West must then learn from the ancient but also new Eastern way of emptying the mind. (quoted in Usui 1966, 234)

This ideology accepted nationalism by depicting the future of Asia as emerging on the strength of anticolonial movements for self-determination. But with a deft, self-essentializing move Konoe declares that this new wave will be guided not by a communist revolution but by a Zen-like denial of the individual. He is thereby able to celebrate the nation in Asia only to submerge it in a higher Asian identity, for he gears the denial of the individual not to a religious understanding of the ultimate emptiness of existence, as Buddhist philosophy might conceive, but to a political priority, that of manufacturing deference to the desires of the Japanese state. Collaborators throughout occupied Asia found themselves formulating their particular nationalisms within the hegemonic trap that Japan set by posing national liberation as being simultaneously the transcendence of the nation by the region, but with Japan standing in as the region's highest representative.[2] Not surprisingly, most collaborators judged it preferable to minimize the ideal of transcendence and play up the theme of liberation from the West, as we shall see in the case of occupied China.

The Creation of the Reformed Government

The Reformed Government was inaugurated in Nanjing on the morning of 28 March 1938. The most senior member of this government by virtue of his position as president of the Executive Yuan was Liang Hongzhi (1882–1946). Liang was a litte-known a politician who had worked with the warlord Duan Qirui in the 1920s but had disappeared into political obscurity following the Northern Expedition in 1927 and the ascendancy of the Guomindang. Second to him, and standing at his side throughout the inauguration ceremonies, was an old-style Cantonese guild manager and political fixer named Wen Zongyao (1876–1947), who would serve as president of the Legislative Yuan. Liang and Wen, together with a former Guomindang official and Green Gang client, Chen Qun (1890–1945), formed the triumvirate that conducted the negotiations from January through March that led to the emergence of the Reformed Government. This regime provides the substance for my inquiry into collaborationist nationalism, not because it was the best known of the puppet regimes (on the contrary, it is almost completely unknown even to scholars of modern China, who are more familiar with its successor, the Reorganized National Government of Wang Jingwei) but because it was the first Japanese-sponsored regime to occupy the capital in Nanjing and as such was the first to come up with a coherent state ideology justifying collaboration.

The task of negotiating this regime into existence proved less straightforward than anticipated. The three Chinese leaders did not wish to appear as puppets, nor did they want their regime to be seen as a temporary political arrangement to be dissolved should Japanese negotiations with the Guomindang be revived, as Japanese leaders hoped they would. They had to present the regime as the core of any new national government to follow and accordingly insisted on appropriating the gestures, rhetoric, and organizational structure of a national regime. Declaring eventual jurisdiction over the entire nation was complicated by the simultaneous existence of the Provisional Government of North China, the other Japanese-sponsored regime in Beijing, which harbored its own aspirations to become the stepping stone to a new national administration. For either regime to claim to be the embodiment of China's national destiny was a bold declaration, given that both ruled by the grace of the Japanese Army and exercised sovereignty only over those areas subject to the latter's military occupation. But territorial sovereignty and national integrity were the standards against which the Reformed Government had to measure itself. A regime unable to do so could not align itself with popular nationalist sentiment or hope to attain legitimacy, especially under occupation.

The sponsoring Japanese agency in the Yangzi Valley, the CCAA, went along with these aspirations/fictions, for it recognized the advantage of backing a regime that could make such claims. Being the sponsor of what might prove to be the next national government could only strengthen its position in competition with the NCAA, its counterpart in North China, to control the political outcome in China. The work of organizing the regime fell to the CCAA's Special Service Department (SSD), the Japanese military agency in Shanghai assigned the task of administering the occupied territories. The SSD played a crucial facilitating role in the process of formulating the ideology of collaborationist nationalism. Its officers participated in intense discussions with the Chinese planners of the Reformed Government with the aim of designing a regime that would not appear to be compromised as a Japanese puppet but could claim legitimacy as the outcome of a genuine process of political nation-building. The SSD recognized the need not just to concede the power of nationalist sentiment but to play to it and within its terms.

The formation of an ideology of collaborationist nationalism has been reconstructed in this essay by drawing on three sets of texts, produced variously by the SSD or by Chinese under its supervision, at three critical points during 1938 and 1939. The first set is from February 1938, when the regime was in the planning stage. The second set is from October 1938, just as Japan's policy in China was about to change. The third set, published in March 1939 on the occasion of the Reformed Government's first anniversary, is a series of public statements by collaborationist officials that make the strongest collaborationist appeals to nationalism that the Reformed Government leaders would make before they were swept aside by the new regime of the Guomindang faction under Wang Jingwei. In sequence, they illustrate an ongoing attempt to enunciate a collaborationist nationalism for occupied China.

February 1938: Reversing Guomindang Rule

A Special Service progress report filed with the Japanese Army in the third week of February 1938 indicates that the Japanese advisers to the Reformed Government were committed to making this regime appear to be a legitimate representative of the occupied nation (Bōei kenkyūjo 1938a). There the SSD outlines an elaborate course that regime formation should follow. The first step would be a planning conference attended by two to three representatives from each province and city within the regime's present jurisdiction plus representatives from North China and Hunan, which at this stage were conceived as separate political entities. (The document provides no sense of how these representatives would be recruited, leaving that problem to the Chinese.) The conference would elect "government delegates" who would be given the authority to inaugurate the regime as soon as possible. Once the regime was in existence, a president would be installed. Not content to leave this process to the vagaries of open negotiation, the SSD provided a flow chart that includes one further element, a secret group of "predetermined government delegates" who would meet in camera and make the real decisions for the conference—presumably under Japanese guidance. As it turned out, the secret group was the only piece of the flow chart that approximated reality at the end of the winter of 1937–38. No conference was called, and no president would ever be appointed. In practice, the SSD could not carry out this considered process of state-building, whether due to lack of potential delegates, the time needed to mobilize them, or the indifference of the Chinese who were willing to work with them.

As the Japanese side worried over the process of bringing a genuine new national government into being in Central China, the Chinese side ignored the niceties of process and turned to the task of developing an organizational structure and formulating ideological foundations for their collaboration. The organizational model appears in a ten-point Political Program, and the ideological orientation of the regime is outlined in the brief and polemical founding manifesto. The Chinese side drafted at least the former,[3] and probably the latter as well, in mid-February. A revised version of the manifesto was released at the inauguration of the regime on 28 March, and the Political Program was formally adopted at the regime's first ministerial conference on 1 April (Zhongguo tongxinshe 1938, 26).

The February draft of the Political Program begins by committing the regime to a constitutional separation of powers (executive, legislative, and judicial, described in terms of the venerable image of the bronze *ding* or tripod) and an end to one-party dictatorship. The second of its ten points espouses the principle of anticommunism to ensure the security of East Asia and to stabilize the "national foundation" (*guoben*). (The reference to *guoben*, a term highlighted by Zanasi in this volume, was removed in the final version of the manifesto released at the end of March.) The third point declares that international relations will be conducted on the principle of the equality of nations and the inalienability of the rights of the nation. On this basis, China would "respond to current world trends and seek peace in East Asia." (This point was subsequently rewritten to read, more narrowly, ". . . further the close relationship between China and Japan and consolidate peace in East Asia.") The fourth, fifth, and sixth points concern restoring public order and reviving the economy by returning people to their former occupations and supporting industrial, commercial, and financial enterprises to augment the "wealth of the nation" (*guofu*). More particularly, the fifth point specifies that economic reconstruction will be carried out "under state direction by broadly absorbing foreign capital, planned in coordination with the economy of the friendly country (*youbang*)," the standard euphemism for Japan.

The seventh point of the Political Program commits the new regime to "basing itself on China's long-established moral culture and absorbing world scientific knowledge in order to nurture an intellectually refined and physically strong national people (*guomin*). The radical education and shallow doctrines of the former [regime] must be fundamentally swept away" (*shallow* was subsequently regarded as a weak term and changed to *bizarre*). The eighth point calls for balancing the budget and lightening the people's fiscal burden by reducing expenses and abandoning reconstruction projects undertaken by the former regime that are not urgently needed; by implication, the modernizing state is to be scaled back to a less interventionist posture. The ninth and tenth points promise efficient administration in the service of the nation by selecting and supervising honest officials and getting rid of superfluous agencies. The ninth also guarantees freedom of speech to ensure that members of the nation (*guoren*) can criticize state policies at any time.

The Political Program was written in the language of the nation (*guo*). The nation it imagines is a unitary body of long standing composed of people who need to be protected and nurtured, not mobilized to engage proactively in the tasks of reconstruction. The economic and educational policies designed to do this largely replicate the settled but vanished world that Guomindang republicanism had destroyed. It is a class world in which ordinary people are to be "returned to their original occupations" and "previously established industrial and commercial enterprises" are to be put back on their feet. The government is republican in organization, inheriting the postdynastic structure of the previous Chinese Republic yet refusing to allow the party-based hegemonies and conflicts characteristic of that regime to resurface. It rules the nation responsibly but minimally, not by establishing "responsible government" but by recommitting itself to the old imperial promise of promoting honest officials and removing the corrupt. Members of the nation can speak out about abuses of power, but at no point can they enter politics on the basis of any interest other than what the government itself understands to be the interest of the nation as a whole—which the preconstituted (and nonconstitutional) state already represents in any case. In this model, state and nation exist as a unity in which neither is subject to a process of coming into being—which of course expresses the point of view of the state, which cannot problematize the nation over which it claims legitimate rule.

In the original version of the Political Program, the name Japan is not present, although it was insinuated into the final published copy. The second and third points refer to the objective of achieving "peace in East Asia" without identifying this as Japan's objective (though in revision the Japanese would see to it that Japan was named in the third point). The fifth point specifies foreign economic cooperation but again without actually naming Japan, using "a friendly country" instead.[4] Even though a euphemism has a way of drawing attention to the thing not named, the framers of the Political Program appear to have wanted to avoid naming Japan lest the entire claim they were making for the sovereignty of the new nation collapse. The Japanese presence was the Achilles' heel of their national legitimacy.

The Reformed Government's founding manifesto, similarly drafted in mid-February and distributed for public consumption at the inauguration,[5] begins by bewailing the corruption, incompetence, and recklessness of politics in "our China." In so doing, it invokes its commitment to virtuous government as the qualification for speaking on behalf of the collective nation. The origin of the present disaster it attributes to the previous regime's insistence on waging a war for which it was not prepared and therefore could not win even at enormous cost (although, again, a euphemism is preferred to naming either the Guomindang or Jiang Jieshi). The government threw untrained people into battle as cannon fodder and then left the country in ruins and the people without a livelihood. Defeat drove the Guomindang to a scorched earth policy and into "collaboration" with the Communists—a collaboration far worse than that called for by the Reformed Government. As evidence that "truly there has been no government as evil as this in the entire history of our China," the manifesto asserts that the two archetypal evil rulers of the second millennium B.C.E., Jie and Zhou, would have been "unwilling" to act as the previous regime had done; and the two rebel leaders who overthrew the Ming dynasty in 1644 would have regarded its conduct as "intolerable."[6] The regime had fled into the interior, yet it still claimed to be the government of the people it had abandoned. "Motivated by righteous anger, a group of colleagues wants to rescue the nation from calamity. We hope to replace the old with the new and revive the fate of the nation." (This last phrase was damped down in late March to read: "to start a new beginning with the people.") The manifesto declares that the Guomindang has forfeited its right to represent the nation by indulging in corruption, gaining a stranglehold on power, and engaging in war. As a result of this misgovernment, the Guomindang regime has abandoned the territory it was charged with governing and failed to protect the people. These failures are construed as justifying the founding of the Reformed Government by disinterested elites who will serve the best interests of the nation by reversing what the Guomindang has done, not just vis-à-vis Japan but in all areas of policy.

As for the difficult question of the new regime's relationship with Japan, the manifesto puts it in the following terms, again with the conscious employment of euphemism:

> Our sole mandate is to restore territorial sovereignty to the prewar situation and return to cordial relations with our neighbouring country (*linbang*) so that the people of our country can avoid the disaster of war. Hereafter countries of the same script and same race should never again turn to killing each other. All should be handled on the basis of the old morality of our country in order to establish lasting peace in East Asia and at the same time to continue to preserve the friendships we already have with the European and American countries.

Japan's relationship to China is presented here in terms different from those sketched in the Political Program. Rather than economic cooperation, it is racial solidarity to which the regime appeals. Race can be represented as a simpler and more fundamental principle of national destiny while being suitably vague in terms of what action it entails. It also suggests a more aggressive international posture, though here it is intentionally softened at the end by the reaffirmation of existing diplomatic relationships with white-race nations (also left unnamed). Shaping the whole thing is a reversion to the way things were and a restoration of the "old" morality of the nation, which somewhat contradicts the assertion of a new beginning heralded at the start of the document.

This first statement of collaborationist ideology is a simple text. Its basic orientation is more elitist than populist: coming to the aid of the people on the strength of personal indignation rather than riding a wave of popular sentiment; getting them back to "living in peace and taking pleasure in their occupations" rather than becoming masters of their fate; and restoring administration rather than building a new order. The nationalism of the appeal is weak and, indeed, is nationalist only to the extent that it declares the fate of the nation to be under threat (though the one explicit reference to the fate of the nation was removed from the final published version). Most intriguing is the rhetorical gesture of celebrating racial solidarity as a basis of national solidarity. As Japan's invasion was what stimulated popular wartime nationalism, the gesture would appear to be laden with liability. The appeal to racial solidarity was intended as a defensive measure to preserve national sovereignty in the face of encroachment by members of another "race," yet it was being voiced in a context in which most people were experiencing ethnic contradiction far more with the Japanese than with Europeans or Americans. Hinting at racial solidarity was an aggressive posture that, under the conditions of continuing Japanese Army activity and strong popular anti-Japanese sentiment, could backfire were its articulation not deftly managed. Yet this appeal would be further elaborated in subsequent statements of regime ideology, as we shall see.

As the parenthetical comments about the revisions to these documents prior to promulgation indicate, the claims that the Chinese framers of the documents sought to make were often in tension with those that the CCAA hoped to hear from its clients. The Chinese concern was to emphasize the primary identity of the Reformed Government as the government of the Chinese nation, not as the agent of another. Cooperation with a neighboring country could be acceptable as a means for stimulating regional security and economic development, but that alone could not stand as a sufficient foundation on which to rest a new national identity. Nor, if at all possible, should the neighbor in question be named, lest the fate of one nation (and of the regime governing it) be tied to the fate of another. Although it is not clear to what extent the Japanese officers of the SSD were involved in rewriting these documents, the numerous differences between the original Chinese drafts and the published versions suggest that the SSD brought pressure to bear to replace the quietly nationalistic posture shading the language of the documents toward a more neutral identification with East Asia. For within East Asia (which was a Western concept that Japan had taken on board far more than China ever did), the particular claims of the Chinese nation in opposition to its neighbors could be made to disappear, or at least be trumped by an appeal to the higher purpose of regional accord. In the end, as we have noted, the Chinese framers of the February documents could not resist this pressure; invocations of the nation were scaled back and Japan was named. The margin for maneuver was small.

October 1938: Revision

In February 1938 the idea of the Reformed Government was still being hopefully imagined. By October, however, only half a year into the short life of the Reformed Government, the political situation had changed. Japan had come to feel that Liang Hongzhi's regime did not carry sufficient weight in political or diplomatic circles to earn it any credit and was casting about among disaffected members of the Nationalist Party for new leaders who could field a more persuasive national regime. The prime minister, Prince Konoe, was about to announce the New Order in East Asia, which would overturn his earlier refusal to negotiate with the Guomindang regime (an extreme position that Konoe had been obliged to adopt the previous January). The new policy would call for an equal partnership between Japan and China, a partnership that could now include the Nationalists as long as they jettisoned Jiang Jieshi.

For our purposes, the most significant and surprising aspect of the New Order was its acknowledgment of the claims of Asian nationalism, as we have noted in Prince Konoe's speech of December 1938, in which he declared nineteenth-century-style colonialism to be dead and pledged Japan to the role of liberating the nations of East Asia, not annihilating them (quoted in Usui 1966, 234). This acknowledgment sprang from a realization that nationalism was indeed a vital force and one with which Japan had to deal. Konoe's adviser on Chinese affairs (and an agent for the Sorge spy ring), Ozaki Hostumi, made this realization even more explicit by explaining at this time that Japan had failed to win Chinese cooperation because it knew how to look for feudalism and imperialism, but not nationalism, in China. Nationalism, Ozaki insisted, "can be found everywhere. You can find it in the Guomindang-Communist collaboration," he pointed out, and "you can find it in the leaders of the puppet regimes." In his estimation: "Nationalism is what has enabled China to keep fighting with all her weakness. It is to be found not just at the state level but at the individual level" (quoted in Boyle 1972, 192–93). The earlier contempt for Chinese nationalism had gone, at least in this quarter.

Concurrent with the enunciation of the New Order in the autumn of 1938 was the beginning of the plan to engage Wang Jingwei in the Japanese cause. The involvement of the Guomindang, either in the Chongqing regime or in the person of Wang Jingwei, posed enormous ideological challenges. Liang Hongzhi had based his ideology on a repudiation of Guomindang policies: its practice of one-party dictatorship, its anti-imperialist interpretation of Sun Yatsen's Three Principles of the People, its repudiation of what were viewed as traditional moral values, and its educational policies favoring modern Western knowledge. Collaborating with Japan was for Liang the means by which China could return to its proper national identity, which the Guomindang had compromised. The possibility of enticing the Guomindang into negotiations or of recruiting a high Guomindang leader like Wang was sufficiently exciting to the Japanese that they were willing to force a rewriting of collaborationist nationalism in a form that did not throw up barriers to those elements of Guomindang ideology that Wang Jingwei might represent. At the same time, however, the SSD did not want to reject outright its first generation of collaborators; it hoped instead to bring the first generation into an alliance with the prospective second. Given the mutual suspicion that infected Liang's and Wang's views of each other, the Japanese advisers found themselves having to employ a stronger hand in guiding their clients' different constructions of the destiny of the Chinese nation into a new mix.

This task is anticipated in a secret SSD document dated October 1938 (Bōei kenkyūjo 1938c). The document opens by stressing the need to revise a mistaken ideology in order to develop correct thinking for reconstructing what it calls "New China." It offers four guiding principles. The first principle repeats the old formulas about letting the people "live in peace and take pleasure in their occupations," declaring reliance on East Asian morality, intensifying a sense of conflict with the Western powers, and concentrating and coordinating ideological work; none of this is new. The third and fourth principles call for such sensible approaches as avoiding high-flying ideas in preference to practical methods and making sure that Japanese ideological work takes account of the actual situation in China. The comments indicate, as Ozaki rightly pointed out, that the Japanese had been reading China according to their own preconceptions rather than dealing with Chinese realities.

Most shocking among the four principles is the second, which declares that the Three Principles of the People are not necessarily unacceptable and even that something may be taken from them in establishing basic concepts. The report later suggests that Japan's ideological work must involve showing the Chinese how the Three Principles had been distorted (by the Guomindang) and how those distortions should be corrected. Since the main thrust of the report is that propaganda work must focus on combating anti-Japanese sentiment, the task was to rework the Three Principles into an ideology that was nationalist without being anti-Japanese. In the light of what was already in place, this was a challenge, not least because Reformed Government leaders Liang Hongzhi and Wen Zongyao had made it clear that they regarded the Three Principles as repugnant.

The resurrection of the Three Principles, however edited or reinterpreted, was an unavoidable condition for drawing Wang Jingwei into the Japanese fold. Later, in a written statement to the Chinese war crimes tribunal, Wang's associate Lin Bosheng (1902–46) stated that in 1938 he had been disgusted with the Reformed Government for banning Sun Yatsen's flag, the national anthem, and the Three Principles of the People. These bans were, he declared, a virtual proscription on words like *nationality* (*minzu*), *independence* (*duli*), *freedom* (*ziyou*), *equality* (*pingdeng*), and even *nation* (*guojia*) (Nanjing shi dang'anguan 1992, 530). Lin represented himself at his trial as a Guomindang loyalist engaged in a kind of recuperation of the nation very different from the abject collaboration of the Reformed Government. With this choice of language, he strove to draw a line between Guomindang nationalism and the allegedly unprincipled collaboration of the Reformed Government. Whether Lin did indeed find the erasure of the Three Principles offensive, and whether Wang and his faction shared his view, are incidental to the point that needs to be made here, which is that the entry of Wang's faction into the Nanjing regime involved profound differences that required careful ideological work to manage, if not resolve. Of course, nationalism is not "mere" ideology; it is a potentially powerful force in shaping the possibilities for political action. As Nicholas Dirks has observed of Indian nationalism under colonialism: "Nationalism is not simply a movement that took place to gain freedom, it is a system for organizing the past that depends upon certain narratives, assumptions, and voices, and that continues to have important stakes throughout the social and political order" (Dirks 1992, 14). Liang Hongzhi and Wang Jingwei both had large stakes in the difficult task of remaking the nation under collaboration. Either pushing Liang's regime aside or forcing it to work with Wang's group required the Japanese to force a new form of collaborationist nationalism that could dovetail with the legacy of Sun Yatsen. Faced with this challenge, the leaders of the Reformed Government chose to strengthen their ideology, not compromise it, as we shall see.

March 1939: The Core of the Nation

A year after the inauguration of the Reformed Government, the Japanese advisers to the regime orchestrated an elaborate set of ceremonies to celebrate the first anniversary of its founding. The public documents that are available from this anniversary are not the brief policy statements of 1938 but a fuller set of personal essays in which all the top officials in the Reformed Government look back over the regime's first year (paginated hereafter to Xuanchuanju 1939, 7–35). By this time, the Japanese were engaged in intense negotiations with Wang Jingwei to create an as yet unannounced regime that would push the Reformed Government aside completely. Living under the threat of being superseded, the authors of the anniversary statements pressed the case for their form of collaboration. They strove to validate what they had done, demonstrate that they had acquired sufficient public credit to survive the transition to the new regime, and if possible set some conditions on the ideological composition of the replacement regime. Their texts also protest the public treatment they had received for the path they had chosen and in doing so communicate a sense of anxiety about their status as collaborators. Liang Hongzhi begins his piece, for example, by complaining that if his critics at the time of the regime's founding "didn't regard me as a puppet, then they pointed at me as a traitor. Such doubts and rumors have arisen that privately I harbor bitter feelings" (7). Gu Cheng, Liang's newly appointed minister of education, writes that when he decided to join the government "my relatives and old friends came up with a hundred ways to block me, and those close to me reprimanded me in all sorts of ways. The short-sighted even damned me as selling out my country. But this is a time of emergency when each must show his benevolence and wisdom however he can" (19). For Gu, the threat to the nation justified collaboration more strongly than it argued against it.

No ground was given to Guomindang ideology. Not one of the authors whispers a word about the Three Principles of the People; instead, they concentrate on keeping up the pressure on Guomindang leaders as the architects of China's mess. Liang Hongzhi declares that these men were "desperate scoundrels plotting to control the nation" (7). Minister of the Interior Chen Qun judges the destruction caused by the war to be unprecedented in Chinese history. He goes further back than 1937 by characterizing China's history since 1911 as one of chaos and since 1840 as a century of falling behind the great nations of the world in military, economic, political, educational, and cultural terms. Chen better than Liang or Gu grasped the idea of economic development that was popular in some Guomindang circles, notably with members of Wang Jingwei's faction such as Chen Gongbo, the subject of Zanasi's essay in this volume and Wang's second in command after his defection to the Japanese. In keeping with this awareness, Chen Qun is the first in this group of authors to use the theme of China's backwardness—in contrast to the temporary damage of war—to identify the leading challenges the Reformed Government faced. He suggests that China's backwardness, although caused by imperialism, was intensified by the Nationalists and Communists. He declares that the active involvement of these two enemies of the Chinese nation—the Others through which he can secure the right of his regime to rule—should be considered a matter of national shame (14).

Chen Qun and Liang Hongzhi both speak of the Reformed Government as the "axis" (*zhongshu*) or core of the nation as it was reemerging from the anarchy of the war. Chen's model for nation-building is explicitly elitist but bottom-up. He depicts the process as moving upward almost automatically from local to regional to national elites. He sees "elders" and their supporters attached to county-level collaborationist administrations acting locally as the core and transmitting the views of local people upward to a conference of representatives, which then transmits the popular views to the government, which is the core of the entire nation.[7] Chen stresses that his regime's policy of anti-communism emerged out of this process: it came from the people. The reality of regime formation enclosed in archived documents indicates that the process followed precisely the opposite path. Policies were set by the highest leadership—though certain elements such as anticommunism probably were handed down from the Japanese—and passed down to those below. In that downward passage, they frequently encountered resistance.

Chen also uses the notion of the core in describing the new personnel being trained to serve the Reformed Government. He reports that the county and police administrations have established institutes to train cadres and policemen "with a view to producing scientific and disciplined modern administrators who will serve as the core [or middle] elements (*zhongjian fenzi*) for building a new modern nation and will promote the modern policies of the Reformed Government" (13). Given the effort elsewhere to align the regime with traditional culture, it is at first surprising to find Chen invoking modernity as the highest aspiration of the nation and characterizing it as a matter of science and discipline. Yet fascist movements elsewhere in the twentieth century regularly combined a voluntarism motivating the individual to embrace the unique values of his culture and to embody the purest meaning of the nation with a discipline that desires to transform the same individual into a faceless servant of the state. This is a modern elitism composed not of traditional literati whom the state has co-opted but of a service elite it has created.

Liang Hongzhi's nationalism has little to do with Chen Qun's sense of modernity—which may help to explain why Chen was one of the few Reformed Government leaders to make the transition to a real portfolio in Wang Jingwei's cabinet. When Liang speaks of the Reformed Government as the nation's core, he does so in the implied context of competition with the Guomindang government, which the people refused to accept and had now driven away. He calls for the people to rally to his core government if the "old nation" is to rise out of the ashes. To achieve this, "it is essential that theory must be made firm, knowledge made correct, and the people made clearly aware of this newly arisen core." Without the active support of "the people of the entire nation," he declares, his government will not be able carry out its task of reconstruction. Concerned that the people will continue to recognize the Guomindang regime as the nation's core, the principal task is to redirect national sentiment in favor of the Reformed Government so as "to unify the mind of the entire nation so that all support the foundation of the nation (*guoben*)." But this ideal is raised only to be postponed, for Liang goes on to observe that "the people of China" (*Zhongguo minzu*) are not readily amenable to such unity because of their habits of passivity and negativity. The ideal would be to achieve the "unified effort of superior and inferior," in the moral language of political linkage from the late imperial era, but that ideal remains elusive. Short of that, the only way to carry out "self-reliance and self-strength-

ening" at this juncture in history is to accept help from China's "good neighbor" (8). Cooperation with Japan, he hoped, would suspend the sense of crisis
and national inadequacy that had plagued China since the rise of Guomindang
and Communist radicalism, hence the language of returning to the core or center of Chinese political culture that he employs at this point in his essay.

By arguing that the Reformed Government, even as it pursues Sino-Japanese cooperation, is the nation's core, Liang declares that China has now become
"an independent and sovereign nation," as he must if he is to claim legitimacy.
He characterizes China's economic relationship with Japan as "a cooperative
division of labor through which both support lasting peace in East Asia." He
insists that economic cooperation is conditional on both parties benefiting
from it, and he regards Japan's assistance as temporary, for to declare otherwise
would be to abandon all claim to national sovereignty. In practice, the national
core of which Liang and Chen speak was hollow. Rather than the elemental
substance of the Chinese nation that has been corrupted and diminished by
reckless westernizers, as they seek to argue, it was a void that the desires of an
imperialist power was filling rather than a meeting point for the forces of
national self-determination.

In his assertions regarding the substance of the regime, Legislative Yuan
president Wen Zongyao stayed away from such difficult metaphors. In an essay
written about the same time, entitled "The Construction of the New Order in
East Asia," he reverts to a classical principle of Chinese warfare—that a general
who loses his army, or a magistrate who loses his county, must take the full
blame—and on that basis calls for Jiang's execution. Indeed, he argues, Jiang
has outdone these feats, for he has lost not one battlefield or one county but an
entire nation. Not to execute him would be to hold the laws of the nation in
contempt (Nanjing shi dang'anguan 1992, 359–60). Wen Zongyao was less troubled than his colleagues in tying collaborationist nationalism to cooperation
with Japan. His anniversary statement, which does little more than plagiarize
the revised Political Program of March 1938, declares the current close relationship between China and Japan appropriate to China's "national circumstances"
(*guoqing*). He declares the ideal of the China-Japan relationship to be not just a
division of labor but a profound trust between the Chinese and Japanese peoples. On the other hand, he is willing to specify that the aid has come not just
from the "friendly country" but from three of its ministries—Army, Navy, and
Foreign Affairs—which were the principal agencies of Japanese military colonialism (10). In doing so, he represents the relationship to be one of state
alliance rather than popular sympathy.

"The Construction of the New Order in East Asia" lays out Wen's understanding of China's collaboration with Japan more fully than the anniversary

text. In this essay, he celebrates the tripartite division of East Asia into China, Japan, and Manchuria. (The anniversary texts remain tactfully silent on Manchuria, an issue that could only further damage the public reputation of the Reformed Government.) For Wen, the New Order represents three achievements for China: revoking colonial status and restoring China's sovereignty, restoring East Asian values and culture, and asserting full racial equality between the yellow and white races. Wen explains these achievements by reciting an account of Chinese history over the previous century from a solidly anti-imperialist viewpoint, emphasizing the Western nations' repeated humiliations and encroachments on Chinese territorial sovereignty. Japan was able to avoid this fate by carrying out a "renovation" (Ch. *weixin*, J. *ishin*, the name the collaborators chose for their government at Japanese prompting) in the Meiji period, which enabled it to join the ranks of the rich and powerful nations. He admits that Japan has attacked China several times but treats those attacks as different in essence: Japan attacked to achieve co-prosperity with China and break the hold of the foreign colonizers, not to encroach on Chinese sovereignty. The best course for the Chinese nation was to become fully East Asian rather than aping the degraded moral values of the West and abandoning its cultural roots. Japan was able to learn from the West so successfully precisely because it did not abandon its "East Asian morality and culture." Throughout the modernization process, the people of Japan preserved their essence of "loyalty to their ruler and love of their nation" (*zhongjun aiguo*). So, too, the Chinese should recognize that China's morality and culture are the finest in the world (Wen ascribes no particular content to these, certainly not the mind emptying that Konoe wanted to celebrate) and use them as a framework for building a modern nation (Nanjing shi dang'anguan 1992, 356–59).

With its denunciation of unequal treaties and its appeal for national renovation and self-strengthening, Wen's collaborationist nationalism is reminiscent of the vision of Chinese modernity outlined in 1901 by Liang Qichao (1873–1929), one of the founding intellectuals of the generation preceding that of Sun Yatsen and the Guomindang. According to the most recent analysis of his historical thought, Liang Qichao envisioned China's modernity as "a historical period in which the Chinese nation, together with all other Asian nations, relates itself to and competes with the Western nations. With traditional despotism drawing to a prolonged end, an unprecedented and more democratic constitutionalism will arise to replace the outmoded political system" (Tang 1996, 44). The Nationalists had failed to sustain the constitutionalism of the century's second decade with which political veterans outside the Party such as Wen liked to associate themselves. Respecting China's location within East Asia, and more particularly its collegial affinity with Japan, would correct the pro-Western tendency of the Nationalists and restore China to a civilized modernity within an Asian context.

From Wen's perspective, the pro-Western stance of the Guomindang represents a colonial mentality that enslaves the Chinese people. Collaborationist nationalism, on the other hand, could claim to free China from its colonial status and allow it to return to its national moral foundations. To complete his argument, however, Wen must abandon Liang Qichao's keen and almost innocent cosmopolitanism for an East-West polarization that, in Liang's analysis, would signal a step backward in China's evolution. Relying on this polarization, Wen blesses China's collaborative relationship with Japan on racial grounds. Liang Qichao had been sympathetic to nineteenth-century European arguments of racial difference, but Wen goes much further when he declares that race is the device that overrides all other discriminations. If colonialism is a racist relationship, as Wen insists it is, then Japan's assistance to China cannot be construed as colonialist because Japanese and Chinese are of the same race. Nor can the Chinese nation be construed as jeopardized by that assistance. Race thus allows Wen to shunt Japan into a position of secondary significance, for, regardless of who has rendered assistance to whom, China's national dignity and identity will inevitably be restored by drawing upon yellow culture instead of white. Race is the category that most smoothly overrides national distinctions, yet it has terrible potential to resurrect them, and that potential is not something to which Wen draws attention.

However elaborated, the arguments put forward by Wen Zongyao and the other leaders in March 1939 share a commitment to the exigencies of state control: that order be restored, that relief for refugees be organized, that China resume its place in the international sphere, and that state-led reconstruction be carried out. Their attention is less on the nation that the people embody than on the state that the leaders control. The one who presents a vision of collaboration that is more nation- than state-based, more focused on the nation as the people than the nation as embodied by the state, is Minister of Education Gu Cheng. Gu's approach to the revitalization of the nation is via the people (*min*) in the spirit of early Republican thinkers such as Sun Yatsen. In this, the longest of the anniversary texts, Gu is concerned to answer the charge that acting on behalf of the people's welfare is treason. He does this by appealing to the idea of the people as the "foundation of the country" (*bangben*):[8]

> There is no nation in this world without people. The former government fled, leaving behind its tens of millions of people. If the new government had not appeared, how would these tens of millions of people have survived on scorched earth? Preserving the people amounts to preserving the

nation. Those who have slandered us as treasonous for preserving the masses are the very ones who have abandoned and slaughtered the people. (19)

Gu subtly reverses the role of the people in the nation: they are not the vessels of sovereignty, as Sun Yatsen might have claimed, but the charges of a state elite self-appointed to rule them.[9] What justifies regime formation is the alignment the elite has made with the people to form the unitary body of the nation. Gu can then conclude with his rhetorical question: "If the people do not survive, where is the nation?"

Gu Cheng seeks to extend his argument—though the effect is to threaten it with incoherence—by turning to the physical body of the nation. He makes a bold claim: "Our group has not given up an inch of territory to anyone, whereas Jiang has retreated pace by pace and lost territory section by section. We have recovered it all" (19). While it may be true that the Reformed Government, unlike the Guomindang regime, was gaining control over more, rather than less, territory, what it was recovering amounted only to portions of the three provinces of Jiangsu, Zhejiang, and Anhui. This was not China, and not even Gu was willing to characterize it as a core, as to do so would expose the absence of the flesh around the core, the large portions of China to which the Reformed Government had no claim. The nation thus remained a romantic ideal projected above the body of the Chinese people, carefully separated from the tangible realities of territorial incompleteness and impaired sovereignty.

Gu seeks to control the troubling element in this situation—Japan's presence—by invoking racial solidarity, not so much with Japan as against the West. Rather than highlighting racial competition between yellows and whites and proposing a natural solidarity with the Japanese, as Wen Zongyao did, Gu reminds East Asians of the disastrous fate of reds and blacks, the most thoroughly colonized of the world's races.[10] To accept an alliance with the white West, as the Guomindang does, is to expose oneself to colonial domination. Collaboration with Japan is, paradoxically, the only means available to China at this time for transcending the collaboration of colonial status and for achieving full national sovereignty. In Gu's view, race had made collaboration essential to the process not of regional harmony but of China's national liberation.

The Limits of Collaborationist Nationalism

Whether those who read these arguments for collaborationist nationalism were swayed by them is beside the point of this essay, and in any case it is impossible to determine conclusively, especially as any answers in the positive were completely discredited as of 1945. Persuasion or its failure does not negate the fact that the regime spoke in the language of the nation and could assume coherence by doing so. Some wartime writers repeated the official arguments aired in the captive press during the occupation, and defendants reinvoked these ideals at the war crimes trials after it was over, but these were particular public contexts that called for particular ideological statements and cannot be used to indicate any degree of popular concurring response. Liang Hongzhi asserted in his anniversary text that "the majority of the people of the nation" sympathized with his policies for national recovery, and that the opposed minority would eventually be convinced as his regime's work came to fruition (9). But one can more readily suppose that an appeal for collaboration on the grounds that to do so would contribute to the protection of the people and the preservation of the territory of the nation was barely plausible under conditions of military occupation. It is nonetheless worth pausing to consider why collaborationist nationalism failed to compete with the nationalism of the resistance when both claimed equally to speak for the good of the Chinese nation. Political circumstances may well have discredited the collaborators right from the start; but let us set those circumstances aside to consider the particular burdens of nationalist discourse, regardless of which side speaks in its terms.

The principal burden of any nationalist discourse lies in its having to compete with other political agendas. As Michael Robinson (1993, 167) has pointed out in the context of Korea, nationalists must "continuously construct and tighten national unity in the face of multiple narratives or competing interpretations of what constitutes the nation." The anxiety that a different vision of the nation is always in competition with one's own is much heightened for those who would defend collaborationist nationalism, for that defense requires arguments in favor of subordinating one's national identity to the hegemony of a foreign power, arguments that are usually weak. Nationalism fetishizes the nation to which one is bound. It resists the idea of bracketing that primary nation with a second, which is what collaboration entails. In the presence of a less contorted and less troubled version of nationalism, the weaker claim, which requires more work to sustain, fails.

Nationalism is nonetheless vulnerable to competition precisely because it is a concept that has no content other than what a particular nation or state elite ascribes to it. Nationalism is not simply "there," like gravity, but requires work to come into being. It must be created through the stimulation of patriotic sentiment, the structuring of political and social institutions that link people together into a single national unit, and the elaboration of an ideology that celebrates the nation as a focus of identity formation.[11] Shy of calling upon popular sentiment in the face of foreign military slaughter, the Reformed Government busied itself with the latter two. It created disciplinary institutions (county governments, police, youth leagues) to simulate the operations of a nation and to stimulate identification with it. And it produced fragments of an ideology tying the fate of the nation to Japan's protection against the encroachments of colonial Western powers and its support in overcoming the corruption and wastage of the Guomindang regime. Together these features sketched out a nation that was socially conservative, politically restrictive, and culturally antique; xenophobic but utterly Asian; in retreat from the alienating conditions of modernity; and appealing to those who regarded the changes of the previous twenty years as distasteful and still available for correction.

The Wang Jingwei regime, which replaced the Reformed Government as it reached its second anniversary in 1940, had to promote a different type of collaborationist nationalism, one that could be made to conform to Guomindang ideology—which meant reversing most of the renovationist elements of its predecessor. The new Reorganized National Government was able to fit into Japan's East Asian vision by emphasizing the pan-Asian elements when it relaunched Sun Yatsen's thought, but it also did what it could to create an impression of sovereignty. Wang's most powerful associate in this project was Chen Gongbo. Chen argued at length for the validity of the new collaborationist nationalism over the old, yet he too was obliged to rest his claims ultimately on an argument of expediency not unlike Gu Cheng's. War, Chen explained in an article published in March 1942 on the second anniversary of *his* regime, is a time when "the survival or demise, disappearance or continuation of the nation" is the most pressing issue. Only by accepting China's position within East Asia and refusing to flee the nation, which is what Jiang Jieshi's faction of the Guomindang had done, could patriotic Chinese guarantee their nation's survival. The nation was at stake, and the duty of the patriot was to ensure that this dreadful outcome be averted (Nanjing shi dang'anguan 1992, 64).

The national destiny for which both styles of collaborationist nationalism yearned was not compelling to most sectors of the elite and had few points of contact with popular feeling. These ideologies found voice because of the destabilization of war, not because they expressed the aspirations of a large but suppressed segment of the elite or the people. But I would suggest that collaborationist nationalism faced a larger structural problem as well. Nationalism in a colonial context is rarely a matter of achieving or exercising total independence, though it may be constructed as such. It usually arises in a struggle to overthrow a colonial power, yet it involves political and cultural compromises with more powerful centers of gravity. Guomindang nationalism embraced anti-imperialism, but its policies promoted beneficial economic and cultural links with certain Western countries, notably Great Britain and the United States and to a lesser extent France and Germany. The urge within the Guomindang to re-create China in the image of a "modern nation" necessitated borrowing and adapting ideologies and organizations dedicated to overthrowing indigenous ideas and practices, resulting in the reproduction of Western nationhood in China. Gu Cheng and his associates idealized East Asia and invoked racial solidarity with other yellow people because the nation they wanted was Asian. Gu declared in his final peroration that "both countries of China and Japan should embody (*ti*) Confucianism and utilize (*yong*) science in order to create the core of our spiritual culture," repeating the old formula that nineteenth-century Chinese had invoked to adjust their relationship to Western forms of knowledge. "We should use our Eastern spirit to fashion Western material so that the world will never again witness the evil that feasted on our flesh and we can proceed together to the realm of Great Unity (*datong*)" (22). He favored associating the Chinese nation with Japan rather than allying it with the West because the Japanese model eschewed objectionable cultural features of the West; it also conformed to familiar notions of harmony and hierarchy.

Under late (and even post-) colonialism, all nationalisms are collaborative in some measure, as the spokesmen for the Reformed Government declared. The surrounding presence of the world system means that no nation can be fully autonomous. Dependent on economic networks established through colonial relationships, late colonial nations must make points of connection and compromise with former (or neo-) colonial powers if their economies are to flourish and sometimes, too, if the political survival of the liberation elite is to be assured. Nationalism is relative, for the nation never achieves a state of absolute separation from other nations. The Reformed Government ideology of the nation could point to the compromises of Guomindang nationalism, but it could not expose its own. It thus fell into the hegemonic trap of Japan's East Asian liberationism: that the nation would be transcended at the moment of its realization.

Collaborationist nationalism failed less because it relied on a vision of the nation that held little appeal (an Asian culture in an interstate system of other Asian cultures) than because the ideological constructions of its architects lay at such a great distance from the unstable social reality in which most people lived. The problem with Gu Cheng's picture of China marching toward a Confucian Heaven hand in hand with Japan was not that the Communists and Nationalists generated more persuasive nationalist discourses. Rather, the elite claim of national independence was contradicted by the palpable fact of Japan's brutal military occupation of China. The daily experience of life in occupied

China precluded any possibility that people would recognize Gu's account as something that made sense or inspired hope. Under other circumstances—of national unity or renewed prosperity, perhaps—it might have, but those circumstances did not arise. Where is the nation? Japan's treatment of the people the Reformed Government claimed to be protecting doomed any search for it in occupied territory. Japan actively contributed instead to a situation in which Nationalists and Communists both were able to make their different nations appear elsewhere, preventing the Reformed Government from attaining the legitimacy it needed to outface the competing nationalisms of its enemies.

NOTES

1. The idea that the nation consists of a "moral consciousness" was expressed by Ernest Renan (1996, 52) in his now famous lecture on the nation, delivered at the Sorbonne in 1882.

2. I am grateful to my student Mike Ouyang for suggesting the phrase "hegemonic trap" to describe this situation.

3. Chinese authorship of the Political Program is confirmed by a draft copy preserved in the archives of the Japanese Self-Defense Ministry, under the title of which has been written in Japanese "proposal from the Chinese side" (Bōei kenkyūjo 1938b). I have found no draft copies of the Political Program or the manifesto in Chinese archives, though the China Number Two Historical Archives in Nanjing (file 2001[2], entry 1) contains a copy of the latter, hand dated 7 April 1938.

4. Instead of the conventional term for state or country or nation (*guo*, the root on which *Zhongguo* is built), the euphemism employs the term *bang*. This term designated the territory of an enfeoffed lord in the Zhou dynasty, one fiefdom among many within the Chinese single-state system of the first millennium B.C.E.. The word was avoided in the Han because it was the given name of the Han founder, Liu Bang, but it came back into use after the Han to designate smaller states beyond China's borders. I am still seeking the origin of the euphemism "friendly *bang*" and the reasons for using it. I suspect it has to do with reducing the sense of difference or distance between Japan and China, which were now fellow *bang* within a common regional unit rather than separate *guo*; it may also have been used to diminish the status of China as a *guo* superior to Japan, just as the Japanese use of the Orientalist "Shina" for China was intended to do.

5. The discussion of the manifesto that follows is based on the printed *baihua* (colloquial) version prepared in anticipation of a 16 March inauguration, which is reproduced in Heiwa hakubutsukan 1990, 178. That inauguration was canceled on 15 March and rescheduled for 28 March. The manifesto underwent changes before being released for the later inauguration, the most important having to do with specifying its relationship to the Provisional Government in Beijing. The same source reproduces the more widely circulated *wenyan* (literary) version of the final text.

6. In the Chinese political imagination, the emergence of the Zhou state from the

collapse of the Shang under its last ruler, Zhou, and the appearance of the Qing state after the rebellions of Li Zicheng and Zhang Xianzhong at the end of the Ming are events of the same type, both ushering in eras of social civility guaranteed by the existence of a state that governed effectively (see Des Forges 1997, 96–98).

7. A Japanese text of the previous June characterizes the Standing Committee of the Political Consultative Conference, on which sat the *yuan* presidents and ministers, as the "core" of the Reformed Government (Zhongguo tongxinshe 1938, 26).

8. Gu Cheng's use of *bangben* rather than *guoben* quietly but puzzlingly demotes China from *guo* to *bang* status. His choice of language might signal a rhetorical attempt to edge away from the harder notion of national sovereignty enshrined in *guo;* see note 4.

9. Vichy France provides an interesting parallel, inasmuch as Philippe Pétain liked to invoke the "people" of the nation in his rhetoric and avoid *république,* whereas Charles de Gaulle invoked the latter but tended to avoid the former (Tournier 1996, 67–68).

10. In matters directly concerning education, which was his portfolio, Gu Cheng continues this theme of fundamental opposition to Western imperialism by deploring the Guomindang's use of foreign textbooks in higher education and calling for the compilation of Chinese textbooks that are more selective in their inclusion of translated foreign knowledge.

11. I have drawn these three indicators of nationalism from the analysis in Robinson 1988 as outlined in Befu 1993, 107–8.

The Incoherent Nation: An Exploration of Chinese "Postnationalism"

Xiaoping Li

Envisioning "Postnationalism"

China's rapid transformation over the past two decades has given rise to a proliferation of inquiries into how recent changes in ideology, economy, and culture have altered the meanings of *nation* and the content of nationalism. Recent observers have problematized conventional paradigms of the nation in an effort to capture the current "complex weave of Chinese nationalist sentiments" (Unger 1996, xviii). This essay participates in this inquiry by considering a major contradiction in the circumstances of China's nation-building, namely, the interweaving of globalism and nationalism. China has always been part of the globe, despite its traditional self-image as a "world" unto itself and its isolation from the capitalist West during the Mao era (1949–76), and changes in the globe have unavoidably produced changes in China. Historically, progressive waves of globalization, in concurrence with the rise and spread of capitalist modernity, coerced imperial China into ascribing to itself the identity of a modern nation-state and a member of the international community. More recently, the operation of global capitalism has compelled post-Mao China to increase its integration with the networks of the global economy. To emphasize globalization's impact on Chinese consciousness and practices is not to assume a simple causal relationship between the two. Rather, China's nation-building process and its global maneuvers are intertwined. From these seemingly contradictory orientations arises the incoherence that some have identified in Chinese nationalism, an incoherence that I shall address through the concept of "postnationalism."

The concept of "postnationalism" is a way of making sense of the incongruity in Chinese sentiment and praxis within the context of globalization processes. Employing a term of this sort must further complicate the already "notoriously controversial subject" of "the national question" (Hobsbawm 1990, viii). Despite, or even because of, the substantial advances made in the theorization of nationalism since it became a subject of Western scholarship, the controversies surrounding nationalism have also grown, especially when "non-Western theorists have encroached regularly on the territories of Western theory, working oppositionally, with and against (both inside and outside) dominant terms and experiences" (Clifford 1989a, 179). Among scholars in Asia who have contested Western theories of nationalism, Partha Chatterjee's (1993) historical inquiry into Indian nationalist movements challenges the notion that nationalism is merely a Western phenomenon exported to the non-Western world, yet his critique of the derivative character of Asian nationalism (1986) reveals the persistent influence of European Enlightenment discourse even in its rejection. More relevant to my discussion of "postnationalism" is Aijaz Ahmad's (1996) observation that, as a consequence of Western imperialist expansion, the non-Western world has become involved in a discourse of a universal modernity that runs against the ideals of nationalism. The nationalist quest for sovereignty, authenticity, and coherence, it may be argued, has proceeded in circumstances in which incongruity has become a defining feature of national existence.

Postnationalism is seldom used as part of the vocabulary that addresses "the national question," though a few theorists of nationalism have noticed the coming of a "postnational" era as nation-states become subject to the shaping power of globalizing forces (Hutchinson and Smith 1994, 11). The concept has yet to emerge as a common heuristic device to make sense of phenomena situated within the global/local nexus. This means that there is a lack of existing models or theoretical paradigms on which to rest my argument. Nonetheless, writing at a time when "knowledge" itself is understood as a site of contestation, I think that it is worthwhile to venture into this new space to present another interpretation of modern China on this basis.[1]

The concept of postnationalism has broad applications. First of all, it expresses the myriad contradictions in contemporary China that arise out of the intersecting trajectories of globalism and nationalism. As the country becomes more involved with the world economy, maintaining cultural and political integrity becomes a major concern of the state, particularly after the Tiananmen Square massacre and the disintegration of the Eastern European socialist bloc in 1989. In general, the Chinese approach has been similar to that taken by some other Asian states and elites. This approach involves the juxtaposition of globalist economic development with the promotion of certain elite-defined postures, be they patriotism, national pride, or so-called Asian values. Economic policy aims at further integrating local production with the global market while at the same time nationalist sentiments are mobilized in the hope of consolidating local social cohesion. The term *postnationalism* seeks to capture the rich contradictions and nuances generated by such nation-based maneuvers in the global capitalist system. It allows us to take into account globalization's impact on nation-states and to make better sense of the (often unintended) outcomes of global and local interactions.

At the end of the twentieth century, it is clear that we can no longer study the nation or nationalism without considering the globe and its processes. Globalization is now broadly acknowledged as the most powerful transformative force, its capital, human, technological, and cultural flows reducing spatial integrity and blurring the boundaries between nations and the divide between the First and Third Worlds (Clifford 1989a). Global capitalism is crumbling the fixity of locations, changing the texture of local life worlds outside of the West, and engineering cultural transformations. As it does so, the study of nations and nationalism faces even greater challenges. Certainly, in the West globalization has "entailed a profound change" in the concepts of "national identity," as minority cultural rights movements in multicultural societies accentuate "the increasingly ambivalent, fragmented, and hybrid character of older and well-established national identities in the West" (Hutchinson and Smith 1994, 287).[2] The nation is no longer seen as a stable, coherent entity. Rather, its transitoriness, ambivalence, and conceptual indeterminacy are underscored (Bhabha 1994b). Globally, the reshaping of culture, national economy, and politics by forces beyond national borders necessarily encumbers scholarly inquiry with a new sense of temporality and spatiality. We see its manifestation in current inquiries into questions of space, time, and global modernities. "Time-space compression" (Harvey 1990: 240) is a key feature of globalization that threatens national identities as it creates "global identifications" (Hall et al. 1996, 621–23).

The concept of postnationalism bridges the otherwise separable inquiries into globalization and nationalism, enabling us to capture what has been largely overlooked by the study of nationalism. What does the term mean? Literally, *postnationalism* denotes "coming after the nation in time." If we follow the suggestion of some theorists of nationalism that we are moving into a postnational era, postnationalism mainly signifies a sense of time derived from the European Enlightenment conception of history. But postnationalism as a condition is broader and more complex than this, for this new historical phase, when local affairs are intricately linked and interdetermined by forces outside of a national territory, is associated with rapid changes pointing to the dilution of nations and nationalisms. But, as Eric Hobsbawm (1990) and others have recognized, nations and nationalism continue to exist and the state remains an organizing entity, although it has been compelled to alter its role (Wallerstein 1991). Yet the ideology of nations and nationalism has increasingly become irrelevant in political, economic, and cultural spheres. To speak of this condition as "postnation" is therefore to speak primarily in terms of spatiality, not temporality. Postnationalism in this sense belongs to a crowd of descriptive/ interpretive terms characterizing contemporary conditions of human and cultural existence—*globalization, transnationalization, postcoloniality, creolization, transculturation,* and *hybridity*—without being reducible to them. It delineates the dual attempt to globalize on the one hand and to hold onto the nation on the other, both of which are moves intended to maintain self-coherence. As a common mode of thought and a major strategy of nation-building today, post-nationalism maintains the nation-state through global maneuvers. This globalist approach understands that the survival and well-being of the nation lies in its reinvention through its close integration into global structures. As a result, postnationalism is essentially schizophrenic: the very embodiment of incoherence and the very source of contradictions we see in nation-based operations in the global space.

Postnationalism's close association with globalization leads me to consider that it is not an emerging phenomenon of an era following nationalism but a condition that became possible with the historic spread of Euro-American modernity. As China's initial phase of "modernization" early in the twentieth century occurred in conjunction with the process of globalization, it is possible to argue for China (as for other former Western colonies such as India) that a postnational condition emerged in the early stage of forging the modern nation-state. In imposing upon China a new order of space and time, the Sino-Western encounter left a lasting ambivalence. As a result, China's search for a coherent, autonomous, and authentic nation has from the very beginning been built upon incoherent, rational, and hybrid articulations and endeavors. The concept of postnationalism is intended, therefore, to throw light on the particular spatiotemporal contexts that have shaped, in fundamental ways, Chinese approaches to nation-building and cultural reconstruction for at least a century. I shall develop this argument later in the essay.

Looking at China in postnationalist terms allows us to explore a body of complex symptoms that have emerged from the processes of China's modernization, symptoms that are linked to the ambivalence and disjunction already mentioned. This essay is less a systematic investigation of historical and contemporary occurrences of these symptoms than a probe of postnationalism as both a condition of twentieth-century China and an interpretive category for understanding cultural production over the last two decades. In the course of drawing on current Chinese discussions centering around culture, modernization, and nation, I shall trace the underlying psychological and strategic schizophrenia back to the turn of the century. To show the value of analyzing modern China in close relation to global transformation, I shall first turn to some recent writings on Chinese nationalism, which I find problematic because of their confinement to a typically nationalist territorial imagination that obliterates or depreciates the role of globalization in the Chinese handling of the "national question."

The Nation Inside and Outside the Globe

Recent scholarship on Chinese nationalism has enriched our understanding by adding new categories to existing analytical schemes (e.g., Unger 1996).[3] It has uncovered nationalism's shifting modes and multiple layers, particularly in the post-Mao era, and has increased awareness that popular culture constitutes a major site where sentiments of all kinds are played out. For example, Lisa Rofel argues that the popularity of the teleserial *Yearning,* which the *New York Times* applauded as "real entertainment" devoid of "socialist politics," seems to unravel the "re-imaged possibilities of national identity" after the Tiananmen Square massacre (1995, 303). On the other hand, the teleserial *A Beijing Man in New York* displays the "newly virile nationalism" that has emerged since 1989. Resonant with a growing disenchantment with the West, it speaks of the sentiments of various segments of the intelligentsia. Geremie Barmé (1994, 275) comments:

> As the children of the Cultural Revolution and the reform period come into power and/or money, they are finding a new sense of self-importance and worth. They are resentful of the real and imagined slights they and their nation have suffered in the past, and their desire for strength and revenge is increasingly reflected in contemporary Chinese culture.

Paralleling this development is the dilution of old forms of nationalism, as political and economic developments in post-Mao China appear to undermine the foundation of the Chinese nation-state. The decline of state nationalism had already begun in the 1980s, when the relationship between Chinese intellectuals and the state deteriorated. As the former came to identify themselves with the "nation" rather than the state, China faced a crisis of national identity (Goldman et al. 1993).[4] Economic change seems to have been the major driver in the diminishing of antiforeign or anti-imperialist nationalism, replacing the old ideological discourse with a transformative "pro-commerce economic nationalism" (Xiang 1993, 104). Not only is the economy playing an important role in the reconstruction of national identity, as Crane (1996) has observed in China's special economic zones, but it is driving regionalism at the same time. An increasingly prosperous southern China with its close ties with the global economy is thus eroding the northern-based, Han-centric mythos of national genesis. An emerging "southern-oriented national identity" characterized "by mercantile openness, international interaction, decentralization, and southern cultural pre-eminence" (Unger 1996, xvii) is inducing what some observers believe is a plural and democratic national identity (Friedman 1994, 1996).

Underlying these analyses is an awareness that the globalist approach is embedded in the "open-door policy," as China actively recruits foreign investment and steadily maneuvers itself into the global commodities market. This policy has complex implications for the Chinese, as Jonathan Unger has noted:

> Under Deng many Chinese have had to come to terms with a world economy in which China is merely the largest under-developed country, far outstripped by its economically sophisticated East Asian neighbours. In this circumstance, feelings of national pride and national identity are being built in diverse ways. Chinese nationalism today seems like Joseph's biblical coat of many colours. It does not consist of a single cloth, a single comprehended sentiment. Rather, it comprises an inter-stitching of state-inculcated patriotic political appeals, Han ethnic identification, and culturalist pride; a confusion of aspirations for national greatness alongside growing sub-national assertions of regional identity; open-minded optimism and anti-foreign resentment. (1996, xvi–xvii)

These new perceptions arise, however, from an analysis that has given insufficient attention to the interpenetration of national and global processes in the reconstruction of China's national and cultural identity. The global and local are both crucial in explaining what Unger sees in the expressions of Chinese nationalism today, namely, the "scenarios that seem diametrically at odds with each other" and the "contrasting trends" that seem to be "simultaneously in progress" (xvii). One of these "contrasting trends," and a source of major contradiction in China today, is the conjunction of globalism and nationalism.

Inquiries into the economy's role in reformulating national identity tell us little of how identities are actually reworked through the interplay of global and local forces.[5] Similarly, culture and cultural production are interpreted within national territories that are presumed to be discrete. Thus, the "national culture" implied in Lanxin Xiang's (1993) proposed remedy for national integration appears to be something coherent, stable, and pure that defies time and infiltration; yet the reality is that the work of making national culture goes on not within in a pure national sphere but in a local/global nexus that extends both well above and well below the nation. For instance, the popular teleserials already mentioned, which some observers have depicted as expressions of nationalism and the search for a national identity, are not merely that but are outcomes of *local* structural and textual incorporations of *global* commercial culture. To make sense of them, we must delineate how the transborder cultural flows enabled by modern technology and other channels of communication multiply contacts with other cultures, broaden the possibility of reinvention, and intensify hybridization; at the same time, we need to grasp how capital accumulation at both the global and local levels restructures the symbolic sphere, alters modes of cultural production, and influences strategies of narration.

The intertwining of globalization and localization produces complex trajectories and unique consequences, particularly in the symbolic realm, as James Watson (1992, 80) has noted of the Democracy Movement. But the experience of the Democracy Movement also testifies to the ambivalent effects of globalization. Global cultural flows threaten to deauthenticize local expressions, but they can also offer new means of political struggle. Culture's capacity for reinvention thus further poses a challenge to the scholarship on nationalism to the extent that it has failed to acknowledge national culture's global dimensions.

(Re)Positioning the Chinese Self on the Globe

Chinese tactics of nation-building in the 1990s have juxtaposed the embrace of globalism with measures to consolidate local sociocultural integrity through the promotion of patriotism, national pride, and "Asian values." The propaganda of globalization and marketization is thus intermeshed with the propaganda of patriotism and nationalism. Central China Television (CCTV) plays a key role in this ongoing operation through prime time entertainment programs that systematically feed students with "patriotic films," recycling Maoist nationalist rhetoric while nonetheless encouraging a globalist outlook. Cultural traditions, reinvented for domestic and foreign tourist consumption, are amplified as essential components of national identity.

Though divided over the commodification of cultural production, cultural elites generally share this schizophrenia and are anxious to participate in the global cultural economy while trying to protect local cultural space. The desire to modernize China on models based largely on Euro-American modernity runs against memories of Western imperialism and antipathy toward current Western (especially American) domination. We can find this disjuncture in the discourse of the so-called neonationalism that has gained popularity particularly among a younger generation of intellectuals and urban youth since the mid-1990s, which champions "national interests" while accepting "globalism" (*shijiezhuyi*) as a fundamental Chinese principle (e.g., Qing 1996). Even though it may reject Western political and economic models, it asserts China's right to "development" on the basis of a discourse of universal progress derived from capitalist modernity.

China in globalization not only bears the imprint of post-Fordism, with its ideology of consumerism and global mass culture, but is producing a transnational elite class of professionals moving about the world according to the tempo of global economic operation (Masao 1996) and capitalists who accumulate flexibly through local connections (Hall 1991; Ong 1993; Sklair 1994). The Chinese segment of this transnational elite class may be less mobile physically and less influential in global affairs than their counterparts in Asian capitalist societies, but they maneuver well beyond the national territory. In an emotional discussion of globalization and nationalism, Han Shaogong (1995, 91) vividly sketches this particular group as

> consumers of brand names, and border-crossers well-informed of commodity and financial transactions. Their cellular phones chase the exchange rate of American dollars, Japan's financial situation, the progress of the Gulf War, Brazilian weather forecasts, Poland's employment rate, and the controversy that occurred half an hour before the G-7 Summit, so that they can decide the direction of their investments. The great Chinese leader's call of "encompassing the world" many years ago is materialized on computer screens today.

The delocalization of the "nation" in the hearts and minds of this emerging class identifies them as one strand of what I call postnationalism—the fluid space of contingency and changeability in which the postnational subject is less bound by ideological and sentimental factors and less influenced by history than by the current materiality of international economic competition. Han comments on this mutability:

> While some Westerners greet the transnational Chinese class as close friends, these Chinese may disappoint them most. They are no longer the sentimental university students of yesterday, dreaming about foreign, exotic places through a few imported Western films. Their increasing wealth has more impact on their logic and attitude, and hence xenophilia can turn into xenophobia overnight. If they are exporting shoes, they

would naturally hate economic blockages imposed by the West. If they plan to set up business in Tibet or Hong Kong, they would of course pay great attention to Western advocacies of Tibet or Hong Kong independence. This is why "anti-Japanese" or "anti-American" sentiments surface from time to time in their salons. (1995, 91)

Their local consciousness of global space is anchored in values that are primarily those of global capitalism. Beneath the contingency and changeability, the constant factor that determines their sense of nationality, as Han suggests, is capital accumulation within and beyond national borders. This intermeshing of flexibility and essentialism is one of the impulses that enliven contemporary postnationalism. The strategic position taken by the state and elite groups suggests that national autonomy, unity, and identity may still remain major concerns, but their achievement is seen as depending upon how the nation-state maneuvers in the jungle of global politics and economic competition among nation-states and regional economic zones. In other words, to reproduce oneself nationally, one must act globally. Accordingly, the postnational condition is essentially schizophrenic: the fissure between the promotion of globalization and the effort to manufacture national cohesion runs through its inherent structure.

Operating within the local/global nexus, Chinese postnationalist thinking today has retained the China-West axis that has long underlain its formation. Historical memories of Western imperialism remain a major structural feature with which the "neonationalists" make sense of the contemporary world and magnify their appeal to nationalist sentiments. The state, too, continues to vacillate between the promotion of globalization and an emotional invocation of Western invasion, all the while encouraging a revisionist historical inquiry that subdues critiques of imperialism and capitalism (Dirlik 1996b). Current discussions of modernization continue to rearticulate East-West as an ambivalent relationship in the 1990s:

> The coerced dialogue between the West and China gave both parties a double identity: the imperialist West was both China's enemy and educator (*xiansheng*); China was both the West's victim and student. Neither those who emphasized enlightenment nor those who favored national salvation could escape the sorrow brought by this ambivalence. (Kong 1995, 114)

If this ambivalence is a key "structure of feelings" in modern Chinese consciousness, it is materialized in Chinese praxis. Indeed, Chinese nationalisms are often *differentially* anti-Western, as their nation-building has involved a selective borrowing and incorporating of foreign ideas and devices. Typical examples are Wei Yuan's well-known slogan in the nineteenth century to "learn from the barbarians to defeat the barbarians" and the advocacy of cultural hybridization in the May Fourth debate over culture. So, too, China's five-year economic plans before the Cultural Revolution were split between an ideology of anti-imperialism/capitalism and economic programs inspired by Western industrialization and the Enlightenment discourse of progress. Nor is post-Mao China's modernization project more self-coherent. Comparison with the advanced West has somehow dismantled the "Maoist world view that gave China a vision and sense of self-worth," as Barmé observes. What has replaced it is a worldview partially rooted in Western ideological discourses: "a crude pre–World War I positivism, a faith in science, material wealth, capitalism, and national strength" combined with a heady shot of West bashing (1994, 274).

With history in mind, I wish to argue that the postnational condition has not emerged only in the present fin de siècle. The embryonic stage of Chinese postnationalism can be dated back to the turn of the century, when China lost territorial, political, economic, and cultural integrity in an earlier phase of capitalist global expansion. This loss of integrity repositioned China for a nation-building project pursued under conditions of capitalism, modernity, and European imperialism that were nationalist and postnationalist at the same time.[6]

Historical Time and Global Space

In his recent book on the "paradigmatic modern Chinese intellectual" Liang Qichao, Xiaobing Tang interprets Liang's historical and nationalist thinking against the background of a global space reconfigured by modernity. Tang builds his analysis using the concept of spatiality "or a given mode of determining spatial organization and relationships" (1996, 6). This analytical focus derives from a larger inquiry that interrogates historical encounters between Europe and its objects of conquest. European conquests and the discourses attached to it asserted Europe's subject-agent position by drawing other societies within the orbit of a new global history. The encounter accorded time with "the qualities of a dynamic, purposeful, and assertive self/subject, whereas space gradually coalesces into a perfect symbol for that which emerges as an opaque, intransigent, and eventually threatening other/object" (225–26). The modernist subordination of space to time established a new temporal order that compressed and hierarchized world space through a universal, historicist time. This hierarchization was played out concretely through orientalism. As Edward Said has shown, the entire body of knowledge about Europe's Other grew out of a relationship of power between two temporalized spatialities: the modern, progressive Occident and the static, exotic Orient. Within this construct, "historicity meant that one human history uniting humanity either culminated in or was observed from the vantage point of Europe, or the West" (cited in Tang 1996, 231). What is significant to the understanding of nationalism in European-colonized spaces is that nationalist discourse is compelled to subscribe to this new ordering of world history and space in its attempt to construct a modern nation-state congruous with the order of modernity. Tang concludes that "the fundamental nationalist historiographical operation is therefore to systematically translate a reinforced spatial particularity into a temporal causality. Here arises a persistent contradiction in nationalist ideology" (232–33).

The new ideology of a universal time came to Liang Qichao with an acute awareness of the worldwide spatial reconfiguration through the institutions of imperialism and colonialism. As Liang put it, China was being thrown onto the "great stage" of world history. The image of the world as one great stage, Tang argues, was a metaphor for the modernist belief that human history had arrived at a new horizon of purposeful and representable totality. Such a special configuration demanded that previous concepts and practices of the self as well as of the community be readjusted in terms of a new scenario of intelligibility and a new field of relations and significance. Not only was the modern "period of transition" an immense stage for national heroes of all sorts, but China as a nation also had to project its own identity and image onto this great spectacle of world space (1996, 27).

This is where Liang Qichao's blueprint for nation-building acquires its postnational character, for he was compelled to shift his vision from a nation based on time (rooted in traditions and history) to a nation based on space (in a world constituted by modern nation-states). Encountering modernity meant coming to terms "with the new global space as an inescapable modern condition" under which "the spatiotemporal horizon of human experience was to be reorganized around the modern nation-state" (13).

By focusing on modernity as a historical event of global scope, Tang avoids the trap of conventional dichotomies through which Chinese nationalism and the process of nation-building are explained. His account asserts the subjectivity of Liang Qichao and the Chinese critical rethinking of modernity as a result of a close engagement with global issues. The Chinese critique of European modernity and the reassessment of the native tradition in the 1920s are thereby seen as having arisen out of a desire to create a "new cultural system of global significance" that would reinvent modernity. Though Liang's proposal for "a new cultural system" clearly rested upon a synthesis of "our [Chinese] civilization" and "Western civilization," his globalist vision understood modernity as a "productive resumption of tradition." Likewise, "affirmation of native culture" had to "go beyond pride in the nation's past to a different vision of history." This, in Tang's view, signifies "a postnationalist cultural politics that questions the world system of nation-states" (1996, 234).

Although Tang has simplified and "romanticized" the scholar, his use of the term *postnationalism* is relevant to my argument. As indicated earlier, I hesitate to do away completely with binaries such as China and West, East and West, and socialism and capitalism. They have served important cognitive functions and are rooted in the material, historical conditions of China's having "experienced the globalization of history and its motive force, capitalism, not as an internal development but as alien hegemony" (Dirlik 1997c, 70). This differential experience of modernity is crucial for understanding China's subsequent embrace of socialism; so, too, for grasping the character of Chinese nationalism. Third World nationalism, as a direct response to an alien hegemony, seeks to counteract the latter through binary opposition. The dichotomies of nationalist thought thus function as devices of predictable differentiation engendering communities, formulating subjectivity, and objectifying outsiders.

The logic of polarity that has animated anticolonial nationalism in Asia has divided the world of social institutions and practices into two domains, as Partha Chatterjee has argued. The "inner" domain of the spiritual bears the "essential marks of cultural identity" in order to preserve "the distinctiveness of one's spiritual culture." By contrast, the "outside" realm of the material is the domain of "the economy and of statecraft, of science and technology, a domain where the West had proved its superiority and the East had succumbed. In this domain, then, Western superiority had to be acknowledged and its accomplishments carefully studied and replicated" (1993, 6). The essentialist style of thought that arises from this logic strips both the "indigenous" and the "Western" of their complexities, treating them as fixities. Its schizophrenic division of space into two domains can be creative in inspiring the urge to syncretize. But terms such as *imitation* or *replication* cannot adequately capture the complex acts of cultural translation between "inner" and "outside"—the interweave of West and East—that have been going on in the operation of modernity and global capitalism. Under this condition, nationalist assertions invariably bear a postnationalist character inasmuch as the search for a coherent, autonomous, and authentic nation is built upon incoherent, relational, and hybrid articulations.

China manifests this irony. Its nation-building began at a time of increasing globalization, which allowed the West to be constitutive of its self-construction as a modern nation-state. Ongoing negotiations with technologically more powerful modern nation-states thus permeated the search for answers to the "national question." A modern Chinese nation could no longer be expected to rest solely upon local formations; it must be constructed according to existing models elsewhere or through a syncretization of indigenous and foreign elements. China's national salvation could claim to be "nationalist" in its objective, but in its approach and execution it was postnationalist in the sense that the "nation" it created could no longer be the nation that nationalists desired, for the crises and needs being handled locally had been globally imposed. Thus, at the moment when Chinese nationalism was born, it immediately acquired a postnational character. This does not signify so much an impending temporal moment as a spatial reorganization of the world and a recomposition of its cultural systems. By this way of thinking, nationalism and postnationalism are better understood as parallel modes of existence in a locale traversed by global forces than as phenomena that belong to different time zones in a linear progression of history.

Mao's revolution brought to China a brief moment of coherence, but China was not able to avoid facing again the disjunction between a homogeneous and progressive time and a local space that the Chinese themselves perceived as static and backward. The failure of Maoist socialism to adapt effectively to accelerating globalization reinscribed on the modernization project two ambiguities: psychologically, an ambivalent attitude toward the Chinese self and the Western Other; and strategically, an uneasy conjunction between nation-building and globalization. These ambiguities have produced a disunified ideological sphere, but they have also given birth to a richly nuanced cultural sphere. In the following section, I shall discuss postnational manifestations in the cultural arena during the 1980s. I seek to demonstrate that the outcomes of Sino-Western encounters have always been overdetermined, but that we must recognize that local needs and conditions have a decisive impact on what is learned, replicated, and borrowed through this encounter. Western knowledge may never have supplanted Chinese knowledge, or even have been understood in more than a superficial way (Li Zehuo 1987; Tu 1991; Leo Lee 1991a), but to absorb it on its own terms may be to expect the wrong outcome. What is revealed in the cultural reinvention of the 1980s is a more genuinely syncretic process in which active appropriations of Western cultural discourses went hand in hand with the reuse of local cultural elements. Identities were simultaneously created and eroded in the dynamic processes of national cultural reinvention and globalization. They became what Paul Gilroy (1993) calls, in his writing on black cultural discourses, nonidentities.

Intertextures of Cultures

Chinese critics today speak candidly of Western influences on what are labeled the "new," "modernist," or "contemporary" literary or artistic works produced in the 1980s.[7] The decade of the 1980s witnessed the search for new conceptions of life worlds and new forms of representation in an effort to debase the authorized doctrine of representation. Once the door to the outside world was open again, global cultural flows facilitated new forms of expression and perspective that numerous state campaigns against "bourgeois liberalization" failed to eliminate. Form, viewed by Bakhtin as active in any structure as a specific aspect of a "message," was fully utilized to evolve alternate conceptions of the Chinese world (Promorska 1968, viii). Modernist experiments were therefore full of political innuendo; they affronted the confines of official canons and conventional cultural taste. More significantly, as in the early days of Sino-Western cultural interaction, learning from the West was seen as an indispensable means to national and cultural rejuvenation. The 1980s, then, resuscitated the very ambivalence that originated from the national crisis. That ambivalence has produced results that resist conventional categories such as "Westernization," "national culture," and "Chinese identity."

It is well known that borrowing from the West enabled the development of cultural discourses in the 1980s. The Chinese avant-garde theater owed its birth in part to the Theater of the Absurd (Tay 1990). So did rock music, which built upon a borrowed repertoire of Western rock and roll (including its bodily representations), although its lyrics drew upon local sentiments and the experience of alienation.[8] Visual artists searched through Western art history of the past hundred years and worked through the techniques and concepts of impressionism, fauvism, cubism, surrealism, dadaism, abstract expressionism, and pop art.[9] A "foreign consciousness" had already appeared in the film industry around the year 1980 in the "splurge of fancy techniques" used by Chinese filmmakers, "as if the film makers were determined to catch up with the technical progress of the West and to show the outside world that the Chinese are capable of performing all the advanced tricks with the camera" (Leo Lee 1991b, 16). A younger generation of filmmakers broke through the cinematic conventions of "socialist realism" by learning from European films and film theory, creating the "new cinema" that radically transformed cinematic language by uncovering the suppressed energy, potency, and spontaneity in the culture of everyday life and offering deviant representations of Chinese realities through formal novelties.[10]

Signs of "Westernization" naturally touched a nerve with orthodox nationalists. The literary and art works characterized by Western-influenced conceptualization and formalist innovations were criticized as lacking "native character" and reflecting no Chinese realities. These discursive contestations and disputes are usually seen in terms of internal struggles carried out in local political terms (e.g., "socialist art" versus "bourgeois tendencies"—a synonym for "modernism"). If we view them in relation to China's historical trajectory of nation-building in a global context, however, they can be seen as manifestations of Chinese postnationalism in the first decade of post-Mao era. The disputes contained the particular cultural resonances of their era, but they carried on the tension between turning West and maintaining "Chineseness" and so embodied the very dilemma of internationalizing while nation-building.

Critics passionately voiced their concerns about national cultural identity in the 1980s but failed to recognize "Chinese cultural identity" as an ongoing reformation that historically has involved absorbing foreign influences. Not only were the avant-garde artists whom they accused of being "Westernizers" no less patriotic than the self-righteous nationalists, but they tried to strike a "competitive balance" with their Western counterparts even as they courted Western ideas and forms (Li Xianting 1993, xvii).[11] The West was a means of achieving a long-cherished collective end: a renewed "Chinese" culture through which the Chinese could carry on a dialogue with Westerners on equal terms. That equality is understood as the best guarantee of China's national power and sovereignty, to say nothing of the artists' own identity in the international art world.

The critics' fear of "total Westernization" is equally unjustified. Wavering between the national and global/Western, the postnationalist cultural project allows negotiation between local agency and conditions and foreign discourses according to local needs. The outcomes of the negotiation can be rather intriguing because they often produce the unintended consequence of localizing Western cultural forms. Indeed, modernist movements in the 1980s bore the imprints of local conditions. Borrowing was selective, and the utilization of borrowed forms was determined by the particular historical juncture, the artists' subjectivity, and the issues with which he or she sought to deal.[12] As Leo Lee points out, "modernism" in literary terms is not "a brand of high modernism in the Western sense" but rather a "modern manifestation of Chinese sensibility." It grew out of some writers' demands for "a new, subjective way of comprehending and delineating reality" (as opposed to the "objectivism and naturalism" of realism)[13] and "a deep-seated frustration of the self in its dealings with the external world, a world so defined and enveloped by the Party's zigzagging shifts of ideology." The "modernist" writers did not go so far as to traverse the "journey from 'high modernism' to 'postmodernism,' from symbolism and the avant garde to decadence, parody, and kitsch." Instead, they established their modernist identities largely by renouncing literary conventions and experimenting with novel narrative techniques derived from the West (Lee 1990, 66).

In this light, "sinicization" is complex. Rather than a sheerly passive adoption of foreign ideas and practices, sinicization is mediated by the shaping power of local political, economic, and aesthetic conditions, which yields unexpected results, and by the agency of the actors who are involved in the cultural translations. To take an example from the "new Chinese cinema," *Yellow Earth* established international fame for Chinese films in 1984 but was heavily criticized by authorities at home for being too "modernist" and "Western." Caught up in conventional notions of representation, the authorities lost sight of an important aesthetic redemption of elements of traditional Chinese style in visual representation. As Ni Zhen (1994) observes, *Yellow Earth*, the cinematography of which appeared so "foreign" to Chinese audiences at the time, in fact entails a transformation of the spatial consciousness and compositional theories of classical Chinese painting into a system of imagistic signification that originated in the West.[14] It does so through a negotiation, a dialogic movement more exactly, between forms of representations invented by two different cultures and discourses:

> By means of the coding strategies of *Yellow Earth*'s iconic signification, there is revealed within the frame of the silver screen the redemption or transformation of the connotations of classical painting discourse; and such terms as "emptiness," "nothingness," and "Great Void," which have specific philosophical connotations in horizontal scrolls, are transformed in the material reproduction of the imagistic world into extensions of things in the movie. This tendency in the filmic rhetoric of *Yellow Earth* naturally leads to a break with the forms of iconic signification found in mainstream Chinese movies. Interestingly enough, this new rupture is a result of insight gained through sensitivity derived from a profound understanding and probing of the classical painting tradition. (74–75)

Rather than submitting to Western cultural rhetoric, avant-garde artists carved out a location for forms of resistance against total Westernization. Although they might have been overwhelmed initially by Western forms and ideas, they later managed to turn them around to suit their own needs. "Westernization" was thus a movement from temporary submission to self-reassertion.

The exploration of Western discourses was accompanied by root-searching gestures that recognized the richness of local traditions. Reusing the indigenous, blended with borrowed cultural elements, was a strategy through which artists tried to formulate their own distinctive identity.[15] Though drawing heavily from the West, artists consciously utilized images of local landscape, Chinese ideographs, and philosophical tenets to construct their works. For instance, the dadaists intermeshed Duchampian methods with Daoist and Zen theories, and the "reconstructionists" employed Western artistic concepts to deconstruct Chinese symbols (Li Xianting 1993, xvi). Hybridity, easily recognizable in other areas of the cultural sphere, was a natural result of what was simultaneously Westernizing and home grounding.[16] What underlies it is a now familiar ambivalence: the awareness that self-renewal lies in going beyond the "national" and the anxiety that one may possibly lose one's national self in the journey into the beyond.

In its disregard for cultural and national boundaries, the postnationalist cultural project has obscured the meaning of "Chineseness" and "Chinese culture." Although it enabled cultural rejuvenation, the project had its limits. As in the early period of modernization, cultural borrowing in the 1980s remained dominated by the power structure that nationalism seeks to repudiate. The very fact that Chinese artists and writers saw the West as a primal source of inspiration and foundation for a modern Chinese nation/culture speaks volumes about the centrality of the West in the construction of the modern world and Chinese subscription to the discourse of a universal modernity. An ongoing obsession with progress reproduced the cultural predicament of the early modernizers by unconsciously masculinizing, fetishizing, and homogenizing the West.[17] This structural problematic of Chinese postnationalism is a source of lasting apprehension.[18]

(Post-)China and Global Capitalism

The postnationalist schizophrenia continues in the 1990s, as intellectuals still see, speak about, and construct the self in relation to a Western Other. Much of the talk about culture and modernization still mirrors the premises of the debates at the turn of the century and in the 1980s, and identity remains one of the key issues, as some worry about the increasing Western presence in intellectual discourse. The search for cultural reconciliation, and particularly for theoretical justification, has anchored itself in the New Confucianism and the assertion of an Asian modernity. The national question has become dominated by a new Chinese sense of self-importance and a desire for strength and revenge. Unfulfilled historical ambitions, anxieties about social disintegration, and an ongoing pressure to adapt to new global situations drive the task of reproducing national consciousness. These pressures have given rise to dissonance in the cultural sphere, especially given the cozy alignment between intellectual and state discourses and the rhetoric of global capitalism.

As China has become the most recent (and now heavily colonized) frontier of global capitalism, cultural production in the 1990s has worked to carve out a niche in the globalized field of cultural consumption. The renewed "culture fever" of the mid-1990s has partially been driven by the commercialization of cultural production (Wang Hui 1995) such that culture is now spoken of in terms of "mass culture," "cultural industries," and "a marketplace of culture." Commercialized cultural production curtails the political and cultural significance of cultural borrowing that we find in the hybridized art discourses of the 1980s. Arif Dirlik notes this when he observes that "for all the claims to 'Chineseness,' neither in motivation nor in form is there anything particularly 'Chinese' about the new cultural products, which are recognizable only as very contemporary products, on a local terrain, of a global consumer culture that erases the distinctiveness of the local by commodifying it" (1996b, 195).

While culture in the modes of capitalist cultural production becomes embodied in commercially successful entertainment, it is not completely devoid of political and ideological content, just as the global postmodern culture, as Hall (1991) calls it, is never innocent. The cultural iconoclasm that arose in the May Fourth era and resurfaced in the 1980s lingers and rearticulates itself in popular cultural texts, where the well-known premise about the repressiveness and cognitive limits of cultural tradition is essentialized through the old binary oppositions of the West and China, tradition and modernity, stagnation and vitality, backwardness and progress, and past and future. The teleserials that aim at modernizing national consciousness construct countryside and city through just these sorts of polarities of values. They represent the nation's future as an extravagant and ambitious urban China, formed by postmodern, global cities hosting transnational economic activities and inhabited by a flamboyant transnational bourgeois class with ravishing, cosmopolitan lifestyles. By contrast, rural China and its agrarian economy are repeatedly targeted as enclosures, the causes of backwardness and stagnant mentality. The peasant class is designated as the bearer of the past and the perpetuators of repressive traditions.

The prominent position given to global cities, the global economy, and the transnational class in these "modernization serials" suggests that antitraditionalism in the 1990s is not what it was earlier in the century. It is now little more than an instrument of modernization and a capitalist-oriented globalization. Absent are the powerful critiques and analyses of the failure of Mao-style socialism and its feudalistic heritage of the 1980s, when writers, filmmakers, and visual artists evoked the images of "wall," "well," and "bondage" as metaphors of repression.[19] Equally lacking is an inquiry into the articulation between elements of native traditions and global capitalism under the new circumstances. In fact, cultural iconoclasm has been, for most of this century, unable to go beyond one-dimensional articulation due to its complicity with the discourses of modernization and globalization. Neither the May Fourth Enlightenment nor the popular teleserial *River Elegy,* aired in the late 1980s, offered a critique of the capitalist West. They have inscribed and reinscribed on the collective Chinese imagination the binary oppositions between Western and Chinese cultures and in so doing candidly championed a modernity based on Euro-American experiences.

This complicity with the Western ideal of national modernity may explain an ironic twist in the current coexistence of tradition-bashing popular cultural texts and an uncritical embrace of the New Confucianism. In the 1980s, Xiao Gongqin, who later became known as a key advocate of neo-authoritarianism, a Chinese version of the East Asian model of development, wrote in *The Predicament of Confucian Culture* of China's "failure to meet the challenge" of Western civilization in the Sino-Western encounter of the late Qing period. Xiao's critique of Confucianism is sharp:

> Nineteenth-century Confucianism lacked any mechanism of self-renewal in the face of the Western challenge, and it was unable to accomplish the transition from traditional thinking to modern thinking. As a result, it continued to react against new situations and crises according to its sinocentric psychology and out-of-date mind-set. In other words, when *internationalism* became a reality in the second half of the nineteenth century, the scholar-officials relied upon exclusion as a major strategy of *national* defense. The huge gap between reality and mentality placed Confucian culture in a predicament from which it was unable to free itself. (1986, 3–4; emphasis added)

This kind of historical interpretation contributed in part to the intelligentsia's initial refusal to accept the "East Asian development model" or the New Confucianism espoused by Western and Asian scholars as well as a number of Asian governments. When the Harvard Confucian scholar Tu Wei-ming went to lecture at Beijing University in the early 1980s, many in the audience rejected his ideas, arguing that Tu knew too little about mainland China's situation and was reviving a tradition from which they were still striving to escape.[20]

However, in the 1990s a new promodernization historiography is emerging alongside the state's efforts to recreate ancient myths, as Dirlik (1996b) observes. Responding to the call of global capitalism and Chinese aspirations for partaking in the global economy, this kind of ideology rewrites China as a historically open, cosmopolitan society even at the cost of validating imperialism. Neo-authoritarianism and the New Confucianism, both derivative of the East Asian development model, revalidate traditions in a way that reproduces "orientalism." The presence and popularity of these discourses denote complex motivations. Neo-authoritarianism, which had immediate political utility after the 1989 state crackdown on demonstrators in Beijing, pursues a cultural program that insinuates a reconciliation with tradition: the path to modernization is to be built in part upon a "controlled or selected introduction of Western institutional civilization" and the reuse of traditional values for modernization (Gu and Kelly 1994, 223).[21] More intricate is the case of the New Confucianism. Though problematic, it is potentially antihegemonic "in the assertion of the relevance of Chinese cultural values against an earlier Euro-American denial of their relevance in the modern world" (Dirlik 1996b, 198). In this sense, both discourses are potentially liberating, for they allow the Chinese intelligentsia to mobilize native cultural traditions to resolve their century-old cultural predicament with the West.[22] In the contemporary context of capitalist globalization, however, the belief that modern East Asia constitutes a successful hybrid space where modern Western elements blend unobtrusively with traditional Asian outlooks and practices only affirms the postnationalist orientation of the state and its elites. Confucianism, now remade "as a different culture of capitalism" (197), poses no challenge to global capitalism but complies with Chinese ambitions to become part of it while apparently reaffirming a Chinese civilizational core (Hou 1995; Peng 1995). Educators can now teach the younger generation Chinese cultural traditions and depict them as crucial to modernization rather than its barrier (Gu and Gao 1995; Kong 1995; Zheng 1995).

To make the situation more complicated, some Chinese scholars have launched critiques of the "cultural radicalism" that has cultivated antitraditionalism since the turn of the century (Chen Lai 1993; Gao 1995). The critique of "cultural radicalism," which aims at establishing intellectual sovereignty as the foundation of cultural reconstruction,[23] argues that the New Cultural Movement of the second decade of this century mistakenly treated political problems as problems of culture. Such "misrecognition" has had a profound impact on the Chinese mind throughout the century and is particularly revealed in the politicization of the Cultural Revolution and the 1980s' "culture fever." The "post-enlightenment perspective," as it has been labeled by others (Chen 1994), is partially anchored in New Confucianism, but it cannot be simply dismissed as native orientalism.[24] It is part of the general cognitive shift away from the binarism that has deeply influenced Chinese intellectual perceptions of world relations to a multiplicity that is closely associated with postmodernist thinking without being derivative of Western theory.

Nonetheless, the ongoing acquisition of Western intellectual perspectives seems to perpetuate the same old dilemma: if continual learning from the West is an indispensable condition of nation-building, how far can one go in absorbing such knowledge without losing one's cultural sovereignty? What happens to one's national identity if one's understanding of local (national) situations is filtered through Western intellectual perspectives?[25] This quandary underlies Chen Xiaoming's warning about an emerging "postcolonial culture" in China:

> It is precisely the excessive accent placed on indigenous culture that gives "postcolonial culture" its character. Only those who imagine an opposing West as a listener and desire the latter's recognition emphasize so much the "otherness" of their own culture. We find this in the success of these film directors—the spokesmen of "oriental (Chinese) culture" such as Zhang Yimou and Chen Kaige. Almost all the advocates of the "otherness" of oriental (Chinese) culture have been encouraged by the West. Rather than holding that contemporary China has an indigenous culture that can carry on a dialogue with the West, I think we have a postcolonial culture that is dragged along by the West. (1994, 14–15)[26]

Another scholar describes contemporary Chinese culture as a "moon culture" (*yueguangxing wenhua*), implying that it simply reflects Western tastes. In using Western theories to analyze Chinese cultural phenomena and expressing themselves through Western jargon, China's critics and writers suffer from aphasia and have lost faith in their own culture (Gan 1996).[27]

More vocal in its critique of contemporary intellectual practices is the so-called neonationalism expressed in such popular books as *China Can Say "No"* and *China Can Still Say "No."* This argument criticizes the nihilist attitude that Chinese intellectuals have toward native culture and their submission to the Euro-American imagination. Championing the supremacy of China's national interests, its West and Japan bashing responds to the premise among Western and Japanese conservatives that China is a threat. Its emotional appeal depends in part on the perception of a Western conspiracy to erode China's sovereignty and cohesion and to impede its opportunity to become a superpower. Nationalism, argue the neonationalists, is primarily "a principle of survival." The right to development is a part of human rights. Assigning themselves the role of spokespersons for the Third World, the neonationalists draw on historical and current global situations to enunciate a savage critique of Western imperialism, domination, and centrism (Song et al. 1996a, 1996b).

Upon a closer look, neonationalism is burdened with its own contradictions and dissonance. Its tones of national chauvinism and cultural superiority blend with cries of national victimization by foreign powers. Although antihegemonic in its opposition to a globalization defined by the interests of the developed world and its affirmation of a "third path" to modernity, it is uncritical in its reliance on concepts such as "development" and "progress." Its conception of global equality hardly transcends a dream that allows China to be the winner in global rivalry. Indeed, its national mobilization sounds very familiar: except for its silence about capitalism, in many ways it reevokes the enthusiasm about development found in the Great Leap campaign of the 1950s.

Despite its ultranationalist appeals, neonationalism builds itself, at the conceptual level, upon a postnationalist program that is complicit with many of the discourses reviewed in this essay: the vision of a "greater China"; an alleged globalist outlook;[28] the New Confucianism's implicit acceptance of Samuel Huntington's (1993a) fallacious thesis on the conflict of civilizations; the acceptance of a universal, historicized time; and a commitment to capitalist modernity despite the repetition of terms such as *socialism*. Precisely because of its alignment with New Confucianism and the European Enlightenment discourse of progress, it is impossible for neonationalism to offer any truly antihegemonic resistance—to launch critiques of global capitalism and China's capitalist transformation and, consequently, to offer an alternative model of national modernity other than that of Euro-American and Asian capitalism. With this failure, Chinese (post)nationalism has in effect abandoned its original goals as it battles to locate China more firmly in a global capitalist system. Entering the global time of capitalism, national space evaporates, leaving nothing but sentimental nostalgia.

Conclusion

"Postnationalism" allows us to make better sense of phenomena situated within the global/local nexus than has been possible when we limit our categories to "nationalism" alone. It denotes the simultaneous dilution of the nation-state and the "nation's" visible symbolic importance in the process of globalization. It delineates the conjunctive attempt to globalize and hold onto the "nation" as a means of maintaining self-coherence and captures the interweaving of globalism and nationalism. The "nation" remains significant in postnationalist constructions of self-identity, yet belief in the nation is driven by the knowledge that to reproduce oneself locally (i.e., nationally) one must act globally. The nation survives in the age of globalization only by its reinvention through close integration into global structures. The postnationalist condition is thus schizophrenic: a tension between promoting globalization and manufacturing national cohesion runs through its structure.

The concept of postnationalism highlights the spatiotemporal context that has shaped Chinese approaches to nation-building and cultural reconstruction. It is not an emerging phenomenon of a coming era to follow nationalism but a condition that became possible with the spread of Euro-American modernity. By thrusting China into a new order of space and time, the Sino-Western encounter in the nineteenth century left a lasting ambivalence in both historical and contemporary circumstances. As a result, China's search for a coherent, autonomous, and authentic nation has from the beginning been built upon incoherent, relational, and hybrid articulations and endeavors. It is this disjuncture that accounts for, to repeat Jonathan Unger's words, "scenarios that seem diametrically at odds with each other" and "contrasting trends" that seem to be "simultaneously in progress" (1996, xvii).

The 1980s postnationalist cultural project was fruitful in borrowing from Western cultural discourses to reformulate cultural identities that defy national borders and put into question conventional perceptions of "national culture." In its contemporary form in the 1990s, however, postnationalism appears more as a strategy employed by the state and elite groups for national survival and economic development in an increasingly interdependent world driven by global capitalism. It operates to dissipate the tension between the demands of global capitalist operation and the local need to sustain national and cultural cohesion. In this regard, the Chinese approach is similar to that taken by other states and their elites in Asia, such as Singapore, which juxtapose globalist economic development with the mobilization of patriotism, national pride, and nationalist sentiments.

The disjuncture underlying the postnationalist reconstruction of nation and culture makes postnationalism both a blessing and a curse. In bringing China into the global economy of production and consumption, it has not only perpetuated the old ambivalence toward the Chinese self and the Western Other but it has incited a sense of urgency and a strong feeling of rivalry. In the 1990s, the language of postnationalism is increasingly ordered by the lexicon of global capitalism. Ironically, a cozy alignment among the Chinese intelligentsia, the state, and global capitalism has turned postnationalism into a practical tool to advance China's goal to assume a more powerful position in the world economy.

NOTES

1. See Mani 1989, Clifford 1989, hooks 1994, and Dirlik 1996a for their insights into the politics of knowledge production.

2. Major works on cultural hybridity and transnational and diasporic cultures include Gilroy 1993, Bhabha 1994a, and Mercer 1994.

3. For instance, feminist scrutiny of the relation between "nation" and "women" in Chinese studies seeks to revise "the most basic categories" (constituted by the dichotomies of China versus foreign and modernity versus tradition) through which sinologists have striven to "apprehend Chinese social relations, institutions, and cultural productions." Scholars argue that gender issues have been "crucial to the way Chinese people have defined their modernity" (Gilmartin et al. 1994, 10). To allow gender "a prominent place in historical and cultural change," feminist inquiries have focused on critiquing the masculine construction of "women" in nationalist discourses in both pre-1949 history and Communist China (Barlow 1993a).

4. The "crisis" thesis is also emphasized by Dittmer and Kim (1993, 286–87), who see post-Tiananmen China "faced with an unprecedented national identity crisis" because "the post-Mao system can no longer cope with systemic problems without infringing on or giving up its identity as a socialist state."

5. Gender analysis needs to examine the interplay of global and local forces that has allowed, at this stage, the articulation of both conventional and modern patriarchies. Functioning as the new orthodoxy of the feminist analysis of Chinese women, the women-nation problematic seems incapable of addressing adequately situations at both the supranational and subnational levels.

6. Tang (1996) uses the terms *postnationalist* and *postnationalism* without elucidating them, though usually it is to denote a spatial condition.

7. For instance, art critic Li Xianting (1993, x) states at the beginning of an introduction to contemporary art in China: "The art concepts utilized in this discussion are largely derived from the aesthetic and conceptual language of twentieth century Western modernism. This acknowledges the fact that the language of modernism has become the international language of art. To a large degree, this reality has dictated the development of modern Chinese art."

8. Personal communication from a visiting Chinese musician, Toronto, 1994. For more information about popular music in post-Mao China, see Jones 1992. His overly political analysis rests upon a simple dichotomy of state control versus popular resistance, neglecting questions concerning music production and cultural borrowing in the context of capitalist transformation and globalization.

9. See writings by Li Xianting (1993) for a discussion of the aesthetic transitions of Chinese contemporary art.

10. Yuejin Wang (1991, 80) evaluates the film *Red Sorghum* as "strikingly rough, forthright, rugged, bold and unrestrained both stylistically and morally to Chinese tastes." It is "a shocking affront to many cherished and received formulas of Chinese cultural praxis; to the deep-rooted Confucian ethical and moral codes of sobriety and decorum; to the ingrained artistic codes favoring strategies of concealment and

restraint; and to the aesthetic taste which prioritizes emotional delicacy and refinement." Rayns (1991) notices the element of ambiguity, new narrative structures, and minimalist dialogues that allow images to carry the burden of constructing meaning. See also Ma Ning 1987.

11. These are Gu Wenda's words. Gu, one of the best-known Chinese artists living abroad, is very conscious of his predicament. The ritualistic atmosphere of his works is a strategy of constructing identity. Other artists whom I have interviewed also maintain such a stance.

12. Local conditions have had a great impact on what is introduced into China. Bertolt Brecht's *Life of Galileo,* Samuel Beckett's *Waiting for Godot,* and Arthur Miller's *The Crucible* were among the first Western plays staged in China in the early 1980s, as this was a time when the Chinese were reflecting upon the absurdity of the Cultural Revolution. The introduction of realism into the visual arts early in the twentieth century was also timed to circumstances in China, for socially committed artists abandoned the tradition of Chinese literati painting in favor of Western realism because of its sense of direct engagement with the world. They hoped that the West's "active" (*dong*) cultural spirit would save and revitalize the "passive" (*jing*) Chinese culture. This movement went against emerging trends in the Western art world, where modernism was moving toward the "possibilities of colour, brushwork, and pure form as a direct expression of the emotions"—ironically, characteristics shared by older literati styles (Li Xianting 1993, vi–xi). For more examples of cultural translation, see Chen's (1991) study of the *menglong* movement and Tang's (1991) discussion of postmodernism in China.

13. The writer Dai Houyin, cited in Lee 1990, 65.

14. Chinese filmmakers who have long worked in that medium have used a variety of strategies to sinicize it and to deal with the "apparent contradictions" underlying the traditional Chinese aesthetic system and the "technical medium of expression" of Western modes of cinematography (Wilkerson 1994, 40–42). Sinicization has often entailed drawing from the aesthetic conventions of Chinese poetry and painting. See, for instance, Woo's (1991) writing on the peculiar features of "Chinese montage"; see also the articles in Ehrlich and Desser 1994.

15. The artistic exploration of native idioms was part of the modernist movement in the 1980s: "native soil painting" appeared in the early 1980s, and the "Back to the Roots" and the "Purified Language" movements emerged around 1987. The former applied elements of Daoist and Zen philosophy, Eastern mysticism, and Chinese literati "ink play" to counter the Western orientation of the "85 New Wave" movement, which sought to discover and transform traditional cultural symbols (Li 1993, xviii–xix; Liu 1994, 56).

16. See Golden and Minford 1990 on the poet Yang Liang; Tay 1990 on avant-garde theater; and Mittler 1994 on contemporary Chinese music. A popular musical genre of the mid-1980s called "Northwest Wind" fused the folk songs of northwestern China with disco and rock rhythms (personal communication from a Chinese musician, Toronto, 1995).

17. By masculinizing the West, I refer to the perceptions of the West as representing the future and advancement, attributes similar to those associated with *yang* in ancient Chinese cosmology—strength, power, and action.

18. Being part of the global world also means submitting oneself to the mercy of Western validation. Trying to become "modern" on Western models entails paying a price. It subjects local practices to the evaluation of the West according to Western standards. In the 1980s, Chinese visual artists often found that they had to defend themselves on the matter of "identity"; their subjectivity and the local and historical materiality that sustained their work were commonly ignored by the West (personal communications from artists and critics from China, Toronto, 1993–94). Critics also see the internationalization of the "new Chinese cinema" as entailing the production of the "Oriental's orientalism," for example, the self-exoticization of filmmakers such as Cheng Kaige and Zhang Yimou (Li 1996; Chow 1995a).

19. The so-called bondage art that appeared in the mid-1980s featured human bodies tied with cloth and plastic tape (Li Xianting 1993, xviii).

20. Personal communication from a friend who was present at Tu's lectures, 1994.

21. Rosen and Zou (1991) trace neo-authoritarianism back to 1986. Gu and Kelly (1994) date it to 1988, especially to Xiao Gongqin. Neo-authoritarianism was a hot topic in academic circles between January and May of 1989. It returned as neoconservatism in 1991 with support from both the "princes' clique" and the CCP elders, for whom it offered "strategic options" that would allow them to maintain central administrative control in a rapidly changing world, particularly after the dismantling of the former Soviet Union. Chinese debates over neo-authoritarianism are surveyed in the 1990–91 winter issue of *Chinese Sociology and Anthropology*.

22. Not all intellectuals have embraced New Confucianism. See Liu Dong's (1993) and Liu Sanfu's (1995) arguments against it and the East Asian development model more generally.

23. Beijing University professor of philosophy Chen Lai argues that Chinese intellectuals repeatedly make the mistake of taking a utilitarian attitude toward scholarship as a means of achieving political ends. Chen's notion of an "autonomous cultural analysis" comes close to Fang Lizhi's idea of the "independence of knowledge." See Chow 1993, 73–90, on Fang Lizhi's call to separate politics from academic work.

24. The term *post-enlightenment perspective* is used by Chen Xiaomin (1994) in his response to Chen Lai's (1993) article.

25. In addition to an acceptance of New Confucianism, there is considerable interest in contemporary Western cultural theory. Some argue that postmodernism and postcolonial theories "have great analytical power when used to interpret contemporary Chinese literature and culture" (Zhang Yinwu 1995, 113).

26. The author of this passage, Chen Xiaoming, describes postcolonial theory and political correctness as examples of "a new and more perplexing Western cultural hegemony produced by an anti-Western cultural hegemony" (1994, 13). Paradoxically, his postcolonial critique of postcolonial theory as Western in origin is decorated with Western theoretical jargon. Chen is of a generation of younger scholars heavily influenced by contemporary Western theories.

27. Critiques of Chinese borrowing of Western theories have contributed little to our understanding of the problems of theoretical transplantation, since the possible deprivation of Western theories of their social and historical specificity and the potential gaps between Western theory and Chinese realities are not the critics' concerns. So far,

inquiries into Chinese transplantation of Western theories have focused on how local conditions circumscribe the reception of Western theory. Questions remain unasked about which specific theories have traveled to China, which local mechanisms of selection and exclusion are in operation, and what produces such mechanisms.

28. The authors declare that neonationalism is "firmly against blind xenophobia and self-enclosure that derive from nationalism. This should be the core feature of Chinese neo-nationalism at the end of the twentieth century" (Song et al. 1996b, 286).

Nation and Postnation in Japan: Global Capitalism and the Idea of National History

Thomas Keirstead

Border Crossings

We seem to be of two minds about nations and their boundaries. On the one hand, they are wonderful things to go beyond. The thought of interactions that are not bound by the nation-state—indeed, that make a mockery of those boundaries—is enticing, whether it be the frisson of smuggling or the seductions of cyberspace. On the other hand, the nation seems a terrible thing to be without. We know from Bosnia, the former Soviet Union, and countless other examples that, however problematic nations may be, when they fail they may release even greater horrors. Likewise, the fervent hope of many a stateless person is to be become a person with a state; the refugee driven from one nation often seeks nothing so much as entry into another.

On the one hand, we recognize nations and their borders as flimsy, paltry things, dependent on some imagined affiliation that can be affirmed or denied seemingly at will by refusing, for example, to speak a certain language or by not paying taxes or simply by declaring or imagining oneself otherwise. Yet, again, boundaries are things that many people would like to invest with real, material presence. In California, a steel wall, barbed-wire fences, and ditches, put there with overwhelming popular support, guard the realm. In Arizona, apparently, there's talk of a magic wall of dust that will tag illegal border crossers with a fluorescent powder, and some civic-minded citizens near Tucson drive into the desert every night to make the border something that, literally, everyone can see: a shield formed by the beams of automobile headlights.

Of course, these same people who give over their nights to erecting a light barrier that lends a visible presence to an otherwise invisible line in the desert are likely to regard international trade as a good thing. They may well think that the technology that has given us the information superhighway is marvelous and liberating, that the wave of the future is a worldwide web of communications that can beam five hundred channels of information even into a truck on a lonely vigil in the desert. In revealing these paradoxes, however, we have not caught this "believer in borders" out in a lie. Throughout the history of capital there has been no great contradiction between capital's international character as an object that necessarily flows, for example, from England to India to China and back again (and has the further boundary-defying capacity to change its form at each stage) and the nation-state. They have worked, and continue to work, hand in hand. Indeed as Thongchai Winichakul (1994) demonstrates in his fascinating study of the development of geographical knowledge in Thailand, the spread of capital, in the form of colonial and quasi-colonial exploitation, demanded the demarcation of national borders. The same, I suspect, is true of capital's new and seemingly more quixotic and elusive progeny: information.

For that reason, I am suspicious of claims that the mode of information (to borrow Mark Poster's term) will set us free, that its shifting, ephemeral, and global nature will mean the end of nations, subjects, genders, and all the other things that bind us. I find that there is a troubling coincidence between the rhetoric of certain prominent strains of theory and the rhetoric of capital: between, on the one hand, the contested, transgressed, multiple, deessentialized, and irrevocably split subject/nation heralded in much of contemporary theory and, on the other, the reveries about the contemporary state of capital to be found in any business fanzine. Capital (information), in fact, seems to be the exemplary poststructuralist subject. Flowing from Zurich to Hong Kong, New York, Tokyo, and Bombay, continuously de- and reterritorialized, capital transgresses boundaries, changes identities, and, given the number of physicists employed by investment banks, exists, if it can be said to exist at all, only as some sort of probabilistic haze. Arguably, the most able practitioners of the kinds of transgressions recommended by theory are the multinational corporations, their managers and gurus. These are the people who, to quote from a recent article in the journal *Public Culture*, "hold out the promise of dramatic liberation—the translation of local knowledges into the single currency of information, universal access to this information for everyone at every moment and, as a result, the ultimate collapse of long-existing barriers based on difference, distance and delay" (Rouse 1995, 353). Yet, despite the rhetoric, these visions of a borderless future are persistently articulated in terms of national or corporate advantage, of America's (say) winning the information revolution.

This suggests to me that it is time to move beyond "subject work," Rey Chow's (1998) term for an area of inquiry that has too long monopolized the attention of cultural studies, namely, the split subject. Subject work has, of course, performed invaluable service by revealing the fissures and contradictions inherent in entities like subjects and nations and by stressing that identities are always multiple and constructed and therefore open to transgression. Valuable though it has been, this work needs to be supplemented with renewed attention to these entities as structures that despite their manifest contradictions govern our behavior and our being. The nation may be an imagined community, but that does not mean that it can easily be imagined away. Similarly, the mere fact of going beyond national boundaries does not mean that we have put them behind us.

In fact, all sorts of things already regularly go beyond national borders: not only goods and capital but a steady stream of immigrants and migrants whose labor is indispensable to the production and circulation of those goods. We should have no need, then, to marvel at the nation's permeability, and we should be wary of any discourse that finds in this fact the harbinger of a new age. What we do need to understand is how the changing nature of capital/information works with ideas of nation and self. We need to consider what kinds of collectivity are possible within the current conjuncture, and we need to consider what resources exist to create them. The pressing issue for me is how we might move from the project of revealing the multiple, split, unstable nature of all identities to "conceptualizing the concrete collectivities through which people act in spheres of politics and culture" (Rouse 1995, 354). What kinds of structures are possible in a poststructuralist world? Or, more specifically, what place is the nation-state to occupy in a world without borders?

Japan and the Rhetoric of Postnationalism

For many commentators, answering this question means divining the fault lines of future global competition. As the ideological certainties of the Cold War fade, and as the rise (especially) of Asia calls Western supremacy into question, concern with how the world will sort itself out in the near future has become almost a fixation. With seemingly millennial urgency, politicians, economists, and pundits of all persuasions have proclaimed the advent of a variety of new world orders. Central to this debate is speculation about the changing nature of the nation-state.

In Japan, fretting about the state of the nation is big business. *Nihonjinron,* or "theories of Japaneseness," is an established genre, accorded its own section in large bookstores. According to Harumi Befu (1993), more than two hundred books of *nihonjinron* were published between the late 1980s and 1992 in addition to countless articles and a number of journals devoted exclusively to the subject. During this period, two issues in particular drove the debate: the question of rice imports, which was brought to a conclusion (of a sort) when Japan agreed to a gradual opening of its rice market in 1993, and the ongoing debate over immigration. In each instance, questions about Japan's involvement in the global economy promoted agonizing over Japan's national identity.

With regard to rice, the Japanese government, with clear popular support, for years resisted pressure from the United States and the European Community to open up its protected agricultural markets; leaders of the Liberal Democratic Party, in particular, had long vowed that not one grain of foreign rice would be admitted to Japan. Japan's reluctance to open its rice markets stands in marked contrast to its overall policy regarding foodstuffs. As Gavan McCormack (1996, 122–23) shows, Japan, bucking the trend of other net food importers like Great Britain, has seen its dependence on imported foods increase steadily over the last thirty years. At present, no amount of self-sufficiency in rice production could hope to offset Japan's reliance on food imports, the total value of which in 1991 surpassed the value of the oil Japan imported. Thus, opponents of rice liberalization, while they persistently raised the specter of a Japan unable to feed itself, also invoked other, more metaphysical kinds of fears: of a people whose sense of identity would be undermined should the rice trade be opened to foreign competition, of a nation that stood to lose its soul. Even advocates of opening the rice market heralded the prospect with hyperbolic claims about the effects such a move would have:

> If Japan . . . were to lift the "rice curtain" by ending protection of its domestic rice market, Asia would be taking its most decisive step in the direction of global leadership. . . . To internationalize this sacred staple would not only internationalize the mythic essence of Japan, it would also revolutionize political culture, which has been founded for the last forty years on rice protectionism. (Funabashi 1991, 21)

Exactly what it might mean to "internationalize the mythic essence of Japan" is not at all clear; what is certain is that the consequences of importing rice would somehow be enormous—and more political and psychological than economic.

Illegal immigration raises similar questions. Like the import of rice, the problem arises in the first instance from Japan's position in the global economy. Since the mid-1980s, large numbers of South and Southeast Asians as well as

Chinese men and women have come to Japan seeking employment, mostly in the construction trade. As the numbers have risen (as of 1992, there were an estimated 500,000 foreign workers in Japan, half or more of them illegal), immigration has emerged as a bona fide social problem (Field 1993, 662; Ozawa 1993, 144). And, while official Japan has for more than a decade preached the doctrine of internationalization (*kokusaika*), the term clearly was not intended to encompass this influx of Asians. Though pragmatists argue that Japan ought to create a guest worker system to handle the problem and take care of Japanese industry's need for cheap labor, no one seems to favor more than a short-term, carefully controlled dalliance with these foreigners (e.g., Ozawa 1993, 146–47). There is no sign, for example, that the Japanese Nationality Act will be amended to allow for easier legal immigration, and popular engagement with the Asian side of internationalization seems limited to an interest in Thai, Korean, and Vietnamese food. Far more often, Asian immigration raises fears of violence and crime, of a carefully ordered society torn apart by people who don't know the language or how to act. For instance, Ishihara Shintarō, while arguing for a more liberal immigration policy, nonetheless feels the need to mention that immigrants may well "bring violence into our safe and peaceful Japanese society" (1990, 94). Likewise, he wonders whether these other Asians might not end up forming their own exclusive communities—"like the Turks do in Germany" (96)—and asks "what would we do if they marry Japanese [women]? We can't very well send the whole family packing" (97).

Behind these worries rest fears of Balkanization and mongrelization, of a nation no longer homogeneous and for that reason no longer cohesive. The debate about immigration in Japan invokes, albeit in an obviously hysterical form, the same threats to the nation-state that Michael Walzer described as the "new tribalism" breaking out "all over the world today" (1993, 164). By this, he means a world in which the very elements that nation-states claim as their foundations—ties of ethnicity, language, religion—are themselves the cause of difficulty. In this scenario, the nation-state is falling prey to the forces that (supposedly) created and sustained it, and the emerging world order will look much like the world we have known—only more so. It will be marked by an intensification of national urges, with the result that there will be more nations, more particularistic in their identity, closer in fact to the fictions of ethnic or religious homogeneity that the nation-state fostered in the first place. Japanese concerns about rice (more properly, about the dangerous vectors imported rice may unleash) and immigration work within a similar understanding of the nation. They suggest that the idea of a multicultural Japan is regarded as an oxymoron and that anything that disturbs the supposed homogeneity of nation-state must lead to its fragmentation.

Other streams of rhetoric about a postnational future present the nation-state as an already outmoded entity. The management consultant Kenichi Ohmae, for instance, maintains that the

> nation-state has become an unnatural, even dysfunctional, unit for organizing human activity. It represents no genuine, shared community of economic interests; it defines no meaningful flows of economic activity. In fact, it overlooks the true linkages and synergies that exist among often disparate populations by combining important measures of human activity at the wrong level of analysis (1993, 78; see also Ohmae 1995a, 1995b).

In place of nations, Ohmae foresees a world of what he calls "region states"—smaller, "natural economic zones ... drawn by the deft but invisible hand of the global market" (1993, 78–79). Although he claims that these region-states are not political entities and pose no threat to existing national governments, his use of the term *state* to describe them suggests otherwise. In Ohmae's scenario, economic globalization will inevitably produce a postnational world, one in which the demands of "natural" economic entities, such as the "Pacific Northwest region state" (Vancouver and Seattle) or the "Great Lakes region state" (Toronto, Detroit, Cleveland), increasingly supersede those of established political units. Governments that do not adjust to the new reality "will be left to reign over traditional political territories as all meaningful participation in the global economy migrates beyond their well-preserved frontiers" (85).

Ohmae is representative of a prominent strain of thought about the way the world is headed. In this view, the ties that matter are not ethnic or religious but electronic and economic. In the words of European Union futurist Riccardo Petrella, the much-heralded technological revolution is producing "an archipelago of technologically highly developed city-regions ... linked together by transnational business firms that bypass the traditional nation-state framework" (Petrella 1991, 59; see also Petrella 1995). As Heidi and Alvin Toffler (1991) put it, the major dividing line in the world of the near future will be between the "wired" and the "unwired." Likewise, the most important connections for Ohmae's region-states are to global trade networks, and his primary example of a region-state is Singapore: a small state defined more by its connections to the outside world than by place or language or any of the other elements that are called on to define most nations. For the wired or connected world, moreover, this scenario promises that global capitalism will produce a kind of economic multiculturalism. The racial, religious, and cultural rivalries so important under a nation-state scheme no longer matter when faced with the prospect of equal-opportunity consumerism. "Where true economies of service exist," Ohmae believes, religious, ethnic, and racial distinctions are not important. . . . Singapore is 70 percent ethnic Chinese, but its 30 percent minority is not much of a problem [to the ethnic Chinese majority] because commercial prosperity creates sufficient affluence for all. (1993, 81)

This line of reasoning has had great appeal in Japan and elsewhere in Asia. Indeed, in Singapore it is one of the foundations of the state. For the past quarter-century, Singapore has been declaring itself "a new kind of city—a Global City. It is a new form of human organisation and settlement that has . . . no precedent in mankind's past history." Singapore is "the city that electronic communications, supersonic planes, giant tankers and modern economic and industrial organization make inevitable" (Wee 1993, 731, quoting a speech delivered by S. Rajaratnam on 6 February 1972). Although few in Japan seem to envision the nation as an archipelago of city-states, the rhetoric is inviting in other respects. The Japanese predilection for robots and technological gizmos is fabled, and Japanese society in general seems to have a great deal invested in imagining itself as being at the forefront of the information revolution. Ozawa Ichirō's best-selling manifesto, *Blueprint for a New Japan*, stresses the need to expand transportation and communications channels by, for example, constructing a mag-lev line that would shrink travel time between Tokyo and Osaka to about one hour and establishing a nationwide fiber-optic data communications network. Similarly, the media are filled with paeans to the information society (*jōhō shakai*), while department store displays overflow with "fuzzy logic" toasters, toilets, and rice cookers and Tokyo has run out of numbers for use with cellular phones. Before remodeling their kitchens, customers are invited to experience the new appliances and layout in virtual reality, and a few years ago a virtual rock star called Haga Yui created quite a stir (Greenfeld 1994, 273). In stressing that the future belongs to the connected and that information is the most valuable form of capital, this particular strand of post-national rhetoric sanctions such investments and fuels the fads.

Of course, more than faddish behavior is behind the eagerness with which Japan has seized on the "information revolution" and its rhetoric. For one thing, in contrast to most models of development, Asia figures conspicuously in writing about the information age. Tokyo, Singapore, Hong Kong and the Pearl River Delta, the Osaka-Kobe megalopolis, and Shanghai figure in almost every analysis as exemplary city-regions. Indeed, in this discourse Tokyo and Singapore, perhaps because of the self-consciousness with which they present themselves as global cities, often serve as models of where older, traditional cities are headed. Factors that once served to define these places as derivative— their dependence on global links, their openness to transnational cultural and economic forces, for instance—now place them on the cutting edge. For much of its history, Tokyo has been deemed, by Japanese and foreign commentators alike, both the emblem of Japan's modernity and the least Japanese of cities, a clear departure from feudal Edo and a bad copy of real cities like New York or London or Paris. Similarly, standard histories ascribe to modern Japan a distinctly hybrid identity. Japan, we have been told repeatedly, is a blend of Asian and Western elements—and it is the Western elements that are usually seen as crucial, for they supply what is "modern" about modern Japan. Because it is a hybrid, dependent on imported (economic, technological, cultural, and political) resources, Japanese modernity is marked as secondary to that of the West, which supposedly developed on its own. The old adage that Japan perfects but never originates captures the essence of these arguments well and has long served to define modern Japan as a pastiche of the West.

Yet it is precisely this ability to adapt other economic and cultural practices that is nowadays celebrated. The globalization—deterritorialization—of capital accrues an advantage to those hybrid sites, like Tokyo, Osaka, and Singapore, that exist in the in-between, that were never really seen as occupying any authentic place. As sites of social and cultural hybridization, they are naturally positioned to manage the interactions—whether moving capital from one region to another or translating management practices from one culture to another—that are the key to today's global economy. As Arjun Appadurai (1990) notes, the ways in which we speak of production (in terms of workers and factories located in such-and-such a place, in terms of national productivity, etc.) mask the actual relations of production, which are increasingly global and transnational. In a sense, though, what this means is that we are beginning to recognize in the economy something we have long held to be the condition of nation-state formation outside a core group of European nations. Places like modern Japan and India we readily recognize as having been formed as much outside the nation as inside it; we see how their modern identities have depended on constructs, such as "Asia" or "the Orient," that are foreign to them. Global power relations—too often comprehended by the banal and misleading term *Westernization*—molded modern Asia: that has been part of the narrative of every Asian nation. Economists, business leaders, and others involved in the production of postnational thought are beginning to discern similar tides of globalization impressing themselves upon nations elsewhere.

In the one case, they produced nations; in the other, they seem to be pushing us past the nation. A striking weakness of this vein of postnational thinking is its failure to differentiate contemporary globalization from the long history of large-scale global interaction. Certainly, the density of communication and exchange is much greater now that it was even a couple of decades ago, and goods and ideas and money chase each other around the globe with breathtaking rapidity. But to what extent have these changes in speed and quantity resulted in qualitative differences? While there is no denying that the changes of the last quarter-century have been enormous, the upheavals we have experienced, and the shock with which we continue to register those upheavals, need to be weighed carefully against the experience of other peoples at other times. Exactly how new are the changes heralded in discussions of the new world order or the new global economy? The displacement of the U.S. textile industry by Chinese and other competition, for example, recalls the destruction of the Indian textile industry at the hands of the British a century or more earlier. And how different is today's globetrotting capitalist from the eighteenth-century "merchant prince" described by John Brewer (1989, 185)?

> The Scot Richard Oswald was typical of this new breed. Together with his compatriots Alexander Grant and John Sargent he presided over business interests in Europe, Africa, America, and Asia. Oswald and his partners invested in Scottish industries—glass works, collieries and rope works— acted as government contractors in Germany during the Seven Years War, built a slave 'factory' at Bunce Island near the mouth of the Sierra Leone River in West Africa (complete, as David Hancock tells us, with its own golf course), owned plantations in the West Indies, speculated in land investment with the Ohio Company and in Nova Scotia and East Florida, and invested in the lucrative gin franchise in Bengal. No scheme better captures the extent of this international empire than Oswald's plan to import Chinese into western Scotland to remedy local depopulation.

One suspects in fact that much of the newness we discern in global exchanges has ultimately to do with point of view. From the perspective of the colonized (or quasi-colonized) regions of the world, economic and social displacement, permeable boundaries and a borderless economy, and a culture overflowing with bizarre hybrids and pastiches of metropolitan culture must seem the norm. Extraterritoriality and loss of tariff autonomy were, after all, key concessions wrung out of China and other East Asian nations under the old treaty system of the nineteenth century. As Doreen Massey (1992) suggests, to find in recent trends evidence for a paradigm shift or the arrival of a new world economic order is to adopt "the point of view of a (relative) elite . . . a predominantly white/first world take on things" (9). More than that, it is to cling to a particularly myopic view of how the so-called First World came about. Numerous studies have demonstrated the intimate relationship between colonialism and national identity in the West (e.g., Said 1978, 1993; Kiernan 1995; Anderson 1991); and varieties of internal colonialism preceded and accompanied overseas expansion. From the outset, the nation-state has been a global enterprise; to charge global enterprise now with threatening to make nation-states irrelevant is questionable to ignore their long and symbiotic relationship.

History and Nation

Not quite 150 years ago, it seemed to many, in Japan at least, that "globalization" was the key to building a strong nation. From its outset, the Meiji state pursued an ambitious program of learning from Europe and America, dispatching its best young scholars abroad for advanced training and bringing hundreds of foreign experts to Japan to assist the nation in all sorts of endeavors, from establishing a modern university to writing a civil code. Fukuzawa Yukichi, perhaps the most prominent intellectual of the early Meiji period, wrote that "intercourse with foreign countries" was the condition under which true independence for Japan might be gained (Fukuzawa 1995, 299–300). And Japan has regularly been singled out for precisely this ability to learn from and assimilate the techniques of the West. In contrast, especially, to China, which (it is said) refused to recognize the advantages to be gained from open intercourse with Western nations, Japan seized the opportunities and made itself into a strong, modern nation. Such "borrowing" extended far beyond specific institutions and embraced clothing and mores, the entire infrastructure of a society.

I would like to focus here on one facet of this infrastructure—the process by which Japan came to be possessed of a recognizably modern history. It is nowadays a truism that all nations must have a history, by which is meant, in fact, one particular kind of history deriving from nineteenth-century Europe (see, e.g., Dirks 1990). This history, which Prasenjit Duara (1995) calls "linear, progressive history," has served "to secure the mystique of the nation" (16), to transform unstable, ambiguous entities into seemingly self-evident collectivities by reconstituting them, via narrative history, as the *telos* of a long, accumulative development. The Meiji Japanese state was certainly alert to the role that history might play in securing the nation: among its first acts, sharing pride of place with administrative and tax reform, was the establishment of an Office of Historiography charged with writing a new national history. In setting up the nation's first department of history at Tokyo Imperial University, the government likewise stressed the contribution that the study of history might make to securing the nation. The charge given Ludwig Riess, student of Leopold von Ranke (1795–1886), who became Japan's first professor of history, was "to give instruction in the regular methods of historical research employed in the West, especially in Germany" (Blussé 1979, 200). The ultimate aim of instruction in history was explicitly national:

> It is my hope that, when we have subjected to the processes of Western his-
> torical scholarship the materials which the Office of Historiography and
> its successors have collected and when we have in that light examined the
> evidence of our country's past and compiled a history therefrom, the for-
> mation of this Historical Society will have proved to have done the state
> some service. (Shigeno [1889] 1991, 200)

A modern history, in which a country's past may speak to its present because the two are linked by a clear chain of cause and effect and in which facts seem to speak for themselves without the intervention of any author, was understood to be an indispensable feature of a modern nation.

The methods that supported the writing of such histories came to Japan as manifestly foreign imports, and this fact makes an examination of Japan's late-nineteenth-century struggles over history extremely useful. Because modern, European-style historiography came on a scene already occupied by other historical traditions, the tensions arising between alternate ways of comprehending the past were clear. Certainly, Japan is not alone in this: even in Europe, the emergence of what we now call history was everywhere marked by struggles among different models. In the case of a nation like Japan, though, we seem much more willing to acknowledge the contradictions. Because we can conjure up for Japan a struggle between East and West, because Japanese historians used precisely the same struggle (and in fact added a third element, China) to establish what was exceptional about Japanese culture, we seem much more ready to recognize the interplay of incompatible elements than we do for those European nations whose particular histories define history in general. While this is clearly a colonizer's view, a view that has its roots in the attitude that reserves for Europe the pure, abstract state of the universal, it also means that Japan ought to be good for the project of, to borrow Dipesh Chakrabarty's (1992) phrase, "deconstructing historiography" and "provincializing Europe."

The third decade of the Meiji era (1888–98) was a fertile time for musings about the role of history in the production of a new Japan. Prompted perhaps by the promulgation of new guidelines for writing history textbooks in 1888 and by the organization of a Department of National History at the Imperial University in 1890, the decade saw an outpouring of writing about history. New journals, some of them publishing two or three issues a month, generated intense interest in the presentation of Japan's past. These journals were part of an explosion of writing in which the shape and nature of Japan's history were of central concern. As they struggled to rework Japan's past into a usable national history, they attended particularly to such fundamental matters as what events and what kinds of events properly belonged to the history of Japan, how these events were to be assembled into a history, and what consequences followed from different ways of recounting the past.

The rise of this modern historical discipline in Meiji Japan is usually described as a three-sided struggle among nativist scholars (*kokugakusha*), advocates of Chinese learning (*kangakusha*), and adherents of the "history of civilization" (*bunmeishi*), that is, Westernizers (see Ōkubo 1988). *Kangakusha* and *kokugakusha* clashed, for example, over the question of whether the government-sponsored official history of Japan should be written in Chinese, following the example of the other official histories (the most recent of which was, albeit, about eight hundred years old at the time), or in Japanese. In a similar vein, representing another leg of the triangle, a scandal erupted in 1892 surrounding the publication of an article that from an avowedly modern, "objective," empiricist position exposed Shinto as a primitive and commonplace form of heaven worship and not the divine expression of the unique essence of Japan (Kume 1891). The article's author, Kume Kunitake, was roundly censured by nativist intellectuals not only for slandering the imperial line and "besmirching a national polity unique in all the world" (Iwashita 1892, 38) but for relying on Western ideas that had no place in articulating Japanese history (Anon. 1892). Likewise, when Shigeno Yasutsugu, a professor at Tokyo Imperial University and director of the government's official history project, suggested on the basis of exhaustive documentary research that a beloved hero of the medieval chronicle *Taiheiki* (Chronicle of the Great Peace) was in fact a fabrication, he was accused of treason by many historians who felt that his alien methods did violence to the nature of Japanese sources (Shigeno 1884; for responses, see Ōkubo 1988, 238–44). Interestingly, when Kume and Shigeno set out to write a Japanese history text for use in the state school system, they seemed to agree. They deliberately avoided the "method used by Westerners of dividing eras into one-hundred-year sections" and opted instead to divide Japanese history according to a more native method into twenty-one ages "based upon political changes" (Kume, Shigeno, and Hoshino 1890).

As these examples suggest, the conflict over how to present the nation's past took shape as a contest between "national" styles of writing history: between Asian modes of historiography, common to nativism and Chinese learning alike, characterized by detailed philological criticism and exemplified by the annals and biographies form of Chinese dynastic histories and the Tokugawa-era *Dai Nihonshi* (Great History of Japan), and a Western style, the distinctive feature of which was held to be cause and effect narrative. Thus, one author, comparing a German history of Germany with a Japanese history of Japan (in English; it was commissioned by the Ministry of Education for the Chicago World's Columbian Exposition in 1893), preferred the former because it attended closely to cause and effect (Mozume 1894). In his opinion, the latter, written in a more purely annalistic style, grew hopelessly confusing when trying to deal with many events occurring simultaneously. Likewise, to Shigeno Yasutsugu, the basic difference between Western and Asian historical writing could be found in the Western adherence to cause and effect narrative: "In arrangement and editing, Western histories are very different from Chinese and Japanese histories. . . . Although they generally follow chronological order, they always fully investigate the causes and effects of events. The most important parts of the text, moreover, frequently incorporate [the author's] conclusions, and thereby stimulate the reader's intellect" (1879, 169). These aspects of Western historiography, he declared, should be incorporated into the writing of Japan's history. Another author asked why fully realized histories (*kanzen naru rekishi*) of Japan were rare and answered his own question with the assertion that few Japanese appreciated what had become established in the West: that history was the science of cause and effect. Only when such an understanding was brought to bear on Japan's inherited historical tradition would the nation have a true history (Sekine 1892).

There is some value to the story of a tripartite contest. It provided the framework within which the participants in the debate staked out their positions, and it established what is still the fundamental division of the discipline into national history (*kokushi*), oriental history (*tōyōshi*), and occidental history (*seiyōshi*; it has since become *sekaishi*, or world history). But there is also something too pat about this effort to sort out the historiographical tangle. Since the denouement of the story is typically the assertion that true national history emerged when Western techniques of narration were joined to the meticulous evidentiary criticism derived from Chinese learning, it echoes too neatly Japan's positioning of itself as mediator between Asian tradition and Western modernity. In this vision, the modern Japanese historian is a man fully conversant with the methods of the West who has also mastered the wealth of detail about the national essence furnished by traditional historiography. But to maintain in this way that history in Meiji Japan issues forth from the confrontation (and eventual reconciliation) of national historiographical styles is simply to reiterate certain commonplace assumptions about the traffic between Japan and the West. It affirms, for one thing, the Meiji-era rendering of the interaction in terms of "Japanese spirit and Western technique" (*wakon yōsai*): the historical discipline in fact offers a paradigmatic case, for its primary aim was to secure the national essence through a marriage of Western methods and indigenous facts. Finally, this stress on conflict between advocates of various national traditions obscures some important, and interesting, areas of agreement. I find it telling, for instance, that Inoue Tetsujirō, a conservative schooled in the nativist tradition, should find nothing problematic about recommending a rigorous course in European history for anyone who wanted to write the history of Japan (1892). Although Inoue's rhetoric makes sharp distinctions between oriental and Western forms of knowledge, his practice of history acknowledges no such division. Historical method, it would seem, can be divorced from its origins and—even to someone as sensitive to national differences as Inoue—transplanted without difficulty from Europe to Japan. Each national history celebrates the singular character of the nation it produces, but history arises, Inoue suggests, from common ground.

In all of the ferment over history that occurred in the 1890s, no one seemed to question the end toward which history must aim and the vehicle that it must use to achieve that end. If there is, for example, fierce disagreement about what constitutes the national essence—Is it to be found in the Emperor? Does it reside in the people? In the landscape?—all are agreed that a strong national sense is history's greatest potential gift to Japan. And if historians argued vehemently about the value of certain sources (or kinds of sources) there seems to be no question among them that narrative is the preferred means. One author, outlining the "three methods of historical exposition"— annals, taxonomy (*ruijūshi*), and cause and effect narrative—asserted that only the last led to "true history" and was essential if "a country were to display its progress toward civilization and enlightenment" (Ariga 1889, 4). Yet another scholar, recalling a conversation that he had at Oxford with the noted Japanologist William Aston, observed that "Europeans and Americans were amazed that a country with as long an imperial tradition as Japan did not yet have a proper history." He blamed the method used in Japan's existing histories for this problem:

> The countries of the Orient were not born yesterday, their experience is not shallow, nor do they lack history. But our existing histories are concerned only with "promoting the good and punishing the bad" (*kanzen chōaku*). They show no interest in elucidating cause and effect. Thus even our Japanese empire, in which the virtues of our national polity and the merits of our customs resound throughout the realm, has no history to compare with those of the Western powers. (Kaneko 1891, 54)

Numerous articles by scholars who belonged to all three camps stressed in a similar manner that narrative is the proper mode for telling history, that in fact it is the only mode that can produce a history suited to the nation. Meiji Japan's debates about history are therefore instructive, if only for what they leave unsaid. Beneath the manifest divisions lies a general, though unstated, consensus that the nation, in order to become a nation, needs a new sense of history, one in which chronology, because it is no longer simply a register of haphazard fragments but a tightly linked chain of causes and effects, will be meaningful in and of itself. But still one wonders how it was, in an atmosphere charged with national rivalries, that cause and effect narrative, associated as it was with the Westernizing "history of civilization," could emerge in the 1890s as *the* mode of writing to assure, as one Mune Atsunori (1896, 25) put it, that "the people will embrace a spirit of loyalty and patriotism." For however much they tried to present one way of reading or writing history as naturally superior, Meiji historians had to contend with the fact that other models existed, models that had the force of a thousand years of tradition behind them and could not be dismissed out of hand.

On the face of it, moreover, the new history ought to have been shaky ground on which to found a nation. Unlike Confucian histories, which could assert that a stable moral system stood behind and guaranteed their unity, or Japanese histories, which were secured by the sanctity of the imperial line, the history Japan learned from the West seemed to rely on nothing but the facts themselves. And one of its primary messages was that things change. Yet this history was called upon to deliver precisely the opposite message. Konakamura Yoshikata, one of the first professors of national literature at the Imperial University, spoke a commonplace when he asserted, first, that "every nation has a character, customs, and other things peculiar to it. Such things do not change. . . . Just as a person's character does not change, the spirit of a country can not be altered. This unchanging, unalterable [character] is what distinguishes me from someone else, is what distinguishes my country from another." Then he continues: "How can we come to know the nation's character? The most important thing is to embrace enthusiastically the study of national history and national letters." If this happens, then it "will cement the bond between the nation and its people" (1890, 38–39).

By juxtaposing these passages, we seem to catch Konakamura in a sleight of hand: maintaining that history, the discipline concerned with how things change over time, can also disclose the unalterable essence that makes Japan Japan. Yet, to be fair, one of the strengths the modern understanding of history claims is precisely this ability to make an object in perpetual motion (say, the Japanese state) yield up an essence that is eternal (the spirit of Japan). The contention that we can make the past meaningful, as opposed to simply eventful, depends on demonstrating that there is an order, a unifying principle, to be found within the chaos of events. This strange power is the key to history's importance in the Meiji nationalist project. And the key to this power lies in the modern discipline's manipulation of time. Writers like Konakamura could maintain without getting caught up in a contradiction that Japan needed its own history and that the basis of that history ought to be Western-style cause and effect narrative because that way of writing time is the condition of possibility for national history—that is, for history that will produce a nation that is both enduring and progressive.

Part of history's utility for national history lies with the "reality effect" it claims to produce, with its seeming ability to find, as Barthes (1981, 4) notes, "in the 'pure and simple' relation of the facts the best proof of those facts." The discipline achieves this effect first and foremost by having the author of a history disappear into his or her text. Linda Orr (1990) points to Michelet's declaration in the preface to his *Histoire de la révolution française*—"I was not the author"—as the "goal of the historian's strategies, the ultimate gesture of legitimation" (76–77). Though historians nowadays may be less reluctant to disavow authorship of their texts, the discipline is still founded on the fiction that historians are (or ought to be) primarily scribes recording and revealing voices, events, peoples, and so on that have lives of their own, that exist apart from the historian's labor. History, as Orr writes, still by and large pretends to record "what speaks all by itself, alone. The events seem to write and read themselves" (75).

This effect helps to account for the transportability of realist narrative. Authored yet authorless, this form of exposition seemed to allow native Japanese materials to speak in their own voices, something other historical styles, with their authors stridently drawing moral lessons from the past or urging Japan to be like the West, could not do. Modern Japanese historians' opposition to so-called Confucian historiography, it would therefore seem, arose not so much because of their aversion to its moralizing character as because the historian had to be present in the history so as to dispense praise or blame. History, in a Confucian mode, is manifestly the work of the historian, and it therefore stands in the way of any notion that history is the record of a preexisting reality. The same could be said of the "history of civilization" school, wherein the too obvious presence of figures like Guizot, Macaulay, and Spencer interfered with the direct transmission of Japan's past. Only when pruned of Confucian exhortation or, depending on the proclivities of the historian, of obvious Western influence, could history promise the nation a real, natural presence that did not depend on anything other than the mere facts of its past. As Hayden White has pointed out, the value of narrativity is that it sustains the fiction that events speak for themselves and that they do so in the form of a story. As he has also noted, however, this naturalization of narrative can only take place if narrative is transformed "from a manner of speaking into a paradigm of the form that reality itself displays to a 'realistic' consciousness. It is [modern historians] who have made narrativity into a value, the presence of which in a discourse having to do with 'real' events signals at once its objectivity, its seriousness, and its realism" (1987, 24). The implication, of course, is that history requires a certain kind of training.

Seen in this light, history's emergence in the Meiji period appears less as a battle between East and West than as an effort to displace these older habits of reading and writing and substitute for them a narrative understanding of the past. Anticipating White by nearly a century, one Japanese writer at least seems to have pinpointed the problem precisely. Writing against "those who insist that we need to rewrite [Japanese] history because our received histories are not very useful, which is to say, not like those of the West," he argues that Japan "does not need to rewrite its old histories. It only needs to change the way they are read." The "essence of history," he further declares, "is to trace the origins and consequences of each and every act." A proper historical sense would therefore emerge in Japan not by casting aside its historiographical inheritance in a rush to imitate the West but by training students to read the old histories so as to discern cause and effect. "It matters not a whit in what style the histories are written," the article concludes, "only how they are read" (Naitō 1889).

Conclusion

The problem facing Meiji nationalist historians was twofold: how to construct a nation from the material of Japan's past and how to insist on that nation's uniqueness. To understand how they accomplished that task, we need to amend the standard account. Meiji historians produced a nation not by "Westernizing" its past or skillfully blending "East" and "West," though these figures are scattered throughout their texts. Rather, they proceeded by restructuring Japan's relationship to its past; they strove to train the Japanese in a different way of appreciating familiar events and heroes so that these monuments all refer to the nation that was to emerge after the Meiji revolution.

The primary instrument for this restructuring, I would argue, was a fundamental, global discourse of the nineteenth century—capitalism. Certainly, the temporality that authorized their histories was a peculiarly capitalist one. The conundrum of capital is that the circulating object somehow creates wealth, that possessions, necessarily alienated in order to become capital, somehow return, augmented in the circuit. This, as Marx demonstrated, in fact engages two circuits. The first, in which a commodity is exchanged for money, which in turn purchases another, different commodity, produces difference; it changes corn into clothing or lead into gold. In the second, which Marx terms the "general formula for capital," "the buyer lays out money in order that, as a seller, he may recover money. . . . He lets the money go, but only with the sly intention of getting it back again. The money, therefore, is not spent, it is merely advanced" (1906, 165–66). Like, in this circuit, produces like.

Time in the modern historical understanding performs a fundamentally similar magic. Its passage generates both difference and essence. In the first instance, corresponding to the Marx's first circuit, an event serves as a kind of commodity, which, acted upon by the historian, becomes the cause of a subsequent event, thereby producing a difference. By this operation, the assassination of an archduke becomes a worldwide conflagration and Gandhi's fasts metamorphose into an independent India. At the same time, however, each event, as the outcome of a prior cause and cause of a later effect, registers a kind of investment, and time's passage thus becomes the equivalent of the circuit in which capital returns further capital: time advances in the same manner as capital—it does not so much flow as accumulate.

Taken together, these two circuits provide the grounds for claiming, as national history did, that history shows that Japan may grow and change yet remain true to its essential character. This kind of operation, to give an example from another region of the discipline, is what enabled Japanese specialists in oriental history, as Stefan Tanaka (1993) has shown, to declare that Japan shares with China a distinctly Asian character—a character that is the basis for establishing Japan's difference from the West—and yet also claim that history has carried Japan far beyond China. Capitalized time is likewise the time of *ishin*, the time of renovation and return proclaimed in the Meiji Restoration, the *Meiji ishin*. It is basic to the Meiji state's proclamation that it represented something revolutionary and yet remained true to primordial origins.

The development of history in Meiji Japan, then, involved at its core the disciplining of time according to the logic of capital. This fact, as I have noted, forces us to reconsider the stories we have told about history's place in Meiji nationalism. It has been customary for some time to concentrate on historians' assimilation of or revolt against the West. This approach seems seriously limiting. I wonder, first, what it can tell us about the Meiji-era struggles over history because it remains firmly within the bounds Meiji politicians and historians themselves set for the debate, which in their estimation was all about national identity. But this way of sorting out the debate is the more troubling because we in the West have made it the peculiar fate of non-Western nations to be forced to carry out these debates about East and West.

From the Meiji period to the present day, attempts to define Japanese identity have regularly revisited the debate over whether Western categories and methods have the right to speak of and for Japan. Thus, the debates of Meiji statesmen over political reform were invigorated by quarrels about what place European models might have in the articulation of the new Japan (Gluck 1985). In 1940, a group of scholars gathered under government auspices to discuss how Japan might overcome the constraints of European-style modernity (Heisig and Maraldo 1994; Sakai 1989). More recently, trade disputes have become an occasion for cultural commentary that on the one side expresses consternation at Japan for refusing to abide by "universally accepted" principles and on the other objects to the distinctly European flavor of these principles and insists that Japan is constituted differently (Ishihara 1991). Meanwhile, it has become textbook *doxa* to portray Japanese history since the Restoration as a series of turns toward or away from the West.

Such histories perform another of the tricks that Marx associates with capital: its ability to hide its workings such that the commodity takes on a life of its own. In capitalism, human labor disappears into the commodities ("congealed labor," "crystallized labor") it produces, creating, as Ann Cvetkovich (1992, 183) notes, "the illusion that capital itself has a body and is capable of reproducing itself independently of human labor." In a similar fashion, the modern historical discipline has given nations lives of their own, such that nations seem to be the logical starting point of history. Nations, that is, have been subjected to the same sort of fetishism that Marx described for the commodity. Both are products of ordinary human labor, yet each, disowning that labor, assumes a paradoxical and, as Marx maintains, "transcendent" character (1906, 75). A table, to use Marx's example, is simply wood worked by human industry into a new form. In the instant the table is put into circulation and becomes a commodity, however, it "stands on its head, and evolves out of its wooden brain grotesque ideas"—namely, that it "rule[s] the producers instead of being ruled by them" (76, 79). It is fetishized as the source and measure of value. As the rhetoric of "founding fathers" and the like attests, nations, too, are the product of human labor and ingenuity. Yet they masquerade as something quite different—instead of having histories, they become the condition of possibility for history, the ground upon which all histories must be based. The nation dictates the character of its people; the product assumes the place of the producer.

One of the odd effects of the modern historical discipline has thus been to exempt the nation from history, to remove it from the vicissitudes of politics and economics and attribute to it a supposedly more primal substance, typically religious, ethnic, or cultural—all entities somehow beyond the reach of time. Intent on isolating from the flow of time those elements that are deemed not to change and thus could serve as the basis for defining a people or a state, history in its most widely accepted form nowadays is not so much a chronicle of change as an examination of the spirit, persisting through the ages, that harbors the true and unique meaning of, say, Japan or Asia.

This brings me back to the issues raised at the outset of this essay. My long excursion through Meiji historiography was intended to make some key points about current debates over nations. First, just as national history always forces us to comprehend global interactions in terms of a competition between nations, postnational rhetoric is hampered by a basic inability to understand these interactions in terms other than the dissolution of nations. It imagines a fundamental tension between the nation-state and largely capitalist forces of globalization, and it is predicated on the idea that these two are in competition, not collusion. Postnationalist thinking conceives of the nation, in other words, in precisely the same way that national history does: as a form of collectivity characterized by natural boundaries and marked by primordial allegiances to a religious, ethnic, or linguistic community.

Second, both nationalism and postnationalism depend on a certain construction of history. History's role in the development of nations has been widely studied, but its importance to postnationalist rhetoric is not widely recognized—in one influential construction, after all, the postnational world is what follows the "end of history" (Fukuyama 1992). A particular understanding of history helped to consolidate the nation-state as *the* normative form of collectivity, and it underwrites as well the ways in which we understand the significance of forces like "globalization" today. The alarm with which Samuel Huntington (1993a, 1993b, 1993c), Ishihara Shintarō, and others greet globalization (e.g., the fear that it is producing "split countries" that cannot endure) is comprehensible only if one believes that it is the role of history to produce discrete peoples, homogeneous national cultures, and other essences. On the other hand, giddy celebration of hybridity per se makes sense only against a backdrop that regards such hybrids as novel, that sees in them a reversal of the historical processes of the past couple of centuries.

Finally, given the affinities between these two supposedly antithetical forms of discourse, we need to look beyond their fixation on the nation to make sense of what is happening now—or in Meiji Japan. As Marx's analyses of production and exchange did for our understanding of commodities and value, so, too, might an analysis of time and history begin to defetishize these entities and return the nation to history. One way to work toward that end might be to recover something of the possibilities present in Meiji discourse. The idea that national history did not come naturally, that people had to be taught to think historically, is an important one. It indicates that other approaches to the past were once plausible and that outcomes other than the nation were genuinely thought (or feared) to be possible. Meiji historians sought to portray the nation as the natural outgrowth of a timeless essence; however, their fears that the nation might not come into (or continue in) existence unless it was repeatedly proclaimed in a certain kind of history reveal that the community called the nation is grounded not in some primordial substance but in a particular historical, political, and economic project.

Bibliography

Ahmad, Aijaz. 1996. "Post-colonial Theory and the 'Post' Condition." Oral presentation at York University, Toronto.

An Ch'angho. 1997. Preface to Sin Ch'aeho [1908] 1997:1–4.

Anderson, Benedict. 1991. *Imagined Communities: Reflections on the Origin and Spread of Nationalism.* Rev. ed. London: Verso. First edition 1983.

Anonymous. 1892. "Kokka no daiji o bakuro suru mono no fuchū fugi o ronzu" (The disloyalty and dishonor of those who unveil national secrets). *Kokkō* 3, no. 9:48–51.

Anonymous. 1910a. "Seishin byōin sankanki" (A visit to a psychiatric hospital). *Jogaku sekai* 9, no. 6: 174–79.

Anonymous. 1910b. "Tōkyō no byōin wo hōmon shite fujin no seishinbyōsha wo kataru" (A visit to the Tokyo asylum and the female psychiatric patients I saw there). *Fujin sekai* 4, no. 10: 38–40.

Appadurai, Arjun. 1990b. "Disjuncture and Difference in the Global Cultural Economy." *Public Culture* 2, no. 2: 1–24.

Ariga Nagao. 1889. "Nihon rekishi jidai bunkatsu ron" (On the division into stages of Japanese history). *Kōten kōkyūsho kōen* 11:1–17.

Arooran, N. K. 1980. *Tamil Renaissance and Dravidian Nationalism, 1905–1944.* Madurai: Koodal Publishers.

Ashcroft, Bill, Gareth Griffiths, and Helen Tiffin. 1989. *The Empire Writes Back: Theory and Practice in Post-colonial Literature.* London: Routledge.

Balasubramaniam, K. M. 1965. *The Life of J. M. Nallaswami Pillai.* Madras: Annamalainagar.

Barlow, Tani E., ed. 1993a. *Gender Politics in Modern China: Writing and Feminism.* Durham: Duke University Press.

———. 1993b. "Colonialism's Career in Postwar China Studies." *positions* 1, no. 1: 224–67.

Barmé, Geremie R. 1994. "Soft Porn, Packaged Dissent, and Nationalism: Notes on Chinese Culture in the 1990s." *Current History* 93, no. 584 (September): 270–75.

———. 1995. "To Screw Foreigners Is Patriotic: China's Avant-Garde Nationalists." *China Journal* 34: 209–34. Rpt. in Unger 1996.

Barthes, Roland. 1981. "The Discourse of History." *Comparative Criticism: A Yearbook* 3: 3–20.

Beasley, W. G. 1987. *Japanese Imperialism, 1894–1945.* Oxford: Clarendon.

———. 1989. "The Foreign Threat and the Opening of the Ports." In *Cambridge History of Japan,* vol. 5, edited by Marius Jansen, 259–307. Cambridge: Cambridge University Press.

Beauchamp, Henry K., trans. and ed. 1906. *Hindu Manners, Customs and Ceremonies by the Abbé J. A. Dubois.* Oxford: Clarendon Press.

Befu, Harumi. 1993. "Nationalism and *Nihonjinron.*" In *Cultural Nationalism in East Asia: Representation and Identity,* edited by Harumi Befu, 107–35. Berkeley: Institute of East Asian Studies, University of California.

Benedict, Carol. 1996. *Bubonic Plague in Nineteenth-Century China.* Stanford: Stanford University Press.

Bernstein, Laurie. 1995. *Sonia's Daughters: Prostitutes and Their Regulation in Imperial Russia.* Berkeley: University of California Press.

Bhabha, Homi. 1994a. *The Location of Culture.* New York: Routledge.

———. 1994b. "Narrating the Nation." In Hutchinson and Smith 1994, 306–12.

Bickers, Robert A., and Jeffrey N. Wasserstrom. 1995. "Shanghai's 'Dogs and Chinese Not Admitted' Sign: Legend, History, and Contemporary Symbol." *China Quarterly* 142 (June): 444–66.

Blussé, Leonard. 1979. "Japanese Historiography and European Sources." In *Reappraisals in Overseas History,* edited by P. C. Emmer and H. L. Wesseling. Leiden: Brill.

Bōei kenkyūjo (Self-defense research institute), Tokyo. 1938a. "Chū Shi hōmen shin seiken jūritsu ikisatsu" (Complications concerning the establishment of a new regime in the Central China Area). February. Shina: Shina jihen: Zempan 315: Chū Shi hōmengun tokumubu (Special Service Department, Central China Area Army).

———. 1938b. "Zhonghua minguo xin zhengfu niding zhenggang" (Proposed political program of the new government of the Republic of China). February. Riku Shi mitsu dainikki (Secret diaries of the army in mainland China), S13–7, entry 30.

———. 1938c. "Chū Shi shisō taisaku yōryō" (Outline of ideological policy in Central China). October. Riku Shi mitsu dainikki, S13–30, entry 51.

Bourdieu, Pierre. 1991. *Language and Symbolic Power.* Cambridge: Harvard University Press.

Boyle, John Hunter. 1972. *China and Japan at War, 1937–1945: The Politics of Collaboration.* Stanford: Stanford University Press.

Breuilly, John. 1982. *Nationalism and the State.* Manchester: Manchester University Press.

Brewer, John. 1989. *Sinews of Power: War, Money, and the English State, 1688–1783.* New York: Knopf.

Brook, Timothy. 1999. "Capitalism and the Writing of Modern History in China." In *China and Historical Capitalism: Genealogies of Sinological Knowledge,* edited by Timothy Brook and Gregory Blue, 110–57. Cambridge: Cambridge University Press.

———. 2000. "The Creation of the Reformed Government in Central China, 1938." In *Chinese Collaboration with Japan, 1932–1945: The Limits of Accommodation,* edited by David Barrett and Larry Shyu. Stanford: Stanford University Press.

Burns, Susan. 1997. "Contemplating Places: The Hospital as Modern Experience in Meiji

Japan." In *New Directions in the Study of Meiji Japan,* edited by Helen Hardacre and Adam L. Kern, 702–19. Leiden: Brill.

Bush, Richard. 1982. *The Politics of Cotton Textiles in Kuomintang China, 1927–1937.* New York: Garland.

Caldwell, Robert. 1849. *The Tinevelly Shanars: A Sketch of their Religion and their Moral Conditions and Characteristics.* Madras: Christian Knowledge Society Press.

———. [1856] 1974. *A Comparative Grammar of the Dravidian or South-Indian Family of Languages.* London: Harrison.

———. 1857. *Lectures on the Tinnevelly Missions: Descriptive of the Field, the Work and the Results.* London: Bell and Daldy.

———. 1875. *The Languages of India in Their Relation to Missionary Work.* London: R. Clay, Sons, and Taylor.

———. 1881. *Records of the Early History of the Tinnevelly Mission.* Madras: Higginbotham.

Chakrabarty, Dipesh. 1992. "Postcoloniality and the Artifice of History: Who Speaks for 'Indian' Pasts?" *Representations* 37:1–26.

Chandra, Vipan. 1988. *Imperialism, Resistance, and Reform in Late Nineteenth Century Korea: Enlightenment and the Independence Club.* Berkeley: Center for Korean Studies, University of California.

Chatterjee, Partha. 1986. *Nationalist Thought and the Colonial World: A Derivative Discourse?* London: Zed.

———. 1993. *The Nation and Its Fragments: Colonial and Postcolonial Histories.* Princeton: Princeton University Press.

Chen Gongbo. 1928a. *Zhongguo Guomindang suo daibiaode shi shenme?* (What is it that the Chinese Nationalist Party represents?). 3d ed. Shanghai: Fudan shudian.

———. 1928b. *Zhongguo lishishang de geming* (China's historical revolution). Shanghai: Fudan shudian.

———. 1928c. "Guomin geming de weiji he women de cuowu" (The crisis of the national revolution and our mistakes). In Chen Gongbo 1936, 4–24.

———. 1928d. "Zai lun disan dang" (Discussing again the third party). *Geming pinglun quanji* 8.

———. 1933a. "Xu sinian shiye jihua chugao" (Preface to the four-year industrial plan). In Chen Gongbo 1936, 121–35.

———. 1933b. "Tongzhi jingji yu zuzhi" (Economic control and organization). In Chen Gongbo 1936, 174–79.

———. 1933c. "Wei shiye jihua gao guoren" (Announcement to the people on the four-year industrial plan). In Chen Gongbo 1936, 136–60.

———. 1934a. "Heyi haiyou lianbanglun" (How can we still have federalist theories?) *Minzu zazhi* 2, no 6:797–804.

———. 1934b. "Tichang shenme de wenhua" (What kind of culture should we advocate?). *Minzu zazhi* 2, no. 8:1117 (1)–1123(7).

———. 1934c. "Geju de tongzhi jingji" (Setting up separatist regimes of economic control). In Chen Gongbo 1936, 187–92.

———. 1935a. "Zhongguo liangshi de ziji" (China's food self-sufficiency). In Chen Gongbo 1936.

———. 1935b. "Yinong liguo shi duide ma?" (Is it correct to establish the nation on the basis of agriculture?). In Chen Gongbo 1936, 167–73.

———. 1936. *Sinian congzhenglu* (Memoirs of my four years in office). Shanghai: Shangwu yinshuguan.

———. 1966. *The Communist Movement in China.* Edited by M. Wilbur. New York: Octagon.

Chen Guangfu. Interview. New York: Columbia University Oral History Project.

Chen Lai. 1993. "Ershi shiji wenhua yundong zhongde jijing zhuyi" (Radicalism in twentieth-century cultural movements). *Dongfang* 1:38–44.

Chen Xiaomei. 1991. "Misunderstanding Western Modernism: The Menglong Movement in Post-Mao China." *Representations,* no. 35 (summer): 143–62.

Chen Xiaoming. 1994. "Fanjijing yu dangdai zhishifenzi de lishi jingyu" (Antiradicalism and the historical predicament of contemporary Chinese intellectuals). *Dongfang* 1:11–15.

Chen Yutang, ed. 1993. *Zhongguo xiandai renwu minhao dacidian* (Bibliographic dictionary of modern and contemporary China). Hangzhou: Zhejiang guji chubanshe.

Ch'oe Kiyŏng. 1991. *TaeHan cheguk sigi sinmun yŏn'gu* (Studies on newspapers during the TaeHan empire). Seoul: Ilchogak.

Chŏng Chinsŏk. 1995. *Inmul Han'guk ŏllonsa* (A biographical history of the Korean media). Seoul: Nanam ch'ulp'ansa.

Chow, Rey. 1993. *Writing Diaspora.* Bloomington: Indiana University Press.

———. 1995. *Primitive Passions.* New York: Columbia University Press.

———. 1998. *Ethics after Idealism: Theory, Culture, Ethnicity, Reality.* Bloomington: Indiana University Press.

Chu Sigyŏng. 1907. "Kugŏ wa kungmun ŭi piryo" (The need for a national language and national writing). *Sŏu* 2 (January):31–34.

Clifford, James. 1989a. "Notes on Travel and Theory." In Clifford 1989b, 177–88.

Clifford, James, ed. 1989b. *Traveling Theories, Traveling Theorists.* Santa Cruz: Center for Cultural Studies, University of California at Santa Cruz.

Coble, Parks M. 1980. *The Shanghai Capitalists and the Nationalist Government, 1927–1937.* Cambridge: Harvard University Press.

———. 1991. *Facing Japan: Chinese Politics and Japanese Imperialism, 1931–1937.* Cambridge: Harvard University Press.

Crane, George. 1996. "'Special Things in Special Ways': National Economic Identity and China's Special Economic Zones." In Unger 1996, 148–68.

Cvetkovich, Ann. 1992. *Mixed Feelings: Feminism, Mass Culture, and Victorian Sensationalism.* New Brunswick, N.J.: Rutgers University Press.

Davey, Frank. 1993. *Postnational Arguments: The Politics of the Anglophone-Canadian Novel since 1967.* Toronto: University of Toronto Press.

Davis, Richard H. 1991. *Ritual in an Oscillating Universe: Worshipping Siva in Medieval India.* Princeton: Princeton University Press.

De Felice, Renzo. 1956. *Mussolini il rivoluzionario (1883–1920).* Turin: Giulio Einauidi.

Des Forges, Roger V. 1997. "States, Societies, and Civil Societies in Chinese History." In *Civil Society in China,* edited by Timothy Brook and B. Michael Frolic, 68–95. Armonk, N.Y.: M. E. Sharpe.

Ding Weizhi. 1995. "Wan Qing guocui yundong lunshu" (On the National Essence Movement in the late Qing period). *Xinhua wenzhai* 6:70–75.

Dirks, Nicholas. 1987. *The Hollow Crown: Ethnohistory of an Indian Kingdom.* Cambridge: Cambridge University Press.

———. 1990. "History as a Sign of the Modern." *Public Culture* 2, no. 2: 25–32.

———, ed. 1992. *Colonialism and Culture.* Ann Arbor: University of Michigan Press.

Dirlik, Arif. 1975. "Mass Movements and the Left Kuomintang." *Modern China* 1, no. 1: (January):46–74.

———. 1996a. "Reversals, Ironies, Hegemonies: Notes on the Contemporary Historiography of Modern China." *Modern China* 22, no. 3 (July): 243–84.

———. 1996b. "Looking Backward in the Age of Global Capital: Thoughts on History in Third World Cultural Criticism." In *In Pursuit of Contemporary East Asian Culture,* edited by Xiaobing Tang and Stephen Snyder, 183–215. London: Westview.

———. 1996c. "Chinese History and the Question of Orientalism." *History and Theory* 35, no. 4 (December): 96–122.

———. 1997. "Modernism and Antimodernism in Mao Zedong's Marxism." In *Critical Perspectives on Mao Zedong's Thought,* edited by Arif Dirlik, Paul Healy, and Nick Knight, 59–83. New Jersey: Humanities Press.

Dittmer, Lowell, and Samuel S. Kim, eds. 1993. *China's Quest for National Identity.* Ithaca: Cornell University Press.

Duara, Prasenjit. 1995. *Rescuing History from the Nation: Questioning Narratives of Modern China.* Chicago: University of Chicago Press.

Dubois, Abbé J. A. [1879] 1989. *A Description of the Character, Manners, and Customs of the People of India; and of their Institutions, Religious and Civil.* 3d ed. Edited by G. U. Pope, with notes, corrections, and additions. New Delhi: Asian Educational Services.

———. [1906] 1959. *Hindu Manners, Customs, and Ceremonies.* 3d ed. Edited and translated by Henry K. Beauchamp. Oxford: Clarendon.

Duus, Peter, Ramon H. Myers, and Mark R. Peattie, eds. 1989. *The Japanese Informal Empire in China, 1895–1937.* Princeton: Princeton University Press.

Eastman, Lloyd. 1990. *The Abortive Revolution: China under Nationalist Rule, 1927–1937.* Cambridge: Harvard University Press.

Ehrich, L. C., and D. Desser, eds. *Cinematic Landscapes: Observations on Visual Arts and Cinema of China and Japan.* Austin: University of Texas Press.

Esherick, Joseph. 1972. "Harvard on China: The Apologetics of Imperialism." *Bulletin of Concerned Asian Scholars* 4, no. 4 (December):9–16.

Fairbank, John K., Edwin O. Reishauer, and Albert Craig. 1968. *East Asia: Tradition and Transformation.* Boston: Houghton Mifflin.

Fang Keli. 1995. "Jicheng pipan, zonghe chuangxin" (Inheriting through critique, creating through hybridization). *Xinhua wenzhai* 11:147–49.

Fang Xiangting. 1934. "The Cooperative Movement in China." *Nankai University Monthly Bulletin on Economic China* 7 (May): 5.

Fee, Elizabeth, and Dorothy Porter. 1992. "Public Health, Preventive Medicine, and Professionalization." In *Medicine in Society: Historical Essays,* edited by Andrew Wear. Cambridge: Cambridge University Press.

Feng Ziyou, ed. 1931. *Wang Jingwei xiansheng wenji* (Collected writings of Mr. Wang Jingwei). N.p.: Dahan ribao.

Field, Norma. 1993. "Beyond Envy, Boredom, and Suffering: Toward an Emancipatory Politics for Resident Koreans and Other Japanese." *positions* 1, no. 3:640–70.

Fitzgerald, John. 1996. *Awakening China: Politics, Culture, and Class in the Nationalist Revolution.* Stanford: Stanford University Press.

Fletcher, Joseph, Jr. 1979. "A Brief History of the Chinese Northwestern Frontier." In *China's Inner Asian Frontier,* edited by Mary Ellen Alonso, 21–51. Cambridge: Peabody Museum, Harvard University.

Foucault, Michel. 1977. *Discipline and Punish: The Birth of the Prison.* New York: Pantheon.

Fray, C. R., ed. 1940. *Cambridge History of the British Empire.* Cambridge: Cambridge University Press.

Friedman, Edward. 1994. "Reconstructing China's National Identity: A Southern Alternative to Mao-Era Anti-Imperialist Nationalism." *Journal of Asian Studies* 53, no. 1 (February): 67–91.

———. 1996. "A Democratic Chinese Nationalism?" In Unger 1996, 169–82.

Fukuda Masayoshi. 1943. *Gotō Shimpei.* Tokyo: Manshū nichinichi shimbun Tōkyō shisha shuppanbu.

Fukuyama, Francis. 1992. *The End of History and the Last Man.* New York: Free Press.

Fukuzawa, Yukichi. [1875] 1995. *Bunmeiron no gairyaku* (An outline of a theory of civilization). Tokyo: Iwanami shoten.

———. 1960. *The Autobiography of Fukuzawa Yukichi.* Translated by Eiichi Kiyooka. New York: Columbia University Press.

Funabashi, Yoichi. 1991. "Globalize Asia." *New Perspectives Quarterly* 9, no. 1: 23–27.

———. 1993. "The Asianization of Asia." *Foreign Affairs* 72, no. 5: 75–85.

Gallagher, John, and Ronald Robinson. 1953. "The Imperialism of Free Trade." *Economic History Review,* 2d ser., 6, no. 1: 1–15.

Gan Chunsong. 1996. "Zhuanxing zhongde wenhua ji qi fazhanzhilu" (Culture in transition and development). *Xinhua wenzhai* 1:152–55.

Gao Ruiquan. 1995. "Lun dangdai Zhongguo jiazhiguan de shiluo" (On the loss of the modern Chinese value system). *Xinhua wenzhai* 3:20–23.

Garon, Sheldon. 1993. "The World's Oldest Debate? Prostitution and the State in Imperial Japan, 1900–1945." *American Historical Review* 98, no. 3: 710–33.

Gellner, Ernest. 1983. *Nations and Nationalism.* Ithaca: Cornell University Press.

Gilman, Sander. 1988. *Disease and Representation: Images of Illness from Madness to AIDS.* Ithaca: Cornell University Press.

Gilmartin, Christina K., et al., eds. 1994. *Engendering China: Women, Culture, and the State.* Cambridge: Harvard University Press.

Gilroy, Paul. 1993. *The Black Atlantic: Modernity and Double Consciousness.* Cambridge: Harvard University Press.

Gluck, Carol. 1985. *Japan's Modern Myths: Ideology in the Late Meiji Period.* Princeton: Princeton University Press.

Golden, Seana, and John Minford. 1990. "Yang Lian and the Chinese Tradition." In

Worlds Apart: Recent Chinese Writing and Its Audiences, edited by Howard Gold-blatt, 119–37. Armonk, N.Y.: M. E. Sharpe.

Goldman, Merle, Perry Link, and W. Su. 1993. "China's Intellectuals in the Deng Era: Loss of Identity with the State." In *China's Quest for National Identity,* edited by Lowell Dittmer and Samuel S. Kim, 125–53. Ithaca: Cornell University Press.

Goodman, Bryna. 1995. *Native Place, City, and Nation: Regional Identities and Networks in Shanghai.* Berkeley: University of California Press.

Goodman, S. G., and Gerald Segal, eds. 1994. *China Deconstructs: Politics, Trade, and Regionalism.* London: Routledge.

Gotō Shimpei. 1890. "Fūten no sei" (Policy toward mental illness). *Tōkyō iji shinshi* (Tokyo medical news). 630:452; 631:511–13.

Gover, Charles E. [1871] 1959. *Folk Songs of Southern India.* Madras: South India Saiva Siddhanta Works.

Grafe, Hugald. 1990. *The History of Christianity in Tamilnadu from 1800 to 1975.* Bangalore: Church History Association of India.

Greenfeld, Karl Taro. 1994. *Speed Tribes: Days and Nights with Japan's Next Generation.* New York: Harper Collins.

Gundert, H. 1869. "On the Dravidian Elements in Sanskrit." *Journal of the German Oriental Society.*

Gu Mingyan and Gao Yiming. 1995. "Xiandaihua yu Zhongguo wenhua chuantong jiaoyu" (Modernization and the teaching of the Chinese cultural tradition). *Xinhua wenzhai* 12:150–53.

Gu Xin and David Kelly. 1994. "New Conservatism: Intermediate Ideology of a 'New Elite.'" In *China's Quiet Revolution,* edited by David S. G. Goodman and Beverly Hooper, 219–33. New York: St. Martin's.

Hall, John A. 1993. "Nationalisms: Classified and Explained." *Daedalus* (summer): 1–28.

———, et al. 1996. *Modernity: An Introduction to Modern Societies.* Oxford: Blackwell.

Hall, Stuart. 1991. "The Local and the Global: Globalization and Ethnicity." In *Culture, Globalization, and the World-System,* edited by Anthony D. King, 19–40. Binghamton: State University of New York.

Hamlin, Christopher. 1994. "State Medicine in Great Britain." In *The History of Public Health and the Modern State,* edited by Dorothy Porter, 132–64. Amsterdam: Rodopi.

Han Shaogong. 1995. "Shijie" (The world). *Xinhua wenzhai* 3:88–93.

Han'guk munhŏn yŏn'guso, ed. 1971–77. *Han'guk kaehwagi kyogwasŏ* (A collection of textbooks from the Korean Enlightenment period). Seoul: Asea munhwasa.

Harsin, Jill. 1985. *Policing Prostitution in Nineteenth-Century Paris.* Princeton: Princeton University Press.

Harvey, David. 1990. *The Condition of Postmodernity.* Oxford: Blackwell.

Hein, Laura, and Ellen Hammond. 1995. "Homing in on Asia: Identity in Contemporary Japan." *Bulletin of Concerned Asian Scholars* 27, no. 3: 3–17.

Heisig, James W., and John C. Maraldo. 1994. *Rude Awakenings: Zen, the Kyoto School, and the Question of Nationalism.* Honolulu: University of Hawaii Press.

Heiwa hakubutsukan, ed. 1990. *Kami no sensō: senden* (The paper war: propaganda). Tokyo: Emiirusha.

Hiruta Genshirō. 1985. *Hayari yamai to kitsunetsuki: kinsei shomin no iryō jijō* (Epidemic disease and fox possession: popular medicine in the early modern period). Tokyo: Misuzu shobō.

Ho, Ping-ti. 1998. "In Defense of Sinicization: A Rebuttal of Evelyn Rawski's 'Reenvisioning the Qing.'" *Journal of Asian Studies* 57, no. 1: 123–55.

Hoare, James. 1994. *Japan's Treaty Ports and Foreign Settlements: The Uninvited Guests, 1858–1899*. Folkstone, Kent: Japan Library.

Hobsbawm, Eric. J. 1990. *Nations and Nationalism since 1780*. Cambridge: Cambridge University Press.

hooks, bell. 1994. "Essentialism and Experience." In *Teaching to Transgress: Education as the Practice of Freedom*, 77–92. New York: Routledge.

Hoston, Germaine. 1994. *The State, Identity, and the National Question in China and Japan*. Princeton: Princeton University Press.

Hou Chi-ming. 1954. *Foreign Capital in China's Economic Development, 1895–1937*. Ann Arbor: University Microfilms.

Hou Yangxiang. 1995. "Ruxue yu xiandaihua: Yang Xiangkui xiansheng fantanlu" (Confucianism and modernization: a conversation with Yang Xiangkui). *Xinhua wenzhai* 5:153–57.

Hough, James. 1824. *A Reply to the Letters of the Abbe Dubois on the State of Christianity in India*. London: Seeley and Son.

Hulbert, Homer. [1905] 1962. *The History of Korea*. Edited by Clarence Weems. New York: Hillary House.

Huntington, Samuel. 1993a. "The Clash of Civilizations?" *Foreign Affairs* 72, no. 3: 22–49.

———. 1993b. "Why International Primacy Matters." *International Security* 17, no. 4: 68–83.

———. 1993c. "The Islamic-Confucian Connection." *New Perspectives Quarterly* 10, no. 3: 19–23.

Hutchinson, John. 1994."Cultural Nationalism and Moral Regeneration." In Hutchinson and Smith 1994, 122–31.

Hutchinson, John, and Anthony Smith, eds. 1994. *Nationalism*. Oxford: Oxford University Press.

Hwang Hyŏn. 1971. *Maech'ŏn yarok* (Hwang Hyŏn's unofficial history). Seoul: Yŏksa p'yŏn ch'an wiwŏnhoe.

Hwangsŏng sinmun (Capital gazette). [1898–1910] 1974. Seoul: Han'guk munhwa kaebalsa.

Inden, Ronald. 1990. *Imagining India*. Oxford: Basil Blackwell.

Inoue Tetsujirō. 1892. "Tōyō shigaku no kachi" (The value of oriental historical studies). *Shigaku zasshi* 24:704–17.

Irschick, Eugene F. 1969. *Politics and Social Conflict in South India: The Non-Brahmin Movement and Tamil Separatism*. Berkeley: University of California Press.

———. 1994. *Dialogue and History: Constructing South India, 1795–1895*. Berkeley: University of California Press.

Ishihara Shintarō. 1990. *Toki no shiosai: Nihon to sekai o meguru chichi to ko to no 14 no taiwa* (Sounds on the shore of time: fourteen dialogues on Japan and the world). Tokyo: PHP.

————. 1991. *A Japan That Can Say No.* Translated by Frank Baldwin. New York: Simon and Schuster.

Iwashita, Masahira. 1892. "Shintō wa saiten no kozoku to'iu ron o yonde sono mō o benzu" (In refutation of the argument that Shinto is an old superstition). *Kokkō* 3, 10:33–44.

Janetta, Ann Bowman. 1997. "From Physician to Bureaucrat: The Case of Nagayo Sensai." In *New Directions in the Study of Meiji Japan,* edited by Helen Hardacre and Adam L. Kern, 151–60. Leiden: Brill.

Jiang Yongjing. 1993. "Guomindang sanjutou Hu Wang Jiang de fenhe" (Alliances among the three Guomindang heads, Hu Hanmin, Wang Jingwei, and Jiang Jieshi). *Zhuanji wenxue* (Biographical literature) 62, no. 3:15–24.

Johnson, Chalmers. 1962. *Peasant Nationalism and Communist Power: The Emergence of Revolutionary China.* Stanford: Stanford University Press.

Johnston, William. 1995. *The Modern Epidemic: The History of Tuberculosis in Japan.* Cambridge: Center for East Asian Research, Harvard University.

Jones, Andrew F. 1992. *Like a Knife: Ideology and Genre in Contemporary Chinese Popular Music.* Ithaca: East Asia Program, Cornell University.

Jones, Eric. 1994. "Asia's Fate: A Response to the Singapore School." *National Interest* 35 (spring): 18–28.

Kailasapathy, K. 1986. *On Art and Literature.* Madras: New Century Books.

Kaneko Junji, ed. 1965. *Nihon seishin byōgaku shoshi Meiji hen, Nihon saiban seishin byōgaku shoshi* (A bibliography of Japanese psychiatry: the Meiji period, a bibliography of forensic psychiatry). Tokyo: Nihon seishin byōin shoshi.

Kaneko Kentarō. 1891. "Kokushi hensan wa genji no kinmu" (Compiling a national history is urgent business). *Kokkō* 2, no. 9: 54–59.

Kaneko Tsuguo. 1982. *Matsuzawa byōin gaishi* (A brief history of Matsuzawa Hospital). Tokyo: Nihon hyōronsha.

Kariya Haruo. 1993. *Edo no seibyō: baidoku ryūkō jijō* (Venereal disease in the Edo period: the spread of syphilis) Tokyo: San'ichi shobō.

Kasza, Gregory J. 1995. *The Conscription Society: Administered Mass Organization.* New Haven: Yale University Press.

Katsu Kaishū. 1971. *Katsu Kaishū zenshū* (The complete works of Katsu Kaishū). Tokyo: Keisō shobō.

Kawakami Takeshi. 1982. *Gendai Nihon byōnin shi* (A history of the sick in modern Japan). Tokyo: Keisō shobō.

Kawamura Kunimitsu. 1990. *Genshi suru kindai kūkan* (Visions of modernity). Tokyo: Seiyusha.

Keene, Donald. 1971. "The Sino-Japanese War of 1894–95 and Its Cultural Effects." In *Tradition and Modernization in Japanese Culture,* edited by Donald Shiveley, 121–75. Princeton: Princeton University Press.

Kiernan, V. G. 1995. *Imperialism and its Contradictions.* Edited by Harvey J. Kane. New York: Routledge.

Kim Key-hiuk. 1980. *The Last Phase of the East Asian World Order: Korea, Japan, and the Chinese Empire, 1860–82.* Berkeley: University of California Press.

Kobayashi Yōtarō. 1991. "'Saiajiaka' no susume" (Re-Asianization). *Foresight* (April): 44–46.

Kohn, Hans. 1944. *The Idea of Nationalism: A Study in Its Origins and Background.* New York: Macmillan.

Kon Satoshi. 1991. *Waarudo apaatomento horaa* (World apartment horror). Tokyo: Kōdansha.

Konakamura Yoshikata. 1890. "Kokushi kokubun kenkyū no hitsuyō o ronzu" (On the necessity of studying national history and national letters). *Kokkō* 2, no. 2: 38–39.

Kong Fanjin. 1995. "Ershi shiji Zhongguo wenxue yanjiu zhong de erge wenti" (Two questions in twentieth-century Chinese literary studies). *Xinhua wenzhai* 6:112–14.

Kong Genghong. 1995. "Wenhua chongtu lilun pingshu"(On 'The Clash of Civilizations?'). *Xinhua wenzhai* 4:157–59.

Koppedrayer, K. I. 1991. "Are Sudras entitled to Ride in the Palanquin?" *Contributions to Indian Sociology* 25, no. 2: 191–210.

Kōseishō imukyoku, ed. 1955. *Isei hachijūnenshi* (A history of 80 years of medical policy). Tokyo: Ōkurashō insatsukyoku.

Kume Kunitake. 1891. "Shintō wa saiten no kozoku" (Shinto is an outdated custom of heaven worship). *Shigaku zasshi* 23–25. Reprinted in *Kume Kunitake chosakushū*, ed. Ōkubo Toshiaki. *Yoshikawa kōbunkan* 3 (1990): 271–96.

Kume Kunitake, Shigeno Yasutsugu, and Hoshino Hiroshi. 1890. *Kokushigan* (Perspectives on national history). Tokyo: Teikoku daigaku zōban.

Kungmin sohak tokpon (A primary reader for citizens). 1895. In Han'guk munhŏn yŏnguso 1971–77.

Kunikida Doppo. 1976. "Byōshō roku" (A sickbed journal). In *Kunikida Doppo zenshū* (Complete works of Kunikida Doppo), vol. 9. Rpt. Tokyo: Gakushū kenkyūsha.

Kure Shūzō. 1902. "Tenkyōin no setsuritsu wa nanika tame ni chichu sururu ya" (Why do we hesitate to establish asylums?). *Ikai jihō* 395:4–5.

Ledyard, Gari K. 1966. "The Korean Language Reform of 1446." Ph.D. diss., University of California at Berkeley.

Lee, James. 1982. "China's Southwestern Frontier: State Policy and Economic Development, 1250–1850." Ph.D. diss., University of Chicago.

———. 1991. "The Southwest: Yunnan and Guizhou." In *Nourish the People: The State Civilian Granary System in China, 1650–1850,* edited by Pierre-Étienne Will and R. Bin Wong, 431–74. Ann Arbor: Center for Chinese Studies, University of Michigan.

Lee Kuan Yew. 1992. "The East Asian Way." *New Perspectives Quarterly* 9, no. 1: 4–13.

———. 1993. "East Asia is North America's Economic Locomotive." *New Perspectives Quarterly* 10, no. 2: 24–29.

Lee, Leo Ou-fan. 1990. "Beyond Realism: Thoughts on Modernist Experiments in Contemporary Chinese Writing." In *Worlds Apart,* edited by Howard Goldblatt, 64–77. Armonk, N.Y.: M. E. Sharpe.

———. 1991a. "Modernity and Its Discontents: The Cultural Agenda of the May Fourth Movement." In *Perspectives on Modern China,* edited by Kenneth Lieberthal et al., 158–77. Armonk, N.Y.: M. E. Sharpe.

———. 1991b. "The Tradition of Modern Chinese Cinema: Some Preliminary Explorations and Hypotheses." In *Perspectives on Chinese Cinema,* edited by Chris Berry, 6–20. London: BFI.

Levenson, Joseph R. 1965. *Confucian China and Its Modern Fate.* Berkeley: University of California Press.

Li Shuyi and Li Xiaobing. 1987. *Wenhua chongtu yu xuanze* (The clash and choices of cultures). Beijing: Renmin chubanshe.

Liu, Wenjian. 1994. "The Dao in Modern Chinese Art." In *China Avant-Garde: Counter-Currents in Arts and Culture,* edited by Jochen Noth, Wolfger Pohlmann, and Kai Reschke, 55–64. Hong Kong: Oxford University Press.

Li Xianting. 1993. "Major Trends in the Development of Contemporary Chinese Art." In *China's New Art, Post-1989.* Hong Kong: Hanart TZ Gallery.

Li Yiming. 1996. "Shiji zhi mo: shehui de daode weiji yu diwudai dianying de suo zhongzhengqin"(The end of the century: society's moral crisis and the death of fifth-generation film). *Dianying yishu* 1:9–13.

Li Zehuo. 1987. *Zhongguo xiandai sixiang shilun* (Treatises on the modern intellectual history of China). Beijing: Dongfang chubanshe.

Liu Dong. 1993. "Zhongguo nengzou dongya daolu ma?" (Can China adopt the East Asian model?) *Dongfang* 1:7–16.

Liu Sanfu. 1995. "Rujiao daode tixi yu shidai wenhua jingshende jiazhi cuowei" (The discrepancy between the Confucian value system and the cultural spirit of our time). *Xinhua wenzhai* 11:148–52.

Luo Dunwei. 1952. *Wushinian huiyi* (A memoir of fifty years). Taibei: Zhongguo wenhua gongyingshe.

Ma Ning. 1987. "Notes on the New Film Makers." In *Chinese Film: The State of the Art in the People's Republic,* edited by George S. Semsel, 63–106. New York: Praeger.

Mahbubani, Kishore. 1995a. "The Pacific Way." *Foreign Affairs* 74, no. 1: 100–111.

———. 1995b. "Why Asia's Balkans Are at Peace." *New Perspectives Quarterly* 12, no. 1: 51–53.

Mani, Lata. 1989. "Multiple Medications: Feminist Scholarship in the Age of Multinational Reception." In James Clifford 1989b, 1–23.

Mantetsu kabushiki kaisha shanhai jimusho (Shanghai office of the South Manchurian Railway Company). 1938. *Chū Shi senryō chiku nōgyō keizai gaikan* (Overview of the agricultural economy in the occupied areas of Central China). Shanghai: Mantetsu.

Mao Zedong [Tse-tung]. [1940] 1967. "On New Democracy." In the *Selected Works of Mao Tse-tung.* Beijing: Foreign Languages Press.

Maraimalai Adigal. 1940. *Saiva Siddhanta as a Philosophy of Practical Knowledge.* Madras: SISSW.

———. [1908] 1980. *Cinthanaik katturaikal* (Reflective essays). Madras: Saiva Siddhanta Works Publishing Society.

———. [1923] 1975. *Velalar nagarigam* (The civilization of the Velalars). Madras: South India Saiva Siddhanta Works.

———. [1929] 1957a. *Kadavul nilaikku marana kolkaikal saivam aaka* (Saivism is consonant with the nature and ways of God). Madras: South India Saiva Siddhanta Works.

————. 1957b. *Comacuntarnayagar varalaru* (The life history of Somasundara Naya-gar). Madras: South India Saiva Siddhanta Works.

Marx, Karl. 1906. *Capital.* Vol 1. Chicago: Kerr.

Masao, Miyoshi. 1996. "A Borderless World? From Colonialism to Transnationalism and the Decline of the Nation-State." In *Global/Local: Cultural Production and the Transnational Imaginary,* edited by Rob Wilson and Wimal Dissanayake. Durham: Duke University Press. Rpt. First published in 1993.

Masaoka Shiki. 1992. *Byōshō roku shaku* (The six-foot-long sick bed). 39th printing. Tokyo: Iwanami bunko.

Massey, Doreen. 1992. "A Place Called Home?" *New Formations* 17:3–15.

Matsumoto Jun. 1980. "Ranchū jiden" (The autobiography of Ranchū). In *Matsumoto Jun jiden Nagayo Sensai jiden* (The autobiographies of Matsumoto Jun and Nagayo Sensai), edited by Ogawa Kenzō and Sakai Shizu. Tokyo: Heibonsha.

Matsumoto Teruo. 1975. *Kindai Nihon ni okeru kazokuhō* (Family law in modern Japan). Tokyo: Kobunkan.

Matsuyama Tōan. 1883. "Eiseihō fukyū no kōsatsu" (On the need to diffuse the public health laws). *Dai Nihon shiritsu eiseikai zasshi* (Magazine of the Public Health Association of Japan) 2:2–6.

McCormack, Gavan. 1996. *The Emptiness of Japanese Affluence.* Armonk, N.Y.: M. E. Sharpe.

Meenakshisundaram, K., ed. 1974. *The Contribution of European Scholars to Tamil.* Madras: University of Madras.

Mercer, Kobena. 1994. *Welcome to the Jungle: New Positions in Black Cultural Studies.* New York: Routledge.

Ministry of Education. 1907. *Kugŏ tokpon* (A Korean language reader). In Han'guk munhŏn yŏn'guso, 1971–77.

Mittler, Barbara. 1994. "Chinese Music in the 1980s: The Aesthetics of Eclecticism." In *China Avant-Garde: Counter-Currents in Art and Culture,* edited by Jochen Noth et al., 80–88. Hong Kong: Oxford University Press.

Miyamoto Shinobu. 1975. *Nihon ni okeru kindai igaku no seiritsu* (The establishment of modern medicine in Japan). Vol. 3 of *Igaku shisōshi* (An intellectual history of medicine). Tokyo: Keisō shobō.

Mozume Takami. 1894. "Rekishi no kakikata, mata rekishi no oshiekata ni tsukite omoeru kotodomo" (Thoughts on the writing and teaching of history). *Kokugakuin zasshi* 1, no. 2: 1–2.

Mune Atsunori. 1896. "Rekishi wa kenkoku no kiso" *Kokkō* 8, no. 4: 25–29.

Nagao Setsuzō. 1983. *Nagao Setsuzō zenshū* (The collected works of Nagao Setsuzō). Tokyo: Shunshōsha.

Nagayo Sensai. 1883. "Eisei gokai no ben" (Correcting the mistaken understanding of hygiene). *Dai Nihon shiritsu eiseikai zasshi* (Magazine of the Public Health Association of Japan) 2:27–33.

————. 1980. "Shōkō shishi." In *Matsumoto Jun jiden Nagayo Sensai jiden* (The autobiographies of Matsumoto Jun and Nagayo Sensai), edited by Ogawa Kenzō and Sakai Shizu, 104–85. Tokyo: Heibonsha.

Naimushō eiseikyoku. 1925. *Isei gojūnenshi* (A history of fifty years of medical policy). Tokyo: Ōkurashō insatsukyoku.

Naitō Chisō. 1889. "Rekishi no dokuhō" (How to read history). *Nihon bungaku* (Japanese literature) 13:5–8.

Nakayama Yasumasa, ed. 1982. *Shinbun shusei Meiji hennenshi.* (An anthology of selections from newspapers, Meiji period editions). 15 vols. Tokyo: Honpo shoseki.

Nallaswami Pillai, J. M. 1895. *Sivajnana Botham of Meikanda Deva: Translated with Notes and Introduction.* Madras: Sri La Sri Somasundara Nayagar.

———. 1913. *Sivajnana Siddhiyar of Arulnandi Sivacharyar.* Madras: Meykandan Press.

Nanjing shi dang'anguan (Nanjing Municipal Archives), ed. 1992. *Shenxun Wang wei hanjian bilu* (Records of the court examinations of traitors of the Wang Jingwei regime). 2 vols. Nanjing: Jiangsu guji chubanshe.

Narita Ryūichi. 1982. "Eisei kankyō no henka ni naka no josei to joseikan" (Women and changing conceptions of women within the changing public health environment). In *Nihon josei seikatsushi* (History of the everyday life of Japanese women), vol. 4: 89–124. Tokyo: Tōkyō daigaku shuppankai.

Nathan, Andrew. 1972. "Imperialism's Effect on China." *Bulletin of Concerned Asian Scholars* 4, no. 4 (December): 3–8.

Ni Zhen. 1994. "Classical Chinese Painting and Cinematic Signification." In *Cinematic Landscapes,* edited by Linda C. Ehrlich and David Desser, 63–80. Austin: University of Texas Press.

Nihon gakujutsu gakkai, ed. 1965. *Igaku* (Medicine). Vol. 24 of *Nihon kagaku gijutsushi taikei* (General history of Japanese science and technology). Tokyo: Daiichi hōki shuppan.

Nihon ishi gakkai, ed. 1979. *Zuroku Nihon iji bunka shiryō shusei* (An illustrated collection of materials on Japanese medical culture). Tokyo: San'ichi shobō.

Nishigori Takekiyo. 1889. *Kami mo hotoke mo nai yami no yō no naka* (In a dark world without God or Buddha). Tokyo: Shunyōdō.

Nolte, Sharon, and Sally Ann Hastings. 1991. "The Meiji State's Policy toward Women, 1890–1910." In *Recreating Japanese Women, 1600–1945,* edited by Gail Bernstein, 151–74. Berkeley: University of California Press.

Numata Jirō and Arase Susumu, trans. 1968. *Nihon taizai kenbunki* (A record of a stay in Japan), by Pompe Van Meedervort. Tokyo: Omatsudō shoten.

Oda Susumu. 1990. *Nihon no kyōkishi* (A history of madness in Japan). Tokyo: Shisakusha.

Ogawa Kenzō and Sakai Shizu, eds. 1980. *Matsumoto Jun jiden Nagayo Sensai jiden* (The autobiographies of Matsumoto Jun and Nagayo Sensai). Tokyo: Heibonsha.

Ohmae, Kenichi. 1993. "The Rise of the Region State." *Foreign Affairs* 72, no. 2: 78–87.

———. 1995a. *Shin Ōmae Ken'ichi repōto* (The new Kenichi Ohmae report). Tokyo: Kōdansha.

———. 1995b. *The End of the Nation State.* New York: Free Press.

Okada Yasuo. 1981. *Shisetsu Matsuzawa byōinshi* (A personal history of the Matsuzawa Hospital). Tokyo: Iwasaki gakujutsu shuppan.

Okada Yasuo and Yoshioka Shin'ichi. 1966. "Sōma jiken toshite mita Gotō Shimpei"

(Gotō Shimpei as seen in the Sōma Incident). *Igakushi kenkyū* (Studies in medical history) 19:990–92.

Ōkubo Toshiaki. 1988. *Nihon kindai shigaku no seiritsu* (The establishment of modern historical studies in Japan). Tokyo: Yoshikawa kōbunkan.

Ong, Aihwa. 1993. "On the Edge of Empires: Flexible Citizenship among Chinese Diaspora." *positions* 1, no. 3: 745–78.

Orr, Linda. 1990. *Headless History: Nineteenth-Century French Historiography on the Revolution.* Ithaca: Cornell University Press.

Ozawa Ichirō. 1993. *Nihon kaizō keikaku* (A plan to reform Japan). Tokyo: Kōdansha.

Peng Yongjie. 1995. "Lun Zhongguo chuantong wenhua de zaisheng wenti" (On the rebirth of Chinese traditional culture). *Xinhua wenzhai* 11:151–53.

Perfetti, Francesco. 1991. *La Camera dei Fasci e delle Corporazioni.* Rome: Bonacci.

Perry, Elizabeth. 1993. *Shanghai on Strike.* Stanford: Stanford University Press.

Petrella, Riccardo. 1991. "World City-States of the Future." *New Perspectives Quarterly* 8, no. 4: 59–64.

———. 1995. "A Global Agora vs. Gated City-Regions." *New Perspectives Quarterly* 12, no. 1: 21–22.

Pillai, K. K., ed. 1957. *Professor P. Sundaram Pillai Commemoration Volume.* Madras: South India Saiva Siddhanta Works.

Pollack, David. 1993. "The Revenge of the Illegal Asians: Aliens, Gangsters, and Myth in Kon Satoshi's *World Apartment Horror.*" *positions* 1, no. 3: 677–714.

Pollock, Sheldon. 1993. "Deep Orientalism? Notes on Sanskrit and Power beyond the Raj." In *Orientalism and the Postcolonial Predicament: Perspectives on South Asia,* edited by Carol A. Breckenridge and Peter van der Veer, 76–134. Philadelphia: University of Pennsylvania Press.

Polanyi, Karl. 1944. *The Great Transformation.* Boston: Beacon

Pomeranz, Kenneth. 1993. *The Making of a Hinterland: State, Society, and Economy in Inland North China, 1853–1937.* Berkeley: University of California Press.

Pope, G. U. 1879. *A Description of the Character, Manners, and Customs of the People of India; and of their Institutions, Religious and Civil, by the Abbe J. A. Dubois, with Notes, Corrections, and Additions.* Madras: Higginbotham and Co.

———. 1886. *The "Sacred" Kurral of Tiruvalluva-Nayanar.* London: W. H. Allen.

———. [1893] 1984. *The Naladiyar or Four Hundred Quatrains in Tamil, with Introduction, Translation, and Notes, Critical, Philological, and Explanatory.* New Delhi: Asian Educational Services.

———. 1900. *The Tiruvacagam or Sacred Utterances of the Tamil Poet, Saint, and Sage Manikka-Vacagar:The Tamil Text of the Fifty One Poems.* Oxford: Clarendon.

———. 1910. "Pura-Porul, 'The Objective,' with an Introduction by J. M. Nallaswami Pillai." *Tamilian Antiquary* 1, no. 4: 1–44.

———. 1973. *Tamil Heroic Poems.* Madras: South India Saiva Siddhanta Works.

Prakash, Gyan. 1990. "Writing Post-Orientalist Histories of the Third World: Perspectives from Indian Historiography." *Comparative Studies in Society and History* 32: 383–408.

Prentiss, Karen P. 1996. "A Tamil Lineage for Saiva Siddhanta Philosophy." *History of Religions* 35, no. 3: 231–57.

Promorska, Krystyna. 1968. Foreword to *Rabelais and His World,* by Mikhail Bakhtin. Bloomington: Indiana University Press.

Pusey, James Reeve. 1982. *China and Charles Darwin.* Cambridge: Harvard University Press.

Qing Xiaoying. 1996. "Guanyu 'bu' de duanxiang" (Thoughts on "no"). In *Zhongguo haishi neng shuo "bu"* (China can still say "no"). Beijing: Zhongguo wenlian chuban gongsi.

Ramsey, Matthew. 1994. "Public Health in France." In *The History of Public Health and the Modern State,* edited by Dorothy Porter, 45–118. Amsterdam: Rodopi B.V.

Ravindiran, V. 1996. "The Unanticipated Legacy of Robert Caldwell and the Dravidian Movement." *South Indian Studies* 1, no. 1: 83–110.

———. 1999. "Caste, Hybridity and the Construction of Cultural Identity in Colonial India: Maraimalai Adigal and the Intellectual Genealogy of Dravidian Nationalism, 1800–1950." Ph.D. diss., University of Toronto.

Rawski, Evelyn. 1996. "Reenvisioning the Qing: The Significance of the Qing Period in Chinese History." *Journal of Asian Studies* 55, no. 4: 829–50.

Rayns, Tony. 1991. "Breakthroughs and Setbacks: The Origin of the New Chinese Cinema." In *Perspectives on Chinese Cinema,* edited by Chris Berry, 104–14. London: BFI.

Redesdale, Algernon Bertram Sidney. 1912. *A Tragedy in Stone and Other Papers.* London and New York: John Lane.

Renan, Ernest. [1882] 1996. *Qu'est-ce qu'un nation?/What Is a Nation?* Translated by Wanda Romer Taylor. Toronto: Tapir Press.

Robinson, Michael. 1988. *Cultural Nationalism in Colonial Korea, 1920–1925.* Seattle: University of Washington Press.

———. 1989. "National Identity and the Thought of Sin Ch'aeho: *Sadaejuŭi* and *Chuch'e* in History and Politics." *Journal of Korean Studies* 10: 121–42.

———. 1993. "Enduring Anxieties: Cultural Nationalism and Modern East Asia." In *Cultural Nationalism in East Asia: Representation and Identity,* edited by Harumi Befu, 167–86. Berkeley: Institute of East Asian Studies, University of California.

Rofel, Lisa. 1995. "The Melodrama of National Identity in Post-Tiananmen China." In *To Be Continued: Soap Operas around the World,* edited by Robert C. Allen, 301–20. London: Routledge.

Rosen, George. 1993. *A History of Public Health.* Expanded ed. Baltimore: Johns Hopkins University Press.

Rosen, Stanley, and Gary Zou. 1991. "Editor's Introduction." *Chinese Sociology and Anthropology* (winter): 1–7.

Rouse, Roger. 1995. "Thinking through Transnationalism: Notes on the Cultural Politics of Class Relations in the Contemporary United States." *Public Culture* 7, no. 2: 353–402.

Rowe, William. 1994. "Education and Empire in Southwest China: Ch'en Hung-mou in Yunnan, 1733–38." In *Education and Society in Late Imperial China, 1600–1900,* edited by Benjamin Elman and Alexander Woodside, 417–57. Berkeley: University of California Press.

Rutt, Richard, ed. 1972. *James Scarth Gale and His History of the Korean People*. Seoul: Royal Asiatic Society.

Said, Edward. 1978. *Orientalism*. New York: Random House.

————. 1993. *Culture and Imperialism*. New York: Random House.

Sakai, Naoki. 1989. "Modernity and Its Critique: The Problem of Universalism and Particularism." In *Postmodernism and Japan*, edited by Masao Miyoshi and H. D. Harootunian, 93–122. Durham: Duke University Press.

Sawada Ken. 1929. *Gotō Shimpei ichidai ki* (A record of the life of Gotō Shimpei). Tokyo: Heibonsha.

Schleiner, Winfried. 1994. "Infection and Cure through Women: Renaissance Constructions of Syphilis." *Jounal of Medieval and Renaissance Studies* 24, no. 3 (fall): 502–55.

Schmid, Andre. 1997. "Rediscovering Manchuria: Sin Ch'aeho and the Politics of Territorial History in Korea." *Journal of Asian Studies* 56, no. 1 (February): 26–46.

————. Forthcoming. *Korea Between Empires: Nation and Identity in East Asia, 1895–1919*.

Schmitthenner, Peter Lee. 1991. "Charles Philip Brown, 1798–1884: The Legacy of an East India Company Servant and Scholar of South India." Ph.D. diss., University of Wisconsin at Madison.

Schram, Stuart, ed. 1974. *Mao Tse-tung Unrehearsed: Talks and Letters, 1956–71*. Harmondsworth: Penguin.

Sekine Masanao. 1892. "Shigaku shiken" (Thoughts on history). *Kōten kōkyūsho kōen* 86:57–64.

Seton-Watson, Hugh. 1977. *Nations and States: An Enquiry into the Origins of Nations and the Politics of Nationalism*. Boulder: Westview

Shigeno Yasutsugu. 1879. "Kokushi hensan no hōhō o ronzu" (How to write national history). *Tōkyō gakushi kaikan zasshi* 1, no. 8: 163–81.

————. 1884. "Sejō rufu no shiden ooku jijitsu o ayamaru no setsu" (The many errors in popular historical tales). *Tōkyō gakushi kaiin zasshi* 6, no. 5: 1–23.

————. [1889] 1991. "Shigaku ni jūji suru mono wa shikō shihei narazarubekarazu" (Those who study history must be unbiased). In *Rekishi ninshiki* (Historical knowledge), edited by Tanaka Akira and Miyachi Masato, 278. Tokyo.

Shimamura Shun'ichi. 1892. "Shimane-ken kitsunetsukibyō torishirabe hōkoku" (A report of my investigation of fox possession sickness in Shimane Prefecture). *Tōkyō igakkai zasshi* (Tokyo Medical Association magazine) 6, no. 20: 981–82.

Shorter, Edward. 1997. *A History of Psychiatry*. New York: John Wiley and Sons.

Showalter, Elaine. 1985. *The Female Malady*. New York: Pantheon.

Shryock, Richard. 1948. *The Development of Modern Medicine: An Interpretation of the Social and Scientific Factors Involved*. London: V. Gollancz.

Sin Ch'aeho. 1908. "Kukhanmun ŭi kyŏngjung" (The importance of national and Chinese writing). *TaeHan maeil sinbo*, 17–19 March.

————. [1908] 1997. "Ŭlchi Mundŏk." In *Tanjae Sin Ch'aeho chŏnjip* (Complete works of Sin Ch'aeho), 2: 251–351. Seoul: Hyŏngsŏl ch'ulp'ansa.

————. 1909. "Tongyangjuŏi e taehan pi'pan" (A critique of Easternism). *TaeHan maeil sinbo*, August 8–10.

Sin Yongha. 1975. *Tongnip hyŏphoe yŏn'gu* (Studies on the Independence Club). Seoul: Ilchogak.

Sivathamby, K. 1979. "Hindu Reaction to Christian Proselytization and Westernization in 19th Century Sri Lanka." *Social Science Review* (Colombo) 1, no. 6: 41–75.

———. 1993. "The Politics of a Literary Style and Ethnic Movement." In *Ethnic Movement in India: Theory and Practice*, edited by G. Palanithurai and R. Thandavan, 115–39. Delhi: Kanishka Publishing House.

Sklair, Leslie. 1994. "Consumerism Drives the Global Mass Media System." In *Globalization and Culture Reader*, 33–38. Durham: Duke University Press.

Smith, Anthony. 1986. *The Ethnic Origins of Nations.* London: Blackwell.

So Wai-chor. 1991. *The Kuomintang Left in the National Revolution, 1924–1931.* East Asian Historical Monographs. Hong Kong: Oxford University Press.

Song Qiang et al. 1996a. *Zhongguo keyi shuo "bu"* (China can say "no"). Beijing: Zhongguo wenlian chuban gongsi.

———. 1996b. *Zhongguo haishi neng shuo "bu"* (China can still say "no"). Beijing: Zhongguo wenlian chuban gongsi.

Spongberg, Mary. 1997. *Feminizing Venereal Disease: The Body of the Prostitute in Nineteenth Century Medical Discourse.* New York: New York University Press.

Sternhell, Zeev. 1986. *Neither Right nor Left: Fascist Ideology in France.* Berkeley: University of California Press.

Stock, Eugene. 1899. *The History of the Church Missionary Society: Its Environment, Its Men, and Its Work.* Vol. 1. London: Church Missionary Society.

Subramania Mudalaiar, V. P. 1909. "A Critical Review of the Story of Ramayana: An Account of South Indian Castes in Tamil." *Tamilian Antiquary* 1, no. 2: 1–84.

Sun Yatsen. N.d. *The Principle of Nationalism.* Taipei: China Cultural Service.

———. [1924] 1953. *Fundamentals of National Reconstruction for the National Government of China.* Taipei: China Cultural Service.

Sundaram Pillai, P. 1909. "Some Mile-Stones in the History of Tamil Literature, or the Age of Tirujanana-Sambhanda." *Tamilian Antiquary* 1, no. 3: 1–65.

———. 1985. "The Ten Tamil Idylls." In *Pattupattu:Ten Tamil Idylls*, edited by J. V. Chelliah, xv–xxviii. Rpt. Thanjavur: Tamil University.

Takagi, Tomigorō. 1938. *Manshū, Hoku Shi, Chū Shi no kōgun imon narabi ni henchi kemmon no ittan* (A visit with the imperial army in Manchuria, North China, and Central China plus observations on the actual situation there). Tokyo: Nihon gaikō kyōkai chōsakyoku.

Tanaka, Stefan. 1993. *Japan's Orient: Rendering Pasts into History.* Berkeley: University of California Press.

Tang Xiaobing. 1991. "The Function of New Theory: What Does It Mean to Talk about Post-modernism in China?" *Public Culture* 4, no. 1 (fall): 89–108.

———. 1996. *Global Space and the Nationalist Discourse of Modernity: The Historical Thinking of Liang Qichao.* Stanford: Stanford University Press.

Tao Xisheng. 1930. "Tongyi yu shengchan" (Unity and production). *Xin shengming yuekan* (New life monthly) 3, no. 1 (April): 1–5.

Tatsukawa Shōji. 1971. *Byōki no shakaishi* (The social history of disease). Tokyo: Nihon hōsoku shuppan kyōkai.

————. 1979. *Kinsei byōsōshi: Edo jidai no byōki to iryō* (A history of early modern writings on disease: sickness and medicine in the Edo period). Tokyo: Heibonsha.

————. 1986. *Meiji iji ōrai* (Comings and goings in Meiji medicine). Tokyo: Shinchōsha.

Tay, William. 1990. "Avant-garde Theatre in Post-Mao China: *The Bus-Stop* by Gao Xingjian." In *Worlds Apart*, edited by Howard Goldblatt, 111–18. Armonk, N.Y.: M. E. Sharpe.

Thompson, Doug. 1991. *State Control in Fascist Italy: Culture and Conformity, 1925–43*. Manchester: Manchester University Press.

Ting, Leonard G. 1936. *Recent Developments in China's Cotton Industry*. Shanghai: Institute of Pacific Relations.

Toffler, Alvin, and Heidi Toffler. 1991. "Economic Time Zones: Fast Versus Slow." *New Perspectives Quarterly* 8, no. 4: 56–58.

Tome Yuki. 1994. "Kindai Nihon no kōshō seido to hasshō undo" (The system of licensed prostitution and the antiprostitution movement in modern Japan). In *Jenda no Nihonshi*, edited by Wakita Haruko and Susan B. Hanley, 461–91. Tokyo: Tōkyō daigaku shuppankai.

Tongnip sinmun (The independent). [1896–99] 1981. Rpt. Seoul: Kabul ch'ulp'ansa.

Tournier, Maurice. 1996. "Français à l'extrême-droite, un mot habité." In *Les mots de la nation*, edited by Sylvie Renaud, 65–81. Lyon: Presses Universitaires de Lyon.

Trautmann, Thomas R. 1997. *Aryans and British India*. Berkeley: University of California Press.

Tu Wei-ming. 1991. "The Enlightenment Mentality and the Chinese Intellectual Dilemma." In *Perspectives on Modern China*, edited by Kenneth Lieberthal et al., 103–18. Armonk, N.Y.: M. E.. Sharpe.

————. 1994. "The Confucian Dimension in the East Asian Development Model." Paper presented at the conference on Economy and Culture in Eastern Asia, Toronto.

Unger, Jonathan, ed. 1996. *Chinese Nationalism*, Armonk, N.Y.: M. E. Sharpe.

Unger, Jonathan, and Anita Chan. 1995. "China, Corporatism, and the East Asian Model." *Australian Journal of Chinese Affairs* 33 (January): 29–53.

Usui Katsumi, ed. 1966. *Nit-Chū sensō* (The Sino-Japanese War), vol. 5. Vol. 13 of *Gendaishi shiryō* (Materials on modern history). Tokyo: Misuzu shobō.

Viswanathan, Gauri, 1989. *Masks of Conquest: Literary Study and the British Rule in India*. New York: Columbia University Press.

Wallerstein, Immanuel. 1991. *Geopolitics and Geoculture: Essays on the Changing World System*. Cambridge: Cambridge University Press.

Walzer, Michael. 1993. "The New Tribalism: Notes on a Difficult Problem." *Dissent* 39, no. 2: 164–71.

Wang Hui. 1995. "Jiushi niandai Zhongguo dalu de wenhua yanjiu yu wenhua piping" (Cultural studies and cultural critique in China during the 1990s). *Dianying yishu* (Film art) 1:12–24.

Wang Jingwei. 1905. "Minzu de guomin" (A national people). In Feng 1931, 1–53.

————. 1930. "A National Economic and Financial Policy." In *The Chinese National Revolution: Essays and Documents*, edited by J. Wang and L. Dang. Beijing: China United Press.

————. [1927] 1935a. "Women yao jianshe zenyang de guojia" (What kind of nation do we want to build?). In *Wang Jingwei wencun* (Various writings of Wang Jingwei), 278–87. Shanghai: Shanghai qizhi shuju.

———. 1935b. "Jianshe" (Construction). In *Wang Jingwei wencun* (Various writings of Wang Jingwei) 275–78. Shanghai: Shanghi qizhi shuju.

———. 1938. "Annei yu rangwai" (Pacify the domestic front while resisting on the foreign front). In *Wang Jingwei xiansheng zuijin yanlun* (The most recent speeches and writings of Mr. Wang Jingwei), 27–33. Shanghai: Zhonghua ribao.

Wang Kewen. 1986. "The Left Guomindang in Opposition, 1927–1931." *Chinese Studies in History* 20, no. 2 (winter): 3–43.

Wang Shuhuai. 1984. *Mianye tongzhi weiyuanhui de gongzuo chengxiao 1933–37* (An appraisal of the work of the Cotton Control Commission, 1933–37). Taibei: Zhongyang yanjiuyuan jindaishi yanjiusuo.

Wang, Yuejin. 1991. "Red Sorghum: Mixed Memory and Desire." In *Perspectives on Chinese Cinema*, edited by Chris Berry, 80–103. London: BFI Publishing.

Wang Xilong. 1990. *Qingdai xibei tuntian yanjiu* (Studies of land colonies in the northwest in the Qing dynasty). Lanzhou: Lanzhou daxue chubanshe.

Wang Zhizhong and Wei Liying. 1989. *Ming Qing xibei shehui jingjishi yanjiu* (Studies of the social and economic history of the northwest during Ming and Qing times). Xi'an: Sanqin chubanshe.

Watson, James. L. 1992. "The Renegotiation of Chinese Cultural Identity in the Post-Mao Era." In *Popular Protest and Political Culture in Modern China: Learning from 1989*, edited by Jeffrey N. Wasserstrom and Elizabeth J. Perry, 67–84. Boulder: Westview

Wee, C. J. W.-L. 1993. "Contending with Primordialism: The 'Modern' Construction of Postcolonial Singapore." *positions* 1, no. 3: 715–44.

Weindling, Paul. 1994. "Public Health in Germany." In *The History of Public Health and the Modern State*, edited by Dorothy Porter, 119–31. Amsterdam: Rodopi.

White, Hayden. 1987. *The Content of the Form: Narrative Discourse and Historical Representation*. Baltimore: Johns Hopkins University Press.

Wilkerson, Douglas. 1994. "Film and the Visual Arts in China: An Introduction." In *Cinematic Landscapes*, edited by Linda C. Ehrlich and David Desser, 39–44. Austin: University of Texas Press.

Will, Pierre-Étienne, and R. Bin Wong. 1991. *Nourish the People: The State Civilian Granary System in China, 1650–1850*. Ann Arbor: Center for Chinese Studies, University of Michigan.

Winichakul, Thongchai. 1994. *Siam Mapped: A History of the Geo-Body of a Nation.* Honolulu: University of Hawaii Press.

Wong, R. Bin. 1997. *China Transformed: Historical Change and the Limits of European Experience*. Ithaca: Cornell University Press.

Woo, Catherine Yi-Yu Cho. 1991. "The Chinese Montage." In *Perspectives on Chinese Cinema*, edited by Chris Berry, 21–29. London: BFI.

Xiang Lanxin. 1993. "Fin de Siècle Beijing: Economic Nationalism versus Political Inertia." *Communist and Post-communist Studies* 26, no. 1: 104–19.

Xiao Gongqin. 1986. *Rujia wenhua de kunjing* (The predicament of Confucian culture). Chengdu: Sichuan renmin chubanshe.

Xuanchuanju (Bureau of propaganda). 1939. *Weixin zhengfu chengli chuzhou jiniance* (Commemorative volume for the first anniversary of the founding of the Reformed Government). Shanghai: Kimura insatsujō.

Yamamoto Shun'ichi. 1982. *Nihon korera shi* (History of cholera in Japan). Tokyo: Tōkyō daigaku shuppankai.

——. 1994. *Baidoku kara eizu e: baishun to seibyō no Nihon kindaishi* (From syphilis to AIDS: prostitution and venereal disease in the modern history of Japan). Tokyo: Chōsō shoten.

Yi Chŏngil. 1908. "Non kungmun" (On national writing). *TaeHan hyŏphoebo* 2 (25 May): 11–14.

Yi Kich'an. 1997. Preface to Sin Ch'aeho [1908] 1997, 259–61.

Yi Kuyŏng. 1985. "TaeHan cheguk ŭi sŏngnip kwa yŏlgang ŭi panyŏng" (The formation of the TaeHan empire and the reaction of the powers). *Kangwŏn sahak* 1 (December): 75–98.

Yi Kwangnin. 1989. *Kaehwa p'a wa kaehwa sasang yŏn'gu* (Studies on the Enlightenment Party and its thought). Seoul: Ilchogak.

Yi Pogyŏng. 1908. "Kungmun kwa hanmun ŭi kwado sidae" (The transition period of national writing and Chinese). *Taegŭk hakpo* 21 (May): 16–18.

Yi Pongun. 1985 [1897]. *Kungmun chŏngni* (Proper principles for the national language). Seoul: T'ap ch'ulpansa.

Yi Sŏngŭn. 1959. "Uri kukki chejŏng ŭi yurae wa kŭ ŭi ŭiŭi" (The history and meaning of the making of our flag). *Kukkasang ŭi chemunje* 2 (July): 177–220.

Yi Sŭnggyo. 1908. "Kukhanmunnon" (On national and Chinese writing). *Sŏbuk hakhoe wŏlbo* 1 (June 1): 20–22.

Yŏ Kyuhyang. 1908. [Unititled.] *Taedong hakpo wŏlbo* 1 (Feb. 25): 52–53.

Yoshimi Kaneko. 1982. "Baishō ni jittai to hasshō undo" (Prostitution and the antiprostitution movement). In *Nihon josei seikatsushi* (History of the lives of Japanese women), edited by Joseishi sōgo kenkyūkai, 223–58. Tokyo: Tōkyō daigaku shuppankai.

Yu Kilchun. 1895. *Sŏyu kyŏnmun* (Observations on my travels to the West). Reprinted in *Yu Kilchun chŏnsŏ*, vol. 1

——. 1908. *TaeHan munjŏn* (A Korean grammar). Reprinted in *Yu Kilchun chŏnsŏ* 5:128–95.

Yu Kilchun p'yonch'an wiwŏnhoe, ed. 1971. *Yu Kilchun chŏnsŏ* (The complete works of Yu Kilchun). Seoul: Ilchogak.

Yuan Senpo. 1991. *Kang Yong Qian jingying yu kaifa beijiang* (Management and opening of the northern border regions during the Kangxi, Yongzheng, and Qianlong reigns). Beijing: Zhongguo shehui kexue chubanshe.

Yun Ch'iho. 1897. "The Whang-chei of Dai Han, or the Emperor of Korea." *Korean Repository* 4:385–90.

——. 1971. *Yun Ch'iho ilgi* (The diary of Yun Ch'iho). Seoul: Tamgudang.

Zanasi, Margherita. 1997. "Nationalism, Autarky, and Economic Planning in 1930s China." Ph.D. diss., Columbia University.

Zani, Luciano. 1988. *Fascismo, autarchia, commercio estero: Felice Guarneri, un tecnocrate al servizio dello "Stato Nuovo".* Bologna: Il Mulino.

Zhang Li. 1981. "Jiangxi noncun fuwu shiye 1934–1945" (Village service enterprises in Jiangxi, 1934–1945). In *Kangzhan jianguoshi yanjiu aohui wenji 1937–1945*. Taibei: Zhongyang yanjiuyuan jindaishi yanjiusuo.

Zhang Pengyuan and Shen Huaiyu, eds. 1987. *Guomin zhengfu zhiguan nianbiao 1925–1949* (Handbook of offices and personnel of the National Government, 1925–1949). Taibei: Zhongyang yanjiuyuan jindashi yanjiusuo.

Zhang Yinwu. 1995. "Dangdai Zhongguo wenxue yanjiu: zai zhuanxingzhong" (Studies of contemporary Chinese literature: in transition). *Xinhua wenzhai* 8:113–14.

Zheng Qun. 1995. "Tigao minzu wenhua sizhi yu xiandaihua" (Elevating national cultural quality and modernization). *Xinhua wenzhai* 3:37–38.

Zhong Heming. 1938. *Riben qin Hua zhi jianjie shi* (History of the espionage behind Japan's invasion of China). Hankou: Huazhong tushu gongsi.

Zhong Xiangcai. 1992. *Zhongguo jindai minzu qiyejia jingji sixiangshi* (History of the economic thought of national entrepreneurs in modern China). Shanghai: Shanghai shehui kexueyuan chubanshe.

Zhongguo tongxinshe (China news agency). 1938. *Ishin seifu shu kikan no gyōsei kikō* (Administrative structure of agencies of the Reformed Government). Shanghai.

Zvelebil, Kamil V. 1992. *Companion Studies to the History of Tamil Literature*. Leiden: Brill.

———. 1995. *Lexicon of Tamil Literature*. Leiden: Brill.

Contributors

Timothy Brook is professor of History, University of Toronto.

Susan L. Burns is assistant professor of History and Asian Studies, University of Texas at Austin.

Thomas Keirstead is associate professor of History, State University of New York at Buffalo.

Xiaoping Li holds a Ph.D. in sociology and teaches at Simon Fraser University, Vancouver.

V. Ravindiran received his Ph.D. in 1999 from the Department of History, University of Toronto.

Andre Schmid is assistant professor of East Asian Studies, University of Toronto.

R. Bin Wong is professor of History, University of California at Irvine.

Margherita Zanasi is assistant professor of Asian Studies, University of Texas at Austin.

Index